PHILOSOPHY OF THE ARTS

'The new edition of *Philosophy of The Arts* provides one of the most comprehensive and pellucid introductions to aesthetics on the market.'
Andy Hamilton, *Durham University*, *UK*

Philosophy of The Arts presents a comprehensive and accessible introduction to those coming to aesthetics and the philosophy of art for the first time. The third edition is greatly enhanced by new chapters on art and beauty, the performing arts and modern art, and new sections on Aristotle, Hegel and Nietzsche. All other chapters have been thoroughly revised and extended.

This new edition:

- is jargon-free and will appeal to students of music, art history, literature and theatre studies as well as philosophy
- looks at a wide range of the arts from film, painting and architecture to literature, music, dance and drama
- discusses the philosophical theories of major thinkers including Aristotle, Hume, Hegel, Nietzsche, Croce, Collingwood, Gadamer and Derrida
- includes regular summaries and suggestions for further reading.

Gordon Graham is Henry Luce III Professor of Philosophy and the Arts at Princeton Theological Seminary. He was formerly Regius Professor of Moral Philosophy at the University of Aberdeen in Scotland. He is the author of *Eight Theories of Ethics* and *The Internet: A Philosophical Inquiry*, both published by Routledge.

PHILOSOPHY OF THE ARTS

An introduction to aesthetics

Third Edition

Gordon Graham

LONDON AND NEW YORK

First published 1997
Second edition published 2000

Third edition published 2005
by Routledge
2 Park Square, Milton Park, Abingdon, Oxon, OX14 4RN

Simultaneously published in the USA and Canada
by Routledge
270 Madison Ave, New York, NY 10016

Routledge is an imprint of the Taylor & Francis Group

Typeset in Sabon by RefineCatch Limited, Bungay, Suffolk
Printed and bound in Great Britain by
The Cromwell Press, Trowbridge, Wiltshire

British Library Cataloguing in Publication Data
A catalogue record for this book is available from the British Library

Library of Congress Cataloging in Publication Data
Graham, Gordon, 1949 July 15–
Philosophy of the arts: an introduction to aesthetics/Gordon Graham.—3rd ed.
p. cm.
Includes bibliographical references and index.
1. Aesthetics. I. Title.
BH39.G67 2005
111′.85—dc22 2005002568

ISBN 0–415–34978–8 (hbk)
ISBN 0–415–34979–6 (pbk)

In memory of
Christina Marie Kennedy (1974–97)
to whom these questions *mattered*

Contents

Preface to the Third Edition

The first edition of *Philosophy of The Arts* appeared in 1997, with a second revised edition appearing in 2000. From the start I have had the benefit of a large number of comments from teachers, students, readers and reviewers. The publisher's suggestion of a third edition has now allowed me to take account of most of them, but the list of people to whom I owe a debt has grown too long to detail. Continued thanks are due to staff at Routledge, who have promoted the book with both enthusiasm and success.

This third edition is a more major revision than the second. It includes a further two new chapters – Chapters 8 and 11 – and what was Chapter 1 in both previous editions has been split into two to allow the material on Kant to be expanded. All the other chapters have been rewritten, and new material added to most of them.

Early versions of some of the themes I discuss were published in papers in the *British Journal of Aesthetics*, the *Journal of Aesthetic Education*, the *Journal of Aesthetics and Art Criticism*, the *Journal of Value Inquiry, Ends and Means*, the *Oxford Handbook of Aesthetics* and the *Routledge Companion to Aesthetics*. All of the material I have used from these papers has been extensively rewritten.

Gordon Graham
King's College, Aberdeen
October 2004

Introduction

The arts are an important part of human life and culture. They attract a large measure of attention and support from states, commercial companies and the public at large. But what makes something 'art', and why should we value it? These are practical questions for civil servants, charitable trusts, private sponsors and educational establishments. They are also theoretical questions with which philosophers have been concerned for more than 2,000 years. Over that long period a number of important answers have been developed and explored, and the purpose of this book is to introduce newcomers to the field of aesthetics and art theory to both the problems and their resolution. Philosophy of art is simply an attempt to answer these questions in a sustained and coherent way, while drawing upon the thinking of the major philosophers who have devoted most attention to them. My intention, however, is not just to provide a textbook for students of philosophy. The book also aims to demonstrate to anyone who reads it – student or non-student – that philosophy of art (or aesthetics) is directly relevant to the study, appreciation and practice of the arts.

Philosophers are not the only people to develop theories of art. Sociologists, musicologists, art critics and literary theorists have done so as well. But what philosophy has to say on these topics is especially relevant to any serious thinking about the value and importance of art. At the same time, it becomes lifelessly abstract if it is too far removed from the arts themselves. That is why, after four chapters on general themes, the book divides into chapters expressly devoted to particular art forms including, for the first time in this edition, the performing arts. The idea is to stimulate an interest in philosophy among those whose principal motivation for approaching these topics is a love of music, painting, film, literature, drama, dance or architecture. Chapter 10 considers at length some recent developments, especially in the plastic arts, and addresses a common concern about modern art – is it art at all? – while Chapter 11 investigates the topical subject of environmental aesthetics. The final chapter of the book explores more complex issues of art theory and, in particular, the Marxist, structuralist and postmodern approaches to art.

One special difficulty about focusing on the specific rather than the general is this: we can only talk meaningfully about paintings, poems, symphonies, and so on if, quite literally, we know what we are talking about. This means that the reader needs to be familiar with the illustrative examples, and it is impossible to be sure of this in advance. So far as I can, I have used the very best-known examples of artworks – for example, the *Mona Lisa*, Beethoven's *Ninth Symphony*, Charles Dickens's *Bleak House*, etc. – but sometimes less well-known examples illustrate the point at issue better. Happily, this difficulty is much less great than it was with the first edition because of the internet, which has become a hugely valuable resource for this purpose. In addition to a complete bibliography, there is a list of websites where collections of artworks, including music, will be found.

Suggestions for further reading have also been reorganized for this edition. At the end of each chapter I have identified more advanced introductory reading, classic writings and major contemporary studies. With one or two exceptions, the advanced introductory reading is taken from two books that have appeared since the first edition was published – the *Routledge Companion to Aesthetics* (now in its second edition) and the *Oxford Handbook of Aesthetics*, both of which are accessible, comprehensive and authoritative. So far as is possible I have identified 'classic' writings from the past, but in a few cases included more recent works. All of them have been the focus of widespread discussion. A third category aims to draw attention to major and important contemporary works, though inevitably this is a tiny selection out of all the available choices. The bibliography at the end includes full details of all these publications, together with works cited in the text. In addition it lists other books and articles that will be of interest to readers following up the topics of the different chapters.

There are a good many introductions to the philosophy of art, and several more since the first edition of this one. The distinctive feature of mine is its focus on the value of art, and the exploration of normative issues in the context of specific art forms as well as the aesthetic appreciation of nature. This approach rests upon an assumption that it is better for the philosopher of art to investigate the question of art's value than to try to arrive at a definition of art, an assumption defended at length in the final chapter. I have put this defence at the end of the book because, though it is logically prior and philosophically crucial to the cogency of my approach, a reader whose interest is primarily in matters artistic can usefully read the book up to that point without going on to engage directly with the rather more abstract philosophical issues involved in defending a normative approach.

The third edition covers several topics that the first and second did not. Despite these additions, however, some interesting questions in aesthetics have inevitably been omitted. This is unavoidable because typically philosophy raises more questions than it answers. The point of an introduction is not to provide a definitive set of solutions to a designated set of problems, but to start the mind of the reader on an exploratory journey of its own.

1

Art and pleasure

The most familiar question in philosophical aesthetics is this: what is art? Why is this question worth asking? The answer has to be that art *matters*. The question 'what is art?' is really the question 'what *counts* as art?' and we want an answer to it in order to know whether or not something should be accorded the *status* of art. In other words, a concern with what is art is not just a matter of classification, but a matter of cultural esteem. There are, then, two fundamental issues in aesthetics – the essential nature of art, and its social importance (or lack of it). Philosophical aesthetics has tended to focus on the first of these questions, almost exclusively in fact. But there is a lot to be said for tackling the second question first. Accordingly, over the course of the next few chapters we will examine four attempts to formulate a *normative* theory of art, which is to say, one that will explain its *value*.

What makes art valuable? A spontaneous answer, even to the point of being commonplace, is this: art is a source of pleasure or enjoyment. For the sake of a label we could call this view 'aesthetic hedonism' from *hedos*, the Greek word for pleasure. The purpose of this chapter is to investigate the adequacy of aesthetic hedonism as a normative theory of art.

Hume on taste and tragedy

Some philosophers have thought that the value of art is *necessarily* connected with pleasure or enjoyment because, they argue, to say that a painting, a poem, a play or a piece of music is good is just the same as saying that it pleases us. The best-known philosopher to hold this view was the eighteenth-century Scottish philosopher David Hume (1711–76). In a famous essay entitled 'Of the Standard of Taste' Hume argues that the important thing about art is its 'agreeableness', the pleasure we derive from it, and that this is a matter of *our* sentiments, not *its* intrinsic nature. 'Judgements' about good and bad in art, according to Hume, are not really judgements at all 'because sentiment has a reference to nothing beyond itself, and is always real, wherever a man is conscious of it' (Hume 1963: 238). In other words, if I like a thing, I like it, irrespective of any characteristics it possesses. 'To seek the real beauty, or the real deformity, is as fruitless an enquiry, as to seek the real sweet or real bitter' (*ibid.* 239). That is to say, aesthetic preferences are expressions of the taste of the observer, not statements about the object, and Hume thinks the wide diversity of opinions about art that we find in the world is confirmation of this fact.

Here we touch upon a question that many people think is central to the philosophy of art – can there be objective judgements of aesthetic value? Hume's essay is widely taken to be the classic exposition and defence of view that they cannot be, that aesthetic opinions are essentially subjective. However, the main discussion of this issue will be postponed to a later stage (Chapter 10), because for the moment we are concerned not with the suggestion that aesthetic appraisals are subjective, but with the idea that, by their very nature, they are connected with pleasure.

As a defence of subjectivism in aesthetics, though, Hume's essay is not really very persuasive. While he observes that aesthetic opinions can differ greatly, he also recognizes that at least some artistic sentiments can be so wide of the mark as to be discountable. If aesthetic appraisal is a matter of feeling, it seems there can be aberrant feelings. The case he considers is that of a minor writer being compared with John Milton, the great poetic genius who wrote *Paradise Lost*. Though, says Hume, 'there may be found persons who give the preference to the former . . . no one pays attention to such a taste; and we pronounce without scruple the sentiment of these pretended critics to be absurd and ridiculous'. What this implies is that, even though taste is a matter of feeling things to be agreeable or disagreeable, there is still a *standard* of taste, and the question is how these two ideas can be made consistent.

Hume's answer is that the standard of taste arises from the nature of human beings. Since they share a common nature, broadly speaking they like the same things. When it comes to art, he thinks, '[s]ome particular forms or qualities, from the original structure of the internal fabric [of the human mind], are calculated to please, and others to displease' (1963: 271). There are of course strange reactions and opinions; people can prefer the oddest things. But Hume believes that the test of time will eventually tell, and that only those things which truly are aesthetically pleasing will go on calling forth approbation as the years pass.

On the face of it, Hume's theory seems to fit the facts. Artistic tastes do differ greatly, yet broadly speaking, most people like and admire the same great masterpieces in music, painting, literature or architecture. Still, contrary to Hume's suggestion, this shared tendency on the part of the majority of people merely reveals a *common* taste, it does not validate any *standard* of taste. The fact that a feeling is shared by many people does not make it rationally obligatory for everyone to feel the same. If an individual has extremely peculiar musical tastes, say, we can certainly regard them as odd, but if Hume is right in thinking that aesthetics is all a matter of feeling, we have no good reason to call them 'absurd and ridiculous'; they are merely different. If we want to say that some views about art are mistaken, we cannot make the mistake rest on human *feeling* about art – it just is what it is – but on something about the art itself.

For present purposes, however, Hume's contention about feeling as the basis of aesthetic judgement is not the main issue, which is rather the connection he alleges between aesthetics and pleasure. Suppose it is true that people declare artworks and performances to be good or bad in accordance with the feeling those works prompt in them. It does not follow that the feeling has to be one of *pleasure*. Hume, along with most of his contemporaries, believed that only pleasure could explain the power of art to attract and hold us. This is why, in another famous essay entitled 'Of Tragedy', he finds it puzzling that people should willingly watch plays, read poems and view paintings that include events which would normally horrify them. His explanation of this phenomenon is that though the horribleness of the events would naturally repel us, it is overlaid with (or even turned into) pleasure by the artistry with which the events are depicted.

> [T]his extraordinary effect proceeds from that very eloquence with which the melancholy scene is depicted. The genius required to paint objects in a lively manner, the art employed in collecting all the pathetic circumstances, the judgement displayed in disposing them; the exercise, I say, together with the force of expression and beauty of oratorial numbers, diffuse the highest satisfaction on the audience and excite the most delightful moments. By this means the uneasiness of the melancholy passions is not only overpowered and effaced by something stronger of an opposite kind, but the whole impulse of those passions is converted into pleasure.
>
> (Hume 1963: 224)

But why is it puzzling that people are attracted by tragedy? The problem arises only because Hume assumes that people must be deriving pleasure from the depiction of horrible events. Perhaps, on the contrary, some people relish *unpleasant* feeling. If so, and if it is on this ground that they commend tragedies, horror films and so on, then Hume is right to think that their aesthetic appraisals reflect sentiment or feeling, but wrong to think that the feeling in question is one of pleasure.

It follows that the connection between art and pleasure is not a necessary one; to say that a work of art is good or valuable on the strength of the feelings it invokes in us, is not the same as saying that we find it enjoyable. Moreover, we might describe it in positive terms – gripping or compelling, for instance – without implying that we derive pleasure from it; the loathsome can exercise a powerful fascination.

Nevertheless, though 'good' does not *mean* 'pleasurable', it still makes sense to claim that art is to be valued chiefly *because of* the pleasure or enjoyment it gives. It is this, I think, rather than Hume's thesis, that most people who believe there is a connection between art and enjoyment mean to assert.

Collingwood on art as amusement

Is it true that art is principally valuable as a source of pleasure and enjoyment? It is worth noting that it is not always natural to speak of 'enjoying' art. People quite easily say this of novels, plays, films and pieces of music, but less easily of paintings, sculptures and buildings. So even if it were agreed that 'enjoyment' often explains the value of art, some further explanation of just what this might mean in the case of the plastic arts and architecture would be needed.

But a more important difficulty is this. To say that art is something we enjoy, tells us next to nothing. People enjoy lots of things – their work, their holidays, their food. When someone says he enjoys his work, we usually ask what it is about the work that is enjoyable, and expect his answer to tell us about what he finds of *value* in it. 'Enjoyment' does no more than signal that he values it. In a similar fashion, the initial claim that art is a source of enjoyment is not in itself informative. It simply leads on to the next question. What *makes* it enjoyable?

It is often assumed (as Hume assumes) that the answer is obvious; things are enjoyable because they give us pleasure. Now the concept of 'pleasure' also needs some clarification, because it can be used in such a general fashion that it means little more than 'enjoyment' in the sense just described, in which case we are no further forward. But getting clear about the concept of pleasure is not as easy as we might suppose. There is a tendency to conflate 'pleasure' with 'happiness' as though they were synonymous, when they are not, and another tendency to think of 'pleasure' as the psychological opposite of 'pain'. Both these tendencies are to be found in the founders of philosophical utilitarianism, Jeremy Bentham (1748–1832) and John Stuart Mill (1806–73), and since utilitarian ideas have had such a powerful influence on contemporary culture, these tendencies have become widespread.

The sense of 'pleasure' we want to examine here is something like 'entertainment value'. The value of art is that it offers us entertainment. This is a thesis that the British philosopher R. G. Collingwood (1889–1943) discusses in *The Principles of Art*, one of the major works of aesthetics published in the twentieth century and one to which we will have occasion to return in a later chapter. Collingwood calls the belief that the value of art lies in its ability to entertain us, 'art as amusement'. While he is partly engaged in the traditional task of philosophical aesthetics – namely defining what art is – his interest is a normative one. The purpose of his book is to arrive at a satisfactory conception of 'art proper' or *true* art, as we might say, and what he wants to show is that 'art as amusement' falls short of 'art proper'. Confusing the two hides an important mistake.

Collingwood does not mean to deny that there are people for whom the arts are a form of entertainment, and it may indeed be the case that, as a matter of fact, they genuinely find amusement in plays, novels, and so on. This is an important point to stress. To claim that 'art as amusement' falls short of 'art proper' does not require us to deny that the arts have recreational value and can entertain us. Collingwood's contention is that if this is *all* we find there, we have missed the thing most worth finding. His analysis of the error in 'art as amusement' is both insightful and persuasive, but best considered in connection with his own, positive theory of art which will be examined in Chapter 3. At this point in the argument, it is sufficient to register a doubt he raises about an important assumption at work. The thesis that art is valuable for the pleasure or amusement we derive from it depends, crucially, on the truth of a factual claim – that we do indeed derive pleasure from it.

Is this actually true? What is at issue here is not a matter of language or belief, but a matter of experience. First, people readily use the language of pleasure and enjoyment in connection with the arts, but it does not follow that the thing they experience is properly called 'pleasure'. Second, for all sorts of reasons people will claim that they enjoy major novels, great masters, the music of the concert hall, and may make this claim quite sincerely. But what they choose to *do* is often a more convincing test of their real opinion than what they feel constrained to *say*. Once we shift our attention to the choices they make, it is not at all obvious that most people find most of what we call art pleasurable in any straightforward sense.

Someone who wants to read simply for pleasure is far more likely to choose a novel by John Grisham than by William Faulkner, though the label 'literature' would be attached to the latter rather than the former. Romantic comedy is a more obvious choice than art film for most people going to the cinema, *just for pleasure*. Channel hoppers wanting an evening's entertainment at home are, by and large, more likely to stop at soap opera than Shakespeare. And who, apart from a very few, would prefer the art gallery to the restaurant if what is in view is simply pleasure?

Such preferences need not prevail universally for the general point to hold; great novels can also be diverting and amusing. But there is this further point to be emphasized. People who, for the purposes of entertainment, choose soap opera over Shakespeare or Grisham over Faulkner, are most unlikely to claim that what they have chosen is artistically more valuable or significant. Probably, they will agree that Faulkner is a far more important writer than Grisham. Even so, his novels provide a much less pleasurable way of passing the time. In the same way 'easy listening' is preferable to Beethoven's late *Quartets*, because it is easy, not because it is greater art.

The fact that personal pleasure and artistic significance can be divorced in this way lends support to Collingwood's contention that the prevalence of 'art as amusement' as the explanation of aesthetic value has distorted people's ability to ask honestly just how much pleasure they derive from 'high' art. Collingwood thinks that there is often a measure of self-deception in people's attitudes, because there is often a conventional pressure to *claim* to enjoy art. But if we are honest most of us will admit that the entertainment value of high art is quite low compared to other amusements.

> The masses of cinema goers and magazine readers cannot be elevated by offering them . . . the aristocratic amusements of a past age. This is called bringing art to the people, but that is clap-trap; what is brought is still amusement, very cleverly designed by a Shakespeare or a Purcell to please an Elizabethan or a Restoration audience, but now, for all its genius, far less amusing than Mickey Mouse or jazz, except to people laboriously trained to enjoy it.
>
> (Collingwood 1938: 103)

Collingwood's judgement on (his) contemporary culture may sound harsh, but he draws our attention to a point of some substance. Forms of entertainment have become more sophisticated over the centuries. What would have amused the 'yokels' in the pit at Shakespeare's Globe theatre must seem a very poor form of entertainment to a generation reared on television programmes like *Fawlty Towers, Friends* and *Blackadder*. These are far funnier than the comic scenes in *Twelfth Night* or *A Midsummer Night's Dream*, and it is only a dogmatic commitment to the belief that great art gives great pleasure that could lead us to deny it.

In any case, there is this further objection. Even if we were to agree, contrary to what has been said, that art can be relied upon to amuse, this would not give us any special reason to value or pursue it. There are many other cheaper and less taxing forms of amusement – card games, picnics, crossword puzzles, computer games, for example. If simple pleasure is what is at issue, on the surface at any rate, art is at best only a *contender* for value, and in all probability a rather weak one.

Mill on higher and lower pleasures

The argument of the preceding section called into question an alleged fact – that people generally derive pleasure from art. But suppose that they do. There is still an important difficulty to be overcome. Not all works of art are to be valued to the same extent. If the value of art did lie in the pleasure we get from it, how are we to discriminate between artworks that differ in quality? How could pleasure explain the difference between, for example, Bach's *B Minor Mass* and Boccerini's *Minuet*, Tolstoy's *War and Peace* and

Graham Green's *Brighton Rock*, or a production by the Royal Shakespeare Company and one by the local amateur dramatic association? If all of them give pleasure, why should we rank some so much more highly than others?

Some people feel tempted to reply that we shouldn't. We ought to respect the fact that different people enjoy different things, and not try to elevate some personal preferences over others. In fact, this appeal to equality has led critics and teachers to abandon, not just the distinction between high and low art, but any notion of a 'canon', i.e. any list of great masters and classic works, whether in music, painting, literature or the theatre. This attack on the idea of a canon is an important aspect of the avant-garde in modern art and will be discussed at length in Chapter 11.

For the moment, though, it is enough to note that most people do go on distinguishing between major and minor writers, painters and composers, and between their greatest and less great works. It is common, furthermore, for both artists and audiences to differentiate between the light and the serious in art, between, for instance, farces and tragedies, Strauss waltzes and Beethoven symphonies, the poetry of Edward Lear and that of T. S. Eliot, the novels of P. G. Wodehouse and those of Jane Austen. Strauss, Lear and Wodehouse were all highly talented, and the works they produced are all to be valued. But they lack the profundity and significance of Beethoven, Eliot and Austen. The question is: how can such distinctions be drawn if all we have to go on is the pleasure we derive from them?

This second distinction – between the light and the serious in art – cuts across the first. Part of the motivation for subverting any 'canon' has been a sense that an unwarranted 'bourgeois' elevation of the art of the gallery and the concert hall has led to a denigration of folk art. But as far as our present concerns go, folk art can sometimes be 'serious' when high art, by contrast, can be frivolous. Many of the folk tales and rhymes assiduously collected by Peter and Iona Opie, for example, touch on themes far deeper than the story lines of many modern novels. It still remains to explain this difference.

One possible answer relies on establishing a difference between higher and lower pleasures, and arguing that the major works of great artists provide a higher kind of pleasure compared to that provided by lighter or more minor works that may still require considerable skill and talent. Can such a difference be elaborated convincingly? John Stuart Mill attempts to do so in the essay entitled *Utilitarianism*. He is not expressly concerned with the question of the value of art, but it is hard to see how any such distinction could be drawn other than in the ways he suggests.

According to Mill, there are only two possibilities. Either we say that higher pleasures hold out the possibility of a greater *quantity* of pleasure, or we say that a higher pleasure is of a different *quality*. The first of these alternatives is plainly inadequate because it makes the value of art strictly commensurable with that of other pleasures. If the only difference is that pleasure in art is more concentrated, it can be substituted without loss by more items affording a lower pleasure. Thus, if what Tolstoy's *Anna Karenina* has over *Friends* or *Neighbours* is *quantity* of pleasure, we can make up the difference simply by watching more episodes of *Friends*. In fact, we don't even have to confine ourselves to similar sorts of thing. Food is often a pleasure, so we could make up for any lack of artistic pleasures, by eating more of the food we especially like.

The implication of this line of thought is that people who have never acquired any familiarity with any of the things that pass for serious art, including the serious elements in folk art, are in no way impoverished, provided only that they have had a sufficient quantity of more mundane pleasures. Pizza is as good as poetry, we might say, a modern version of a famous remark by Bentham. Most of us would want to dissent from such a judgement, but whether we do or not, the fact of this implication is enough to show that the pleasure theory of art understood in this way is inadequate since it cannot show art to have any special value at all.

Mill thinks that 'it is absurd that . . . the estimation of pleasures should be supposed to depend on quantity alone' (Mill 1985: 12). Instead he appeals to the respective quality of different pleasures.

> If I am asked, what I mean by difference of quality in pleasures, or what makes one pleasure more valuable than another, merely as a pleasure, except its being greater in amount, there is but one possible answer. Of two pleasures, if there be one to which all or almost all who have experience of both give a decided preference, irrespective of any feeling of moral obligation to prefer it, that is the more desirable pleasure. If one of the two is, by those who are competently acquainted with both, placed so far above the other that they prefer it . . . we are justified in ascribing to the preferred enjoyment a superiority in quality. . . . On a question which is the best worth having of two pleasures . . . the judgement of those who are qualified by knowledge of both, or, if they differ, that of the majority among them, must be admitted as final.
>
> (Mill 1985: 14–15)

According to Mill, this higher quality of pleasure more than compensates for any diminution in quantity and will in fact offset a good deal of pain and discontent. In a famous passage he concludes:

> It is better to be a human being dissatisfied than a pig satisfied; better to be Socrates dissatisfied than a fool satisfied. And if the pig, or the fool, is of a different opinion, it is because they only know their own side of the question.
>
> (Mill 1985: 14)

Whether Mill's account of higher and lower pleasures is adequate for his purposes in *Utilitarianism* is not the question here. Rather we want to ask whether the same strategy can be used to explain the difference in value that is attached to light and serious art. And the answer plainly seems to be that it does not. This is chiefly because, as we know, tastes differ in art, and consequently the test he proposes cannot be used to adjudicate between competing responses to kinds of art.

Let us take the case of grand opera versus soap opera as both a test and an illustration. Wagner's *Ring Cycle* is an astonishing amalgamation of three major artistic forms – musical, visual and dramatic – on an immense scale. In the estimation of many people, it represents one of the greatest artistic achievements of all time. Television soap operas like *Dallas* are also very protracted, continuing through a vast number of episodes, and they combine the visual and the dramatic. But generally speaking they have poor dialogue and hackneyed plots. No one heralds them as major artistic creations, and the names of their script writers and directors are virtually unknown.

Employing Mill's test, then, it ought to be the case that a competent judge who has seen both will prefer grand opera to soap opera. Suppose that someone who has seen both and is asked to judge, expresses a preference for grand opera. How are we to tell that they are a competent judge? The mere fact that they have seen both will not suffice, because tastes differ, and it may be the case, therefore, that the preference expressed does not arise from the perception of a higher pleasure, but from a liking for grand opera. Someone else, asked the same question, who has also seen both, might have a taste for soap opera and so express a different preference.

Consequently it has to be Mill's majority test that must do the work. Now if we assume (almost certainly without foundation) that majority opinion among those who have seen both favours grand opera, we still have no reason to infer from this that the works of Wagner generate a higher quality of pleasure than episodes of *Dallas*. The larger number of votes for the former may signal nothing more than that taste for grand opera is in the majority. Suppose (more plausibly) that the vote goes the other way, and the majority express a preference for soap opera. We can conclude that more people get more pleasure from soap opera than grand opera, (which seems almost certainly true to me). What we cannot infer is that the normal estimation that puts grand opera on a higher scale than soap opera, artistically speaking, is mistaken. We cannot show that beer is *better* than wine simply by showing that more people prefer it. The suggestion that we can, just begs the question in the present context. The fact that people really enjoy soap opera does not make the dialogue any more sophisticated or the plots any less hackneyed.

It might be said that construing Mill's test in terms of taste ignores an important suggestion: higher pleasures involve the higher faculties; this is what makes them of a higher quality. Such seems certainly to be Mill's view, and it is what justifies him in discounting the opinions of the fool and the pig. Their experience is of a lower order and hence their pleasures are too.

Applied to the subject of art, what this implies is that serious art engages aspects of the mind that lighter art does not address, or even attempt to.

In general this seems to be true. Great art – literary, musical, visual, dramatic – tends to make considerable demands on us, of attention and concentration – whereas light art is much less demanding. However, it is not clear how this would make a difference to the relative value of the two *in terms of pleasure*. It is easy to accept Mill's claim that there is more to human life than eating, sleeping and procreating, and it seems to follow that human beings can expect to enjoy a range of pleasures that are closed to pigs, because human beings have innate endowments of mind and emotional capacity that pigs do not. But these evident differences give us no reason to think that the engagement of a higher capacity brings a different kind of pleasure that can be ranked higher. Pigs cannot do crosswords, and fools cannot while away the time with mathematical 'brainteasers'. Such activities undoubtedly engage higher faculties, but this of itself does not give us reason to think that the pleasure we derive from them is of a more valuable 'higher' kind than the pleasure to be found in, say, sunbathing or ice cream. We can define 'higher' pleasures as those that involve the higher faculties if we choose, but this is mere stipulation. It does not help us to identify a distinctive property that would validate the claim that crosswords and the like are more significant or important than other pleasurable pastimes.

The nature of pleasure

So far it has proved impossible to ground the value or importance of art on pleasure or entertainment value. The concept of pleasure with which Mill is operating is one of a mental or psychological experience that different things can cause in us roughly opposite to pain. Since it is a commonplace that there are different kinds of pain – some much more intense than others – the idea of discriminating between pleasures in terms of their intensity seems plausible. But arguably, this is a mistaken understanding of the nature of pleasure. An older understanding that goes back to Aristotle holds that pleasure is not itself an experience, but something that *supervenes upon* experience. What this means is that the pleasure we derive from an activity is not an after-effect of the activity, in the way that being slightly drunk is the after-effect of a few glasses of wine. Pleasure, rather, is the manner in which we engage in that activity. If I play a game for pleasure, this is to be contrasted with playing it for money, or because I am compelled to, or because I can think of nothing else to do, and it means that I am playing it for the sake of the game itself. What I enjoy when I play tennis for pleasure is not an experience called 'pleasure' which arises as I walk off the court, an experience that might be compared with the 'pleasure' generated by music as I leave the concert hall, say. What I enjoy is the business of playing *tennis*.

This alternative account of pleasure leads to an important shift in the line of thought we have been examining in the course of this chapter. If enjoyment or pleasure in the arts is a mode or manner in which we engage with them – whether as artists or as spectators – then it is in the arts themselves that their value is to be found and not in the pleasurable feelings that may or may not arise from them. We can repeat and refine the question with which we are concerned. Is there an intrinsic feature of the arts that gives them special value, and if so what could it be? One longstanding answer is 'beauty', and this will form the central topic of the next chapter.

Suggested further reading

Advanced introductory reading

Routledge Companion to Aesthetics (second edition), Chapter 4
Oxford Handbook of Aesthetics, Chapter 44

Classic writings

David Hume, 'Of the Standard of Taste' and 'Of Tragedy'
R. G. Collingwood, *The Principles of Art*, Chapter 5
John Stuart Mill, *Utilitarianism*

Major contemporary works

Jerrold Levinson, *The Pleasures of Aesthetics* (1996)

2

Art and beauty

Beauty and pleasure

In the previous chapter we explored the idea that the value of the arts lies in the pleasure we derive from them and saw that such a view is insufficient to explain what is special about the arts over other sources of pleasure, and what makes some artworks serious and others light. Accordingly, we are still in search of something that will enable us to explain art's special value.

To have reached this point is not necessarily to have put the concept of pleasure behind us, because some philosophers have thought that what is special about art is a distinctive kind of pleasure – 'aesthetic pleasure'. The Polish philosopher Roman Ingarden, for instance, urges us to recognize that aesthetic pleasures 'have a special character of their own and exist in a different manner from the pleasures deriving from a good meal or fresh air or a good bath' (Ingarden 1972: 43).

What could this pleasure be? One obvious answer is – the pleasure that accompanies beauty. It has been observed from ancient times that it seems contradictory to describe something as beautiful and deny that we are in any way pleasurably affected by it. The same thing would not be true of a large range of concepts that can be used without any personal evaluative implication or overtone. Colour words are like this. People do often prefer one colour to another, and can even be said to have a favourite colour. But we can't know this from their use of colour words alone. If I describe an apple as 'red', you cannot draw the inference that I favour it in some way; perhaps I only like green apples. But if I describe it as a *beautiful* red apple, you can tell at once that I regard it in a positive light.

Whereas we can apply colour words like red and green without committing ourselves to a favourable estimation of the things we apply them to, we automatically praise something when we call it beautiful, and criticize it when we describe it as ugly. But this raises an important philosophical question. What is the connection between a purely descriptive term like 'red' or 'green' and the evaluative term 'beautiful'?

There are two possibilities that philosophers have discussed at great length. The first is that the connection is purely subjective. That is to say, whereas terms like red and green identify real properties of the apple, the term 'beautiful' says something about the person who uses it. This is the view embodied in the familiar saying that 'Beauty lies in the eye of the beholder' and it is exactly the view we found Hume espousing in the previous chapter – 'To seek the real beauty, or the real deformity, is as fruitless an enquiry, as to seek the real sweet or real bitter' (1963: 239).

Now there are two principal objections to such a view. The first is one that Hume's Scottish contemporary Thomas Reid brought against him. If saying 'This is a beautiful red apple' means 'I like/love/value/prefer this red apple', why don't I just say that? Why cast my opinion in such a misleadingly objective form, as though it *were* about the apple, when in fact it is about me, and my feelings towards it? The other objection is this. If judgements of beauty are purely subjective, why does anyone bother to argue about them? '*De gustibus non disputandum*' an ancient Latin saying goes – 'There can be no disputing over matters of taste'. If I say, I like the taste of avocado, whereas you do not, how could there be any point in arguing about it? I can't give you *reasons* to like the taste of avocado; you just don't. But when it comes to judgements of beauty then people *do* argue. What is more, for the practical purposes of buying paintings and sculptures, judging flower competitions, awarding fashion prizes, granting scholarships, they *need* to argue. We want to award the prize to the most beautiful roses, we want to choose the most beautiful painting submitted in the competition, we want to buy the most beautiful recording of a piece of music, etc.

In the face of these objections, subjectivists about beauty need not concede defeat. But what they must do is add to their account what is called an 'error theory'. If they want to interpret beauty statements subjectively, they must also explain why ordinary language and practice seems to be in error about them. Why do human beings go on speaking in a misleadingly 'objectivist' way about beauty? Why do they engage in arguments that cannot in the end be any more than simple confrontations? And why do they run competitions that cannot have any rational outcome? A philosophically astute subjectivist can offer answers to these questions, but it seems more desirable not to have to answer them in the first place. In other words, the need for 'error theories' of this kind seems to give the alternative, objectivist account of beauty a natural advantage.

However, it also faces two important difficulties. The first trades precisely upon that fact that people do disagree over judgements of beauty. If beauty were an objective matter like the colour of a thing, why would there be so much disagreement? Furthermore, this disagreement is to be found not just between individuals, but across times and cultures. Different cultures have different ideals of beauty and these ideals change as time passes. Surely, if beauty and ugliness were real properties of objects that we discover in the way we discover chemical properties, say, there would be a steady convergence of opinion over time? A second objection is this. Everyone agrees that beauty attracts and ugliness repels. That is to say, an important part of judging something to be beautiful or ugly lies in human response to an object and not just the nature of the object itself. But how could an objective property in and of itself be guaranteed to move us? Surely, for any property that lies purely in the object, we can regard it with either enthusiasm or indifference.

It is possible to reply to this second objection by acknowledging that 'beauty' is not like 'red' or 'green'. Beauty is inferred from more basic descriptive properties, in the way that 'guilty' and 'innocent' are. Someone accused of a crime really is either guilty or innocent. It is not enough for people, even the majority, simply to believe that they are. But guilt and innocence are not properties that can be seen by an eyewitness. They have to be *inferred from* the observations of eyewitnesses. The same is true of judgements of beauty, someone might allege. Beauty is a 'higher order' property, so to speak, whose presence we infer from other more directly observable properties.

The trouble with this reply, however, is that the analogy is hard to sustain. In the case of guilt and innocence, the law provides us with principles (laws) by means of which we can infer one or the other from the evidence of eyewitnesses. But what are the equivalent laws or principles of beauty? There do not seem to be any. We can *say*, if we wish, that aesthetic properties like 'beauty' are inferred from non-aesthetic properties like 'red', but what is to validate these inferences?

Kant on beauty

It seems then that between subjectivist and objectivist accounts of beauty there is a stand-off. Some aspects of the way we talk and act support a subjectivist interpretation, and others support an objectivist interpretation. How then are we to judge between them? This is the problem addressed by one of the greatest modern philosophers, and possibly the thinker who has had the most enduring influence on contemporary ideas of art and aesthetics – Immanuel Kant (1724–1804). The motivation behind most of Kant's philosophy was the pressing need to resolve certain fundamental antinomies. An antinomy is a conflict between two contradictory propositions both of which appear to be provable by reason. For instance, human beings have free will and can choose what to do. At the same time they are physical objects subject to deterministic laws of nature. By focusing on the first we can prove that the second cannot be true; but by focusing on the second we equally prove that the first cannot be true. How is such an antinomy to be resolved?

The stand-off we have just been considering with respect to the nature of beauty can be interpreted as an antinomy of sorts. It seems that the ascription of beauty can equally well be interpreted as an exercise of rational judgement *and* as an expression of personal sentiment or feeling. But both cannot be true and so we seem to have a philosophical impasse.

It is principally this problem that Kant addresses in *The Critique of Judgement*, his great work on aesthetics first published in 1790. This was a late work of Kant's because earlier in his philosophical career he had thought that aesthetic appreciation was purely subjective, simply a matter of pleasure. Kant draws a sharp distinction between feeling and reason, and on the face of it experience of pleasure cannot be rational or irrational, any more than a pain can be rational or irrational, because it is part of our sensitive rather than our intellectual nature; either things give us pleasure or they don't. But Kant came to the view that the aesthetic is a *special* kind of pleasure precisely because it in some sense transcends mere individual preference. Aesthetic pleasure, or pleasure in the beautiful, is something we can expect others to experience at the same time as ourselves. That is not to say that everyone *does* share the pleasure that is to be found in beautiful things. It means, rather, that pleasure in the beautiful is a pleasure it is proper to commend to others. To this extent, appreciating the beautiful is an act of mind as well as a matter of sensuous feeling, and that is why it is correct to speak of aesthetic *judgement*. The task of *The Critique of Judgement* is to give an adequate account of its special character.

The Critique of Judgement is Kant's third critique. The first, *The Critique of Pure Reason*, is concerned with how human minds can have knowledge of the world outside them, how science is possible if you like. The second, *The Critique of Practical Reason*, is an attempt to discern the principles that make action rational and morality possible. The third *Critique* accounts for the aesthetic by locating it in relation to these other two. Kant places aesthetic judgement between the logically necessary (mathematical theorems for example) and the purely subjective (expressions of personal taste). Though the proposition 'this is beautiful' does indeed have the appearance of a cognitive judgement, that is a judgement about how things are, Kant agrees with Hume that expressing such a judgement 'cannot be other than subjective'; that is, arising from a feeling of approval (§1. These numbers refer to sections of *The Critique of Judgement*). But in contrast to Hume, he rejects the view that the experience of beauty is *merely* subjective. This is because, although Hume thinks that the attribution of 'beauty' to an object reflects a sentiment or feeling within us, Kant is aware that this is not how it seems to us. As with a judgement about fact or necessity,

> [the person who declares something to be beautiful] can find as reason for his delight no personal conditions to which his own subjective self might alone be party . . . [and therefore] . . . must believe that he has reason for demanding a similar delight from everyone. Accordingly he will speak of the beautiful as if beauty were a quality of the object and

> the judgement logical . . . although it is only aesthetic and contains merely a reference of the representation of the object to the subject.
> (§6)

In plainer language the idea is this: while it is true that beauty needs to be appreciated subjectively, when we see beautiful things we are aware that the pleasure we derive from them is not a function of something peculiar to us, some 'personal condition to which our own subjective self might alone be party'. Beauty is subjective, but it is not merely personal, as the expression of a preference is when we refer to something of which we happen to be especially fond – a tune that has personal associations, for example, or a favourite dish. Kant gives the example of a preference for 'Canary-wine'. Someone who expresses a preference for the light sweet wine from the Canary Islands over the heavier port that comes from Portugal, does no more than express a personal liking, and has no reason to expect others to share this preference. But in declaring an object to be beautiful, we think we have a 'reason for demanding a similar delight from everyone'.

An aesthetic judgement is thus to be distinguished as one that falls between the universally necessary (or 'logical') and the merely personal. But it occupies another middle ground as well, the middle ground between being merely pleasant or agreeable and being demonstrably good or useful. Delight in the beautiful is neither of these. Suppose I fancy a particular hat. This is a matter of my finding it attractive. Suppose, though, I also think it especially good at keeping my head warm and dry. This is a demonstrable matter; it can be shown to be true or not. In this second case, my judgement (Kant believes) arises 'from the concept' of the end that is to be served – hats are for keeping out moisture and for retaining heat. Once a given end or purpose is specified, then whether something is good (i.e. useful to that end) is not a matter of *taste* but a matter of *fact*.

Now the aesthetic case does not seem to fit either of these exactly. Beautiful objects don't merely catch our fancy. They seem more significant than that. But neither do they seem to have any special purpose; art is not design. So the distinguishing characteristic of the aesthetic must lie in this: it is free but not purely fanciful. In Kant's terminology an aesthetic judgement is 'disinterestedly free'. It has, in one of his most famous expressions, 'purposefulness without purpose' (§10). When I find something beautiful, it is purposeful, but it does not have some specific purpose that might make it useful to me.

Aesthetic judgement is thus to be distinguished (1) from a judgement of fact because it is subjective, (2) from the merely subjective because it commands the assent of others, (3) from a judgement grounded in practical rationality because the beautiful has no practical purpose, and (4) from the merely fanciful or superficially attractive because it has the mark of purposefulness. What sort of judgement is it that falls between these alternatives?

Kant's answer is – a judgement arising from the 'free play of the imagination'. In contemporary English this expression suggests a greater degree of licence than Kant intends, perhaps, because imagination is often confused with fancy. If the two are different it is because imagination, unlike fancy, is constrained or disciplined in some way. But what way? The answer cannot be truth or fact, since these *determine* our judgements and thereby undermine their freedom. I am not free to decide what causes cancer, as I am free to choose what coat to wear. The crucial point is that while the play of the imagination has to be free, it must also be able to command universal assent just as a claim to knowledge or usefulness does.

To explain this curious double nature, Kant postulates a *sensus communis* (or 'common sensitive nature') among humans that is invoked and appealed to when a judgement of taste is made (§§22 and 40). This shared sense is not the same as shared knowledge about the objective properties of classes of things, like the knowledge that aspirin relieves pain, say. If it were, it would lose what is distinctive to aesthetic judgements, their subjective 'freedom'. That is why aesthetic judgements are not about classes of things at all, but about individual objects. In Kant's language, judgements of taste must be 'invariably laid down as a singular judgement upon the Object'. So, when I declare something to be beautiful, I am not placing it within a general category of 'beautiful things' as I place 'aspirin' within the category 'painkiller'. I am focused upon and 'delighting' in this particular object. 'Delight' in the beautiful is fixed upon an object. Instead of an intellectual classification, it consists in contemplation of the object itself.

The aesthetic attitude and the sublime

So far this exposition of Kant has focused exclusively on the business of judging something to be beautiful, but in *The Critique of Judgement* Kant is also concerned with 'the sublime'. The sublime is found most obviously in nature. So too are beautiful things, of course. Indeed, at many points Kant seems more interested in natural than artistic beauty. But whereas a flower, say, strikes us as beautiful because of its delicacy and the interplay between colour and form it displays, a mighty waterfall such as Niagara Falls impresses us by the sheer chaos of its power. The same sort of contrast is to be found in art. The delicacy of a Tudor cottage with oriel windows, say, contrasts with the black forbidding appearance of a castle like Caernarfon in Wales. Similarly, while 'beautiful' is exactly the right word to describe the slow movement of Mozart's *Clarinet Concerto*, it seems a poor, or even erroneous description of a symphony orchestra playing at full volume the high Romantic music of Tchaikovsky or Mahler.

Though these examples are to this extent contrasting, they can also be construed as having something in common – namely the kind of attitude they invite, an attitude whose key element is a feature identified by Kant – disinterestedness. When we look at the oriel window from an aesthetic point of view (it is said) we are not concerned with its functionality, the extent to which it lets in enough light for reading by, or is difficult to clean. Such practical concerns are set aside. So too, when we stand beneath the raging cataract, we set aside any question of how we are to negotiate a crossing or harness its power for the purpose of generating electricity. But more importantly from the point of view of appreciating its sublimity, we also detach ourselves from it emotionally. We apprehend its fearfulness, certainly, but without actually feeling the sort of fear that would make us run away; we savour its power without any anxiety that we might be swept away. It is the sort of apprehension brilliantly expressed in William Blake's famous poem:

Tyger! Tyger! burning bright
In the forests of the night
What immortal hand or eye
Could frame thy fearful symmetry?

To describe the tiger's 'fearful symmetry' as beautiful seems inadequate. This is because, while the tiger does indeed have beautiful fur and is superbly proportioned, much more impressive is the ferocity of the creature as it suddenly appears at night in the forest. If we are to experience this awesomeness, or sublimity, we need both to be able to distance ourselves from any fear we might feel, and at the same time contemplate its fearfulness.

These two concepts – 'contemplation' and 'distance' – are the principal elements in what has come to be known as 'the aesthetic attitude'. The idea of distance received its most influential exposition at the hands, not of a philosopher, but a psychologist, Edward Bullough. In an article published in 1912, Bullough introduced the term 'psychical distance' in order to identify a distinctive psychological state that was, as the title of his article states, 'a factor in art and an aesthetic principle'. His most famous example is that of a dense fog at sea. Such a condition is usually apprehended as a cause of fear and anxiety. But according to Bullough, we can also view it in a psychically distant way, one that allows us to free ourselves from this practical attitude and contemplate the fog in and of itself, as a visual and perhaps tactile phenomenon.

Bullough's essay was especially influential, but it is simply one attempt to give both precise expression and a psychological basis to an idea that has proved to have widespread appeal. This is the idea that aesthetic experience consists in a special state of mind – the aesthetic attitude – and it has two major implications. First, it locates the aesthetic primarily on the side of the observer or audience. 'The aesthetic' is not a type of thing, but a way of seeing or hearing or touching (or tasting possibly). Second, this way of viewing the world makes anything and everything aesthetic, potentially at any rate. If the heart of the aesthetic is a distinctive attitude, then whatever this attitude can be and is applied to, will constitute an aesthetic experience.

Both these implications are of great significance, not merely in philosophy but in the arts themselves, and the coherence of the concept 'aesthetic attitude' is of crucial importance to modern art, as we shall see in Chapter 11. For the moment, however, it is best to explore two major difficulties that arise for the concept in general. The first is this: can we actually specify such an attitude adequately? If the aesthetic attitude is a special state of mind, what state of mind is it?

This is the question that the philosopher George Dickie addressed in an essay that has been very widely discussed – 'The Myth of the Aesthetic Attitude'. As the title makes plain, Dickie argued that all the major attempts to delineate such an attitude precisely (including Bullough's) fail. He subjects to close scrutiny both the ideas of 'distance' and 'disinterestedness'. Dickie thinks that there is no identifiable psychological experience of 'being distanced' into which we are induced 'when the curtain goes up, when we walk up to a painting, or when we look at a sunset' (Dickie 1964: 57). But if there is no identifiable state, then 'being distanced' just means 'focusing our attention on' something we do, but not something we need a special technical term to describe doing.

It might be agreed that the aesthetic attitude is not a special psychological state, but that it is still marked out by its 'disinterestedness', that is its being divorced from practical purpose. But Dickie argues that this suggestion trades on a confusion. From the fact that some practical interests do indeed distract us from focusing on works of art as art – wondering about the investment value of a painting for example – it does not follow that we can avoid distraction only by having no purpose at all. On the contrary, certain purposes will cause us to concentrate on the work more intently – a playwright watching a rehearsal with a view to rewriting the script is one of the examples he gives.

In short, Dickie presents a convincing case against the idea of a distinctive state of mind that we could call 'the aesthetic attitude' and which constitutes the heart of aesthetic experience.

Art and the aesthetic

A second objection to the concept of the aesthetic attitude is this. If aesthetic experience is the application of a distinctive attitude to an object, then the aesthetic has no necessary connection with art. Suppose (to return to Kant) that a special delight arises from 'the free play of the imagination on an object'. This object could be a picture, a statue, a poem or a piece of music, but it could equally well be a sunset, a mountainside or a rose (an example Kant several times considers). All that the Kantian aesthetic requires is that judgements of taste, beauty, sublimity and so on express themselves as singular judgements upon an object. While finding something beautiful is not purely a subjective matter, since it commits us to believing that others will also find the object in question beautiful, even so there is no restriction on what it is we can find beautiful. Natural objects seem as fitting an object for aesthetic delight as anything an artist might create. What then is the connection between art and the aesthetic?

Kant addresses this point (to a degree) when he says 'nature is beautiful because it looks like art, and art can only be called beautiful if we are conscious of it as art while yet it looks like nature' (§45). Though this goes some way to explaining why aesthetic judgement is appropriate to both nature and art, it still confines us to the point of view of someone *looking at* beautiful things. It identifies the essence of the aesthetic with a consciousness of the appearance of objects, which is to say, art appreciation. But what about art *making*?

Artistic production, according to Kant, also arises from a free act of the imagination. Here again, he attempts to bring out the distinctive character of creative activity by contrasting it with other mental operations. Art is different to science, the acquisition of knowledge, because it requires practical skill. But though it is practical, we can differentiate it from craft or design because the nature of the things it produces is not determined by a functional concept. The structure of a piece of furniture or a piece of machinery, say, is determined by the function it has to serve. Since artworks have no such function, they are not 'determined' in this way. Artistic 'genius' (to use Kant's term) has to be *free*. At the same time it is constrained by the need for its productions to look 'natural', or uncontrived. So far so good, but we are still left with this question: what is the connection between the artist's creative act of imagination and the contemplative act of aesthetic judgement?

Aesthetic judgement, according to Kant, is merely a critical, not a productive faculty. While 'a natural beauty is a *beautiful thing*; artistic beauty is a *beautiful representation* of a thing' (§48, emphasis in original). What this tells us is that both nature and art can engage aesthetic judgement, since both can be beautiful. But it is the special task of art to engage the aesthetic attitude by producing representations of things.

One question is whether this does not confine art too narrowly to figurative painting. Lyric poetry is often beautiful, but surely it is expressive rather than representative? Kant does extend his account of art beyond figurative painting with the concept of 'aesthetical ideas' (§49). These are non-visual representations of non-physical things such as love, or death or envy, which it seems clear the literary arts can embody, including, even, lyric poetry. Perhaps a more difficult case is music. Music can be beautiful, but can it be the representation of anything? And surely architecture is functional rather than representative?

These are all questions to be returned to in future chapters. For the moment it is enough to note that while this seems a plausible way to distinguish natural beauty and artistic beauty, it does not explain the special value of art. In the spirit of Kant we can agree that beauty is to be valued for its own sake and not to be reduced to or explained in terms of something else – knowledge or practical usefulness, for example – but we still have to bridge the gap between the value of *beauty* and the value of *art*. Since the world contains beauty without any creative activity on the part of human beings, what does art add? If we already have beautiful things, why do we need beautiful representations? Why is it not sufficient for us to uncover and conserve the beauty that is to be found in the natural world? The appeal to beauty, or even more broadly 'the aesthetic', leaves unexplained the value, if any, in artistic creation. It also leaves unexplained the multiplicity of art forms. If we already have painting, why do we need poetry?

Gadamer and art as play

An attempt to overcome this difficulty is to be found in an essay by the German philosopher Hans-Georg Gadamer, whose title in English is 'The Relevance of the Beautiful'. Gadamer aims to explain the value of art by building upon Kant's conception of the beautiful, while at the same time acknowledging that '[t]he approach to art through the experience of aesthetic taste is a relatively external one and [for that reason] . . . somewhat diminishing' (Gadamer 1986: 19). By his estimation, Kant's great advance was to see, first, that aesthetic taste is not a *purely* subjective matter but something which claims universal assent; second, that it arises not from any concept of the understanding but from the free play of the imagination; and third, that the ability to play freely is the peculiarity of artistic 'genius'.

On the basis of these three propositions, Gadamer thinks that we can forge a much closer connection between aesthetic appreciation and art making than Kant does. As Kant explains it, the mark of genius lies in activity that is productive, but not useful, and which is not bound by any functional concept or repeatable process of manufacture. Free creative activity is not determined by rules, and even artists cannot explain what makes their creations 'right'. Now Gadamer observes that one consequence of this is that 'the creation of genius can never really be divorced from the con-geniality of the one who experiences it' (Gadamer 1986: 21). What he means by this is that, since imagination lies at the heart of art making, the realization of the artwork requires an act of imagination on the part of the observer as well as the maker.

> A work of art . . . demands to be constructed by the viewer to whom it is presented. It is . . . not something we can simply use for a particular

> purpose, not a material thing from which we might fabricate some other thing. On the contrary, it is something that only manifests and displays itself when it is constituted by the viewer.
>
> (Gadamer 1986: 126)

Consider the case of a painting. Leonardo produced the *Mona Lisa*, but what exactly did he produce? The answer, at one level, is a physical object made of wood, canvas and pigments of various sorts, a unique object without any function. But this is not the level at which it is a work of art, of course. The work of art is not a physical object at all, but an image – of a woman with a faint enigmatic smile. To appreciate this, however, we have to see this image for ourselves. If, for some reason, we can only see the thing that Leonardo produced as a physical object, he has failed to present us with the outcome of his imagination. Whereas aesthetic judgement can simply 'play' on the beauty of natural objects, in order to play on beautiful representations, it must first see them *as* representations. This is why aesthetic judgement and artistic production go hand in hand. The artist's creativity needs its audience for its very existence.

In this way Gadamer forges a plausible connection between art and the aesthetic. We might still ask what special value attaches to art above natural beauty. Gadamer's answer is that the deliberate creations of the artist provide 'the experiences that best fulfill the ideal of "free" and "disinterested" delight' (Gadamer 1986: 20). What is the mark of 'best' here? We must look, he thinks, at 'the anthropological basis of our experience of art', the way that art connects with our fundamental nature.

This connection, it turns out, is to be found in play. It is a fact about our anthropology that, in common with some other animals, we engage in play. By nature children engage in those activities essential to physical survival – crying for food, falling asleep, reaching for the things they want. But they also *play*. In thinking about play, we usually contrast it with work and for this reason generally accept that play can be characterized as activity without purpose. But, as Gadamer points out, it is a deep mistake to suppose on the strength of this characterization that play is *trivial* activity and work is *serious*. This is a *different* contrast.

Play is not 'mere diversion' because activity without a purpose need not be pointless. Play has no 'output' but it can be *structured*. In the case of established games like chess or soccer, and even in the simple games of small children, there are rules and goals established within the play itself. For instance, the aim in soccer is to put the ball in the net. Viewed *extrinsically* – from the outside – this amounts to nothing of any consequence and has no value. What value could there be in getting a leather ball to cross a line? This is the sense in which the game is purposeless. But viewed *intrinsically*, that is within the terms of the game itself, the ball crossing the line *is* an achievement, namely a *goal*. Within the game of soccer scoring goals is what lends focus and point to the rules of play and calls for the skill that may be exhibited in it.

Play can be serious, not in the sense that it is professionalized, but in the sense that it demands, solely for its own purposes, the best temperaments and the finest skills of which human beings are capable. Now Gadamer thinks that art is a kind of play, in which together artist and audience join. What is distinctive about great art is the challenge it presents to the viewer to discern a meaning within it. This is not a meaning that can be conceptualized or explicated in language (to this extent Gadamer follows Kant closely) but is rather symbolic. The challenge is to realize fully in our own imaginations the constructs of the artist's imagination and these constructs are symbolic – 'the picture of happiness', for example, rather than a photographic record of a happy occasion. The artist's task is to engage the audience in a creative free play of images whereby symbolic representation is realized.

In making the symbolic central to art, Gadamer here concurs with another distinguished and influential twentieth-century writer on aesthetics, the American Suzanne Langer. In a book entitled *Feeling and Form*, Langer advances the idea that though the 'meaning' of art is not explicable in the way that the meaning of a scientific hypothesis is, this should not be taken to imply that it is either meaningless or merely an expression of subjective feeling. Works of art have *symbolic* meaning, and what we find in art is a meaning that consists in 'the creation of forms symbolic of human feeling' (Langer 1953: 40).

To this Gadamer adds the idea that the realization of symbol is a communal activity. It requires cooperative activity, and this activity – of play – is something in which all and any may engage. (This is Gadamer's interpretation of Kant's *sensus communis*.) But why should we value this special kind of play? His explanation is novel and interesting. We discover in art, according to Gadamer, the same kind of universality we discover in festivals, and the important thing about festivals, according to Gadamer, is that they *punctuate* the flow of time.

> We do not describe a festival as a recurring one because we can assign a specific place in time to it, but rather the reverse: the time in which it occurs only arises through the recurrence of the festival itself.
>
> (Gadamer 1986: 41)

Thus, everyday events are located before or after Christmas, for instance, not the other way around. Christmas is the 'marker' relative to which other days take their significance. Gadamer thinks that we have *two* fundamental ways of experiencing time. One is 'the abstract calculation of temporal duration' (*ibid.*) and the other is 'festival' time. In festival time we get, as it were, a taste of eternity. In an elegant summary he says this:

> [I]n the experience of art we must learn how to dwell upon the work in

> a specific way. When we dwell upon the work, there is no tedium involved, for the longer we allow ourselves, the more it displays its manifold riches to us. The essence of our temporal experience is learning how to tarry in this way. And perhaps it is the only way that is granted to us finite beings to relate to what we call eternity.
>
> (Gadamer 1986: 45)

This compelling final sentence offers us the right kind of explanation for the value of great art by making it a vehicle to the most profound sorts of experience. At the same time, there is a vagueness about it. What kind of relation to eternity is it that art offers us?

Let us leave aside some very important questions about the meaning of 'eternity'. Is there such a dimension? Philosophers have often argued that eternity is an incoherent idea, that we can attach no sense to it. We might, however, preserve the main elements of Gadamer's theory of 'art as play' with something less ambitious. A recent and widely discussed book on aesthetics is Kendall Walton's *Mimesis as Make-Believe*. Walton also thinks that art is a kind of play, and he develops this thought by construing artworks as 'props' in a game of make-believe. The value of art lies in the value of playing this game.

> Make-believe – the use of (external) props in imaginative activities – is a truly remarkable invention. . . . We can make people turn into pumpkins, or make sure the good guys win, or see what it is like for the bad guys to win. . . . There is a price to pay in real life when the bad guys win, even if we learn from experience. Make-believe provides the experience – something like it anyway – for free. The divergence between fictionality and truth spares us pain and suffering we would have to expect in the real world. We realize some of the benefits of hard experience without having to undergo it.
>
> (Walton 1990: 68)

Walton's theory has much more to it than this, but importantly it offers us an explanation of the value of artworks that relies on a less elusive idea than that of 'relating to eternity'. By offering us imaginative experience, works of art give us the benefits of that experience without the cost that would normally attach to it. The play of art is not real life, but it has to do with real life and so may enrich it.

Art and sport

The contention that art is a kind of play is, as we have seen, a theory with important strengths. Still the game of make-believe is not literally a game, only metaphorically, so one way of asking whether the metaphor is adequate or not, is to look at a literal use of 'game', namely sport. Sport is a variety of play, but for the reasons Gadamer gives, it is wrong on this ground alone to regard it as mere diversion or entertainment. Some sport is light-hearted, certainly, but some is serious. *Serious* sport is possible because it can provide a structured, self-contained activity in which human strengths and weaknesses, both physical and psychological, can display themselves. The important point to stress, however, is that in sporting contests the display and appreciation of these strengths – prowess, dexterity, stamina, intelligence, ingenuity, courage, integrity, forbearance, determination, and so on – is not for the sake of something else but for its own sake. Different games require different skills and mentalities, but all provide not merely occasions for, but vehicles for, the realization of these distinctly human capacities.

It is because of its connection with these sorts of achievement and expression that sport has a value greater than the pleasure which arises from amusing diversion. As with art, this feature of sport justifies expenditure of time and money on a scale which, if devoted to more mundane pleasures, would be regarded as straightforward indulgence, or even waste. Of course people can overestimate the importance of sport, and perhaps they often do, but someone who tries to remind us that 'It's *only* a game' has, on at least some occasions, failed to see just what role sport can have in the realization of human excellence. In short, sport is free play of the sort that Gadamer isolates and analyses. What then is the relevant difference between sport and art?

Following Gadamer's analysis, we might be inclined to argue that, whereas art involves a cooperative act of creation on the part of both artists and audience, sport is participant-centred, and the audience mere spectators. But, as Gadamer himself implies, this is not so. The significance of a sporting occasion is often determined by spectator participation as much as sporting endeavour. What makes a win a victory or a loss a defeat is a function of spectator expectation and involvement. Moreover, sporting occasions have that character of festival that Gadamer finds in art, and hence the underlying universality that Kant's common sense possesses. It is precisely because the individual can get swept up in the whole community's involvement that the appeal of sport crosses almost every boundary. It is for this reason too that sporting events can have the character of national contests, triumphs and defeats.

The self-contained and universal character of sport also allows it to create 'festival time'. Wimbledon, the Superbowl, the US Masters and the Olympic Games punctuate the calendar in the way that Christmas, Hanukkah, Ramadan and Kum Mela do for Christians, Jews, Muslims and Hindus. The timing of ordinary everyday events is related in terms of them, not the other way about.

But if all this is true, if sport no less than art can provide us with activity that has 'purpose without purposefulness' and communal occasions of 'festival time', why is art to be valued distinctly from sport, or even as better than sport?

It is clear that Gadamer means us to regard art as an especially valuable form of play, but we have found nothing in his analysis that gives us reason to discriminate between art and sport in this respect. If both Gadamer's analysis and the subsequent argument are convincing, there is a conflict here with the widespread belief that art is of higher (or at least more enduring) value than sport. That this belief is indeed widespread can hardly be doubted. Though sportsmen and women are often fêted as much as artists and performers, in the longer term the great figures of sport are not ranked alongside the great figures of art. There are indeed sporting equivalents of Maria Callas and Lawrence Olivier – Martina Navratilova and Cassius Clay perhaps – but there are no sporting equivalents of Shakespeare or Mozart. Great creative artists such as these take their place beside historically significant philosophers, scientists, religious figures and political heroes; great sportsmen and women do not.

We could dismiss this differentiation as mere convention or cultural prejudice, and conclude that there is no difference in value between art and sport. Or we can endorse this evaluation and seek some explanatory justification of it. Where might such an explanation lie? What we need is a further differentiating feature. Here is one: art can have content whereas sport cannot. That is to say, a play or a book or a painting can be *about* something, but it would be senseless to speak of a game of tennis or football's being about anything. Furthermore, though there are performing arts (about which more will be said in Chapter 8), most artistic activity results in an art object, an abiding *work* of art. Games do not. Even in the age of VCRs and DVDs, when games can be recorded for posterity, leaving aside special benefits like acquiring a better mastery of the techniques of the game, there is relatively little to be gained from viewing them repeatedly. Nor could a particular game be played again in the way that a drama can. The difference is this: the drama has a meaning that can be explored; the game, however compelling to watch, has none.

Walton, in the parts omitted from the passage quoted previously, speaks of exploration and of insight.

> The excitement of exploring the unknown will be lost to the extent that we construct the worlds ourselves. But if we let others (artists) construct them for us, we can enjoy not only the excitement but also the benefits of any special talent and insight they may bring to the task.
> (Walton 1990: 67–8)

Exploration and insight are not terms that naturally apply to games, just as it would be odd to speak of games as profound, shallow or sentimental, descriptions that are easily applied to works of art. We can only use these terms where it makes sense to speak of content or subject matter, and this implies once more that art, unlike sport, has *communicative* import. We cannot give an adequate account of art or its value without taking account of the fact that artworks have something to communicate. But what? Here we come to another important debate in the philosophy of art, namely the nature of artistic communication, and of all the rival theories on this point, one has been dominant – the view that art communicates emotion. It is to this theory that the next chapter is devoted. Before that, it is useful to retrace our steps by way of a summary of both this chapter and the previous one.

Summary

The commonplace view that the value of art lies in the pleasure we get from it has been found to be deficient on a number of grounds. First, it is not clear that what is commonly regarded as the finest in art is, except for those 'laboriously trained to enjoy it', a real source of amusement. Second, if art's value is pleasure, this makes it nearly impossible to explain the various discriminations that are made within and between forms and works of art. Third, it is hard to see how the pleasure theory could sustain the sorts of evaluative distinctions that are made between art and non-art in the cultural and educational institutions of our society. We might try to amend the pleasure theory by formulating a distinction between pleasures, and classifying art as 'higher', but as the examination of Mill showed, no such distinction seems to be sustainable. A further manoeuvre is to try to isolate a distinctive 'aesthetic pleasure', the pleasure we derive from beauty. Following Kant, we can see how focusing on beauty can provide us with a middle position between mere personal pleasure on the one hand and a scientific description of fact on the other. Furthermore it is an analysis that can be extended to include the sublime as well as the beautiful. Yet in the end, the Kantian aesthetic lays all the emphasis on the mental state of the observer whose imagination may as freely play on nature as on art, leaving obscure the connection between art appreciation and art making. And in any case, there are serious doubts (famously articulated by George Dickie) as to whether the concept of 'aesthetic attitude' inspired by Kant is not a myth.

It should be noted that nothing in the argument so far should be taken to imply that art proper cannot be entertaining, or give us pleasure. Nor does the argument deny that paintings and pieces of music are beautiful and are often valued chiefly for this reason. All that the argument so far has shown is that if the chief value of art resides in pleasure or beauty, art cannot be given the high estimation we commonly give it.

Gadamer, building upon Kant's aesthetic, offers us a more sophisticated version of a similar theory – art as play. Play is not mere diversion but is (or can be) a serious and important part of human life. In Gadamer's analysis it may even be shown to have a semi-religious significance, while by Walton's account it is a game which has the benefits of experience without the usual costs. To identify art as a kind of play, therefore, is to attribute a high value to it. Yet if art is nothing more than play, this means that we cannot, as we customarily do, draw a distinction between the importance of art and the importance of sport. Sport can be no less 'serious' than art in Gadamer's theory. In itself, of course, this is no refutation. However, combined with the further observation that art, unlike sport, can communicate something, that it can mean something, there does seem to be reason to look further and to ask whether this element of communication might not justify the attribution of greater value to art. One familiar suggestion is that art communicates emotion, and this is the idea we examine next.

Suggested further reading

Advanced introductory reading

Routledge Companion to Aesthetics (second edition), Chapters 5, 20, 24
Oxford Handbook of Aesthetics, Chapters 5, 18

Classic writings

Immanuel Kant, *The Critique of Judgement*, especially sections 1–17
Hans-Georg Gadamer, *The Relevance of the Beautiful*
George Dickie, 'The Myth of the Aesthetic Attitude'

Major contemporary works

Roger Scruton, *Art and Imagination* (1978)
Kendall Walton, *Mimesis as Make-Believe* (1990)

3

Art and emotion

It is frequently said that what matters most in art is emotion, both the feeling of the artist and the emotional impact of a work on its audience. If pleasure is a commonplace explanation of the value of art, expression of emotion is the commonplace view of its nature. This is a view to which we can usefully give the label 'expressivism'. This distinguishes it from a closely similar term 'expressionism', a name widely used for a school of painting based on the principle that painters ought to express emotion in their pictures. The two terms and the ideas they invoke are obviously connected, but expressivism is a theory that applies to art in general, and not merely to the visual arts. It is a view closely allied with nineteenth-century Romanticism – the belief that true art is inspired by feeling – and the extensive influence of Romanticism well into the twentieth century explains, at least in part, the widespread acceptance of aesthetic expressivism. In this chapter, the connection that expressivism makes between art and emotion will be explored, first in what might be called an everyday version, and then in the more sophisticated version that is to be found in R. G. Collingwood's *Principles of Art*. In both cases, the crucial question will be taken to be: can the appeal to emotion explain what is valuable and important about art?

Tolstoy and everyday expressivism

Not infrequently, great artists theorize about their work. This is unsurprising, but what is more surprising is that even the greatest of creative artists can take a very simple-minded view of art. One of the best-known instances of this is Leo Tolstoy, the Russian literary giant. As well as his many novels, Tolstoy wrote a short book called *What is Art?* and in it the everyday conception of expressivism is set out with striking naiveté.

> Art is a human activity consisting in this, that one man consciously by means of certain external signs, hands on to others feelings he has

> lived through, and that others are infected by these feelings and also experience them.
>
> (Tolstoy in Neill and Ridley 1995: 511)

In these few words, Tolstoy captures a picture of artistic activity that is very widely shared: artists are people inspired by an experience of deep emotion, and they use their skill with words, or paint, or music, or marble, or movement, to embody that emotion in a work of art. The mark of its successful embodiment is that it stimulates the same emotion in its audience. It is in this way that artists may be said to communicate emotional experience.

This picture of the relation between artist and audience is often just taken for granted. Even more famously than Tolstoy, the poet Wordsworth (in the Preface to his *Lyrical Ballads*) held that 'Poetry is the spontaneous overflow of powerful feeling', and it is not unusual to hear this quoted as a statement of the obvious. Yet, we do not have to think very long about this view before serious difficulties arise. Many of these were lucidly catalogued by the American philosopher John Hospers in an essay entitled 'The Concept of Artistic Expression' and again, at greater length, in Alan Tormey's *The Concept of Expression*. They can be listed as follows.

First, in attributing the origins of artistic production to emotional experience we appear to be determining *a priori* – by definition – what can only be determined *a posteriori* – by experience and investigation, namely the causal conditions under which works of art come to be. That is to say, the expression theory seems to assert *in advance of* considering any facts that emotional experience caused Shakespeare, Haydn, Leonardo, Christopher Wren and countless other artists to create in the way that they did. Of course, in response to this objection of assertion in advance of the facts, the doctrine espoused by Tolstoy and Wordsworth could be construed as a purely factual one – the origin of artworks has always been found to be emotion. But on this interpretation it appears to be empirically false; many celebrated artists have expressly denied that emotion lay at the heart of their work.

Second, by focusing upon the *origins* of a work as the criterion by which it is to be normatively classified as 'Art', the expressivist theory seems to involve a version of what is called the 'genetic fallacy'. This is the fallacy of assessing the merits (more usually the demerits) of something by referring to its cause. Hospers puts the point in this way:

> Even if all artists did in fact go through the process described by the expression theory, and even if nobody but artists did this, would it be true to say that the work of art was a good one because the artist in creating it, went through this or that series of experiences in plying his medium? Once the issue is put thus baldly, I cannot believe that anyone could easily reply in the affirmative; it seems much too plain that

> the merits of a work of art must be judged by what we find in the work of art, quite regardless of the conditions under which the work of art came into being.
>
> (Hospers 1969: 147)

Third, in looking for an originating emotion we appear to be ignoring the difference between simple and complex works of art. There are indeed cases where the attribution of an overriding emotion to a work of art is quite plausible. For example, Gustav Mahler's *Songs of a Wayfarer* (for which Mahler wrote both words and music) is easily thought of as the outpouring of emotion, and it is not difficult to identify a single emotion that each song expresses. But this sort of attribution is much less plausible when it comes to complex cases. In a complex work with a great array of characters in a variety of relationships – the range of emotions and attitudes represented is so wide that it is impossible to say that any one is the emotion that the work expresses. What emotion lies at the heart of, or is expressed by, novels such as George Eliot's *Middlemarch* or Thackeray's *Vanity Fair*?

This question is not easy to answer, but this does not mean that it is unanswerable. It might be claimed with some plausibility (to change the example) that Joseph Conrad's *Nostromo* is an expression of his deep pessimism. Since it is a novel with a complex plot and a wide range of disparate characters, if this is plausible it must be possible to regard a complex work of art as the expression of a single emotion. However, the change of example is significant. The fact that the question is reasonably easy to answer in the case of *Nostromo* does not make it any easier to answer with respect to *Middlemarch*. Moreover, as *Nostromo* is probably exceptional it is doubtful if we can give any easy answer for nearly every major work of art.

Consider Shakespeare's tragedies. It might be thought that these are works primarily expressing one emotion – jealousy in the case of *Othello*, for example. But if Othello (the character) symbolizes jealousy, Iago equally symbolizes malice. Which is *the* emotion of the play? In any case, the point of calling them tragedies is to focus attention not on their emotional content, but on the structure of their events. There is usually a high degree of emotion represented in a tragedy, but the tragic element, properly so called, is to be found in the interplay of character and event. In Sophocles' classical tragedy – *Oedipus the King* – it is forces beyond his control that makes Oedipus, despite his best efforts, bring plague on the city of Thebes. When it turns out that it is he who has killed his father, the horror he feels, so powerfully expressed by Sophocles, is the outcome of the tragedy, not its source, or its meaning.

So too with other art forms. The impact of Romanticism, especially in composition, can distort our perception of music and lead us to suppose that the expression of emotion is the key to music. But Romantic music is not the paradigm of all music. In a toccata and fugue by J. S. Bach, for example, it is structure that is important, and the complexity has more to do with mathematics than emotion. On the surface at any rate, this is true of nearly all Baroque music. Yet it would be absurd to dismiss it as valueless, or of less artistic merit, just because it is not Romantic.

Fourth, doubts can be raised about the emotional content, not merely of specific works of art, but of *forms* of art. It is easy to find plausible examples of emotional expression in poetry, opera and the theatre. But is it plausible to suggest that works of architecture express emotion? It seems obvious that Edvard Munch's famous painting *The Scream* has depression as its subject matter, but this gives us no reason whatever to extend expressivism to the abstract painting of Piet Mondrian (though there is a school known as 'abstract expressionism'). And, despite the influence of Romanticism, there are arguments against the idea that music without words expresses emotion, a topic to be taken up again in Chapter 5.

Hospers' doubts about expressivism have gained such currency that they are sometimes regarded as little more than preliminaries to the real issues. But even if they could be laid aside, there are further difficulties. How is emotion supposed to be embodied in a work of art, exactly? It is clearly a requirement of the expressivist theory that it must be embodied in some way or other. This is because for any given work, it could be true *both* that its creation arose from an emotional experience, *and* that it drew an emotional response from the audience, while at the same time being *false* that emotion was the content of the work. For instance, imagine that a singer past his prime, and somewhat despondent because he feels his powers failing, tries again to sing with the sort of vigorous jollity for which his performances were previously admired. He fails, however, and his failure causes his admirers to be equally despondent, saddened to hear how feeble his talents have become. But the song he has chosen to sing is not a sad one. So it must be the case, if expressivism is to be true, that emotion is to be found not merely in the artist and in the audience, but also in the work itself. Yet, if we say, in this case, that though the singer and the audience were feeling sad, but the song was feeling happy, this seems unintelligible. A song can't feel anything. In what sense then is happiness present, when the singer and the audience are sad?

In reply, the proponent of expressivism might draw a distinction between 'being an expression of happiness' and 'being expressive of happiness'. The song does not *express* anyone's happiness. How could it, since all the people are sad? But it is *expressive of* happiness in general. This is an important distinction that we will examine more closely in a subsequent section. For the moment, however, we can note that drawing it constitutes a major modification to the everyday version of expressivism, because it implies that artworks can be described in emotional language, without being directly connected to anyone's emotion. This is a major modification to Tolstoy's account of art and emotion.

We have found an important gap in expressivism's conception of the relation between artist and artwork. But there are also problems in the role that the Tolstoyan story assigns to the audience. Is it true that we are guilty of a failure of appreciation if at the end of Mahler's songs we are not filled with *Weltschmerz* (world-weariness)? Must we grieve to the degree that Leontes does in *A Winter's Tale* if we are to understand the remorse that follows his jealousy? Must we in fact feel jealous ourselves during the first part of the play? The answer to these questions is obvious – No. If it does not seem obvious, this is because we are misled into generalizing from two cases – sadness and fear. It is often true that sad and solemn poetry tends to induce sadness (though not always). It is certainly the case that horror and fear can be induced in an audience by films and plays. The shower scene in Alfred Hitchcock's *Psycho* is one of the most famous examples; John Ford's play *'Tis Pity She's a Whore*, when Giovanni appears holding a human heart and covered in blood, is another. Once we generalize from sadness and fear, however, to all the other emotions – jealousy, despair, romantic love, hatred, patriotism, contempt, spite, and so on – expressivism's account of an audience's involvement becomes completely implausible. Perhaps it is true that anyone completely untouched by a nostalgic work cannot really be said to have appreciated it. But can we only be said to understand and appreciate a portrayal of racist loathing if we have felt slightly racist ourselves? Even in the relatively simple case of gaiety, expressivism seems to fail because it is jokes that induce laughter in audiences and readers, rather than actors on stage being amused by them, or episodes in novels that describe people laughing. What this example makes plain is that the successful portrayal of an emotion in a work of art does not depend on generating the same emotion in the audience.

It might be replied that art has to have impact, and an artwork that aims at a portrayal of any of these emotions, even those of a violent or evil nature, has to count as a failure if it leaves an audience as uncomprehending as before. In fact, this reply signals another important move away from the naive expressivism Tolstoy describes. It invokes the idea that a work of art should alter our *understanding* of emotion, but not that it does so by making us *feel* it. Understanding often generates sympathy, and so it can be true that those who come to a better understanding of an emotion come to feel differently about it. This change in feeling, though, is brought about through the intermediary of the understanding; it is not induced directly.

Aristotle and *katharsis*

So far we have seen that the everyday version of expressivism is too simplistic as a description of the relation between art and emotion. It is also inadequate as an explanation of the value of art. Even if art making was an outpouring of emotion and art appreciation a reciprocal experience of the emotion outpoured, there is this further question. What is so good about the outpouring of emotion?

One suggestion appeals to the idea of 'katharsis' or purging. This is the theory that by arousing emotions in us and giving us objects upon which to vent them, the artist purges us of emotional disturbances that might otherwise erupt inconveniently in ordinary life. The concept of katharsis can be found in both Plato and Aristotle, but it is with Aristotle that it is especially associated. In the *Poetics*, an imperfect text of some lectures on tragedy and epic poetry, Aristotle advances the view that their value derives at least in part from their ability to focus the audience's feeling of fear and pity in a way that relieves them of these feelings. Furthermore, it does so harmlessly, in the sense that the feelings are purged without the necessity of the negative actions that normally accompany them.

It should be observed straight away that Aristotle cannot be said to have a general theory along these lines. First, the *Poetics* is not a work about art, but only two forms of it – tragedy and epic poetry, although Greek tragedy included music. Second, it is incomplete. We know about, but do not possess, a second volume on comedy, and perhaps Aristotle had something quite different to say about it. Third, the word 'katharsis' only appears twice. Of course, there is nothing to stop us generalizing where Aristotle did not, and expanding upon his suggestive remarks. The key element to generalize is the idea that the value of art lies in the contribution it makes to our mental or psychological well-being. Art enables us to rid ourselves of emotions that would otherwise be disruptive or destructive by providing us with imaginary rather than real objects to vent those emotions on.

The considerable appeal of this idea, especially in the twentieth century, has relied heavily on what is in fact a very questionable conception of the emotional life of human beings. This is sometimes called (dismissively) the 'pressure cooker theory' of emotions, and its critics point out that emotions are not a set of forces confined within the human heart. Such an idea pre-dates modern psychology and continues to trade on the ancient doctrine of 'humours'. According to this doctrine, love is to be found in the heart, anger is the blood boiling, literally, and hatred is produced by bile in the spleen. We continue to use these metaphors, but have long ago abandoned the theory that underlies them. Why then would we try to continue with Aristotle's conception of katharsis, which was framed in a world where something like the doctrine of 'humours' was thought to be true?

But let us ignore these important reservations, and suppose that there is some more sophisticated version of the idea that art can relieve us of emotions that would otherwise spill over into ordinary life. Even if there is some truth in this, it cannot unequivocally explain the value of art, since it works two ways. If art can purge us of harmful emotions, it can purge us of beneficial ones as well. Thanks to art we don't hate or hurt as many people as we might, but we don't help as many either. Once relieved of my pity by actors in the theatre, I am less likely to pity the people in the Oxfam posters I pass on my way home. The net effect of katharsis, in short, is neutral as far as the purging of emotion goes.

An alternative to katharsis is arousal, though the two are often combined (and even confused). On this view, art is to be valued not (or not only) for relieving us of emotion, but for stimulating emotional experiences within us. In the previous section, of course, we encountered some serious objections to making emotional response on the part of an audience a key feature of art. Even if such objections could be overcome there is reason to wonder why, taken in isolation, there is something to be valued in the arousal of emotion. If by the skilful use of language someone proves highly effective in arousing race hatred in her audience, this does not seem to warrant admiration of her performance or emulation of her style.

Amongst the most successful uses of pictures, actions and words for the arousal of emotion is pornography. It is plainly the purpose of pornography to arouse a specific emotion – lust – in its audience. The fact that it does so, however, does not either make it art or give us reason to value it. This is partly for the same reason as the racism example; arousing lust in people can have negative consequences. But more important for present purposes is the fact that lust can be powerfully aroused by the crudest of methods. When Penguin published D. H. Lawrence's novel *Lady Chatterly's Lover*, a court case ensued because, the prosecution alleged, the novel was pornographic. The defence called witnesses to testify to its being art. What was at issue, however, was not whether the novel contained scenes likely to stimulate lustful thoughts and feelings, but whether it did so in a seriously artistic way. The crucial question about artworks is not whether they arouse emotion, but how they do this, if they do. Their value lies in the *way* this is done, not in the mere fact of its *being* done.

Expression and imagination

A major part of Hospers' argument against expressivism is that it attributes states of mind to artists when it has neither evidence nor reason to do so. In this connection he remarks that 'Shakespeare could hardly have gone through the experiences of Hamlet, Macbeth, Iago, Cleopatra, Lear, Goneril, Prospero and Coriolanus in one lifetime, but what difference does this make as long as he could present us with a series of vivid, powerful, convincing characterizations?' (Hospers 1969: 149). The point is that what matters is not Shakespeare's experience, but his imagination. It does not matter whether Shakespeare ever felt rage and frustration like Lear's; it only matters whether the character of Lear convincingly portrays it.

Behind this thought lies the most damaging objection to expressivism. It not only ignores the value of imagination; it actually eliminates it. Tolstoy's picture – to repeat – is one in which the artist undergoes an emotional experience of some kind and uses an artistic medium to communicate this emotion. He here captures an important aspect of nineteenth-century Romanticism, which emphasized within this picture the importance of sincerity. An artist's first duty is to be true to his or her own feelings. The mark of great art is the honesty and depth of feeling that it expresses. One consequence of this is that pretended feeling is to be deplored. From such a point of view it is shocking to discover that John Donne composed his immensely powerful poem of grief, *The First Anniversary* (1611), on 'the occasion of the untimely death of Mistress Elizabeth Drury' as a means of currying favour with her influential family. The sentiments he expresses in it he could not possibly have felt, since he never knew her.

Now the implications of this example point in two directions. For Romanticism, plainly, the historical fact must diminish the poem. Donne was insincere. On the other hand, it is equally reasonable to applaud Donne for being able to give such powerful expression to grief when he himself had not felt anything like it. Very few of us can give convincing expression to things we have never felt. The great thing about artists, it might be said, is that the fertility of their imaginations enables them to overcome this limitation.

Now as the example of Donne illustrates, it is a strange consequence of expressivism that it denies aesthetic value to imagination. If expressivism is true, then an artist is really a psychological reporter, simply recording and relaying fact about internal feeling. But if this truly were the case, the artist's activity would have nothing creative about it. It is in the *absence* of feeling that imagination is called for, and imagination is the mark of artistic creativity. The trouble is that expressivism cannot accommodate this kind of creativity.

Croce and 'intuition'

The account of art and emotion that Tolstoy appears to subscribe to, and which I have called 'everyday' because it is so widely believed, has been shown to be defective on several counts. However, the idea that there is some special connection between art and emotion can be founded on a philosophically more sophisticated analysis. One such analysis is to be found in the work of the highly influential twentieth-century theorist of art – the Italian philosopher Benedetto Croce. The clearest statement of Croce's view appears in an essay entitled 'What is Art?' Its title is undoubtedly a self-conscious reference to Tolstoy's book of the same name and some commentators have held that by choosing the same title Croce wanted to indicate just how different his view was from that of Tolstoy. But it is not altogether easy to see just where this difference might lie. According to Croce, and in words that have become the defining slogan for his theory of art, art is essentially *intuition* and

> what lends coherence and unity to intuition is intense feeling. Intuition is truly such because it expresses an intense feeling and can arise only when the latter is its source and base. Not idea but intense feeling is what confers upon art the ethereal lightness of the symbol.
>
> (Croce 1965: 25)

This is expressed in more philosophical language than the passage from Tolstoy quoted above, but it says something very similar. The most striking difference is the absence of any reference to art's effect upon the audience, a feature of expressivism to which we will return.

When Croce says 'Art is intuition' what does he mean and why does he say it? In answering these questions it is best not to start with the first. The term 'intuition' has not caught on widely in art theory, and its everyday meaning is unhelpful. But it is sufficient if we take it, for the moment, to be simply a marker for whatever it is that is special and distinctive about art. Croce, along with many other theorists, is primarily interested in pinning down the distinctively aesthetic. Accordingly his method is what theologians in another context call the *via negativa*, the method of determining the nature of something by making clear what it is *not*.

Croce's first distinction is between art and physical fact. This may seem an odd contrast to draw, but it reflects the inherently plausible claim that art cannot be identified with its physical embodiment; there is more to a painting than pigments on canvas, and it is in this 'more' that the real painting lies. Second, Croce denies that art has anything 'utilitarian' about it. Again this captures a common thought. A painting might prove useful, as an investment perhaps, but this usefulness would be quite tangential to its aesthetic value, and someone who regarded it solely as an investment would have no interest in it 'as art'.

Most people accept this distinction, but Croce adds the further contention that being productive of pleasure is also a utilitarian end, and hence to be discounted. Here, more people would be inclined to disagree, since they see art as intrinsically connected with pleasure. Croce, however, points out that if we also agree (as the arguments of Chapter 1 showed) that the fact that a thing gives pleasure is insufficient to make it art, we must invoke a distinguishing and distinctive 'aesthetic pleasure', and hence still require an explanation of what marks off 'the aesthetic' (the topic we examined at length in Chapter 2).

The next thing that art is not is 'a moral act'. 'Art', says Croce, 'does not originate from an act of will.' This is because while it makes sense to say that an artistic image or portrayal can be *of* something morally praiseworthy or blameworthy, it makes no sense to say that the image is *itself* either of these things. To try to do so would be 'just as valid as to judge a square moral or a triangle immoral' (p. 13).

Finally, and most importantly, Croce wishes to deny that art 'has the character of conceptual knowledge'. It is here that the meaning of the term 'intuition' becomes somewhat clearer. Conceptual knowledge (and under this label we may include philosophy, history and science) is founded upon a distinction between reality and unreality, so that it must compare its hypotheses with 'the world out there'. 'In contrast, intuition refers precisely to the lack of distinction between reality and unreality – to the image itself – with its purely ideal status as mere image' (p. 14). The idea is (and once again this has a natural plausibility) that a work of art, unlike a scientific theory say, is sufficient unto itself; to understand its meaning and value we need only look at the work itself and can ignore the world beyond the work. Whether it represents that world in a lifelike way (*à la* Courbet and the Realists) or grossly distorts it (like Dali and the Surrealists) is irrelevant to its aesthetic worth, which is apprehended without mediation – hence the language of 'intuition'. Art is 'non-logical'.

So much for the *via negativa*. Art is not physical, utilitarian, moral or productive of knowledge. What then does this leave? One approach to this question asks about the value of art. If artistic images are not constrained by external reality, practical value or a moral purpose, what makes them more than idle fancies? Or as Croce puts it 'what function belongs properly to the pure image in the life of the spirit?' (p. 21). The answer stated briefly is that properly artistic images are 'symbols'.

> Art is symbol, all symbol, that is all significant. But symbol of what? Signifying what? Intuition is truly artistic, is truly intuition and not a chaotic accumulation of images, only when it has a vital principle which animates it and makes for its complete unity.
>
> (Croce 1965: 23)

And so we arrive at the doctrine quoted at the start – 'intense feeling is what confers upon art the ethereal lightness of the symbol'. In short, the images of art proper are symbolic expressions of feeling.

How good are these arguments of Croce's? The considerable support his view has attracted derives, I think, from the plausibility of two elements in his *via negativa* – that art is essentially non-physical and non-utilitarian. That is to say, it seems evidently wrong to identify a picture, say, with the physical constituents used to embody it, or to locate its significance and value in its usefulness. On their own, of course, these insights do not constitute a conclusive proof of the expressivist contention that art is essentially linked to feeling. Moreover, it is not hard to show that at least the theory Croce advances is no less vulnerable to the objections Hospers brings against expressivism than is Tolstoy's simple assertion. What Croce's account of the matter does show, however, is that expressivism does not have to rest on either bald assertion or gut feeling; there is a philosophical case to be made for it. So instead of rehearsing the Hospers-type objections already considered, then, we should look instead for a version of expressivism that draws on the sophistication of Croce while at the same time avoiding the more obvious objections. We find just such a version in R. G. Collingwood's *The Principles of Art.*

Collingwood's expressivism

Collingwood's version of expressivism is expressly based on both an admiration for Croce's aesthetic and an awareness of the defects to which everyday expressivism is prone. In *The Principles of Art*, he repudiates most of the features of the everyday version of expressivism. Art, in his view, is not concerned with the arousal of emotion at all. Indeed he draws a sharp distinction between art proper, and the use of art to arouse feelings and emotions. One instance of this is the use of art for purposes of amusement or entertainment, something already considered in Chapter 1. Another is the arousal of emotion with an eye to bringing about practical effects. Perhaps a little oddly, Collingwood calls this 'art as magic'. The sort of thing he has in mind is the way that A. C. Benson's poem 'Land of Hope and Glory' set to music by Elgar is often used at political rallies to rouse patriotic feeling (though Collingwood's own example is not this but the poems of Rudyard Kipling).

Neither of these is art proper, because they use the media of art (paint, poetry, music and so on) as *means*. Art can be used in this way of course – in advertising and propaganda for example; when it is, it is reduced to a kind of technology or craft, a device for doing something else that need not be in any way artistic. If emotional stimulation is the sum of what art has to offer, art can be replaced by other forms of magic and amusement without significant loss. The value of a craft, a means to an end, resides entirely in its products, so that other means to the same end will do just as well. Computer graphics programs can replace cartographers, for example, so if the artists were craftsmen like cartographers, in principle they too could be dispensed with. It is a presupposition of Collingwood's philosophy of art that the nature and value of art has to be explained in a way that makes it of unique value. Without cartography the world is a poorer place only so long as there is not some other technique for producing good maps. Without art the world would be a poorer place, and nothing could make good the loss.

The simple version of expressivism, then, is mistaken in the emphasis it lays on emotional stimulation. This is just one important mistake. Another is its supposition that the relevant emotion is one that pre-exists the work of art and is to be found independently in the life of the artist. That is to say, Collingwood thinks it is wrong to imagine that a work of art is merely the translation into paint, music or words of an emotional experience the artist has had before ever the work of creation has begun. According to Collingwood, the original emotion is nothing more than an indeterminate 'psychic disturbance'. This indefinite experience is gradually identified and refined in the process of creating the work until the artist can recognize it as the emotion it is. An example might be a general uneasiness that is gradually identified as anger, rather than, say, anxiety. It is also wrong to suppose that even this vague 'psychic disturbance' must be temporally prior to artistic activity. The activity of feeling and the activity of creating, though 'not identical . . . are connected in such a way that . . . each is conditional upon the other' (Collingwood 1938: 304), which is to say that neither can be isolated or identified without the other. In other words, we can only identify the emotion when it has come to realization through the work of art.

Towards the end of *The Principles of Art* Collingwood adapts to his own use the terminology of 'impressions and ideas' made famous by David Hume. An 'impression' is a sense experience of any kind – a sound, a sight, a smell – and an 'idea' is a concept which has intellectual but not sensual content. According to Collingwood, each act of imagination has an impression, or sensuous experience, at its base, which by mental activity is converted into an idea. 'Every imaginative experience is a sensuous experience raised to the imaginative level by an act of consciousness' (Collingwood 1938: 306). He means by this that the sensual and emotional experience contained in a work of art is not 'raw' felt experience, but experience mediated by the thought and imagination of the artist.

A major objection to naive expressivism, we saw, is its inability to accommodate the importance of imagination. In Collingwood's aesthetic, by contrast, imagination plays a central role. In fact, art proper as he describes it has two equally important elements, expression and imagination. It is by imaginative construction that the artist transforms vague and uncertain emotion into an articulate expression. The process of artistic creation is thus not a matter of making external what already exists internally, which is how the simple model construes it, but a process of imaginative discovery. And since the psychic disturbance with which it begins is the artist's, art is a process of *self*-discovery. Herein, in fact, lies it peculiar value – self-knowledge.

> Art is not a luxury, and bad art is not a thing we can afford to tolerate. To know ourselves is the foundation of all life that develops beyond the mere psychical level of experience. . . . Every utterance and every gesture that each one of us makes is a work of art. It is important to each one of us that in making them, however much he deceives others, he should not deceive himself. If he deceives himself in this matter, he has sown in himself a seed which, unless he roots it up again, may grow into any kind of wickedness, any kind of mental disease, any kind of

> stupidity and folly and insanity. Bad art, the corrupt consciousness, is the true *radix malorum* [root of evil].
>
> (Collingwood 1938: 284–5)

This is a striking panegyric to the value of art, and attributes very great importance to it. Two thoughts spring to mind, however. If 'every utterance and every gesture' is a work of art, this, on the face of it, leaves 'art' in the more restricted sense in which it is commonly understood, of no special interest or value; anyone and everyone is an artist. Furthermore, if the end of art is self-knowledge, knowledge of our own emotional states, artistic creation seems to be of consequence only to its creator and art becomes a form of introspection. The implication of both points is that we no longer seem to have any reason to devote special attention to a Leonardo or a Shakespeare. Their works are not unique expressions of emotion and, in any case, as such, they are primarily of value to the artists themselves.

Both these inferences are natural, but nonetheless mistaken. Collingwood is aware that his account of art and the artist may easily be construed in this way, and as a result he devotes a whole chapter to the relation between artist and community. In it he argues that it is not 'what *I* feel' that the artist identifies and articulates, but 'what *we* feel'.

> The artist's business is to express emotions; and the only emotions he can express are those which he feels, namely his own. . . . If he attaches any importance to the judgement of his audience, it can only be because he thinks that the emotions he has tried to express are . . . shared by his audience. . . . In other words he undertakes his artistic labour not as a personal effort on his own private behalf, but as a public labour on behalf of the community to which he belongs.
>
> (Collingwood 1938: 314–15)

To this extent Collingwood shares Kant's supposition of a *sensus communis*, and it is for this reason that art is socially important. It is not merely artists, but the whole community of which they are a part, that come to self-knowledge in their work. This is why 'Art is the community's medicine for the worst disease of mind, the corruption of consciousness' (Collingwood 1938: 336). Second, it is wrong to think that the work of art consists in a material object – a painting or a book. This is not because some works of art are not obviously material at all – a dance for instance – though that is an important objection, but because, being acts of imagination, works of art must be recreated in the minds of their audience. This claim has sometimes been interpreted in rather startling ways – as though it implied that art is all in the mind. But Collingwood is making the point that since, for instance, the same poem can appear in many different books, and the same piece of music can be played at different times and on different instruments, the work of art cannot be identified with its physical manifestation. It can only be said to exist if it exists in the active apprehension of a work by an audience. Collingwood expressly rejects any conception of audience as passive spectator: 'Art is not contemplation, it is action' (Collingwood 1938: 332), and the function of the audience is 'not a merely receptive one, but collaborative' (Collingwood 1938: 324). This is one of the very few points in which he concurs with Gadamer, whose theory otherwise he must regard as mistaking art proper for art as amusement.

Expression vs expressiveness

The Principles of Art advances beyond the commonplace version of expressivism. Even so, there is reason to inquire more closely into how far Collingwood really overcomes its defects. At least one of the objections set out earlier – the difficulty of attributing an emotion or even a set of emotions to many works and some forms of art – is no less an objection to Collingwood's theory, despite its sophistication. But let us leave that difficulty aside, because there *are* substantial objections to the Tolstoyan view which Collingwood's theory can be made to answer. It is clear, for instance, that his version of expressivism does not attribute to artists' independent, identifiable emotional states of which their art is the expression. What it attributes (if anything) is an undifferentiated 'psychic disturbance', and we can only take an interest in this in so far as it is realized in the work of art. This is why Collingwood thinks art criticism must be centred on the work rather than the artist. Whereas the commonplace version invites us to scrutinize the artist's history and psychology, Collingwood is scathing about criticism that has been reduced to nothing more than grubbing around for historical titbits about painters and poets.

Still, if there is no way the emotion of an artist expressed in the work can be specified or even apprehended independently of that work, what reason is there to call the work an expression of emotion? Why reason back from the work to the artist's emotions at all? And if, with Collingwood, we acknowledge that what we find in a work of art is 'wholly and entirely imaginative' (Collingwood 1938: 306), why not conclude that the emotion presented to us is presented indifferently as to ownership? It is not *anyone's* and hence not the artist's. This is the line of thought that leads the eminent English literary critic Helen Gardner, in a slightly different context, to reject similar reasoning about Shakespeare's religious beliefs:

> No other dramatist shows, I think, such imaginative response to the quintessentially Christian concept of forgiveness, or gives such memorable expression to it. But . . . one cannot argue from this [to any conclusion about Shakespeare's own religious beliefs]. Shakespeare is our greatest poet of human nature, and all we can say is that if his

> play requires that a character should speak as a Christian he enters imaginatively into Christian experience and feeling with characteristic understanding and sympathy.
>
> (Gardner 1983: 72; brackets added)

The point can be generalized. Emrys Jones, another critic, writes, 'Shakespeare's wholehearted submission to the principle of rhetorical dialectic – his willingness to lend a voice of the utmost eloquence to every point of view – is his dramatic secret' (Jones 1978: 15).

It is worth observing that this 'apersonal' view of poetic imagination is not open to refutation by appealing to the 'depth' of the emotion to be found in a work. Depth of this sort can just as plausibly be construed as evidence of the imaginative power revealed in the work, as it can be taken to be evidence of the poet's having sincerely felt the emotion in question.

There is much to be said for making the imaginative treatment of emotion, rather than the personal expression of feeling, the hallmark of art, and it has important consequences for expressivism. Collingwood argues that a specific emotion cannot be attributed to the artist independently of the work, and that imaginative power is an indispensable part of the artist's endeavour. This implies that the artist's peculiar gift is not a special capacity to *feel*, but a special capacity to *imagine*. To accept this view of art, however, Collingwood must abandon an important element of expressivism, one to which he holds throughout, namely, that 'the artist's business is to express emotions; and the only emotions he can express are those which he feels, . . . his own'.

In a similar fashion, the audience's emotional experience also ceases to be important once we examine Collingwood's expressivism closely. The everyday version, it will be recalled, holds that emotion is transmitted from artist to audience by being aroused in the audience. Collingwood argues vigorously that to try to arouse emotion through the medium of art is a profound mistake. Nevertheless, given that the artist's expression of emotion is itself an experience of emotion, and given further that audience participation is a collaborative realization of that experience on the part of both artist and audience, it seems to follow that the artist's emotion is aroused in the audience. In order to avoid this apparently inevitable conclusion, Collingwood must argue that the audience's collaborative activity, like the artist's own, is 'wholly and entirely imaginative'. It follows that what anyone actually feels on reading a poem or watching a play is as wholly irrelevant to a proper appreciation of it as the psychological history of the author. If imagination rather than feeling is what matters, it is as much a mistake to try to determine the merits of a work of art by audience 'reaction' as it is to judge the work on the author's 'sincerity'.

To understand this point, we have to return to the distinction mentioned earlier between 'being an expression of' and 'being expressive of'. Some writers sympathetic to expressivism have argued that the errors in the everyday theory arise from a confusion between the two. 'Being an expression of emotion' implies that there is someone whose expression it is. 'Being expressive of' does not imply any possessor, either artist or audience. For instance, someone can cry 'Aahh' in pain. This is an expression, but being largely inarticulate is not expressive. Later when the pain is gone, it might be described as 'climbing to a crescendo' before the cry. This is expressive of the pain but not an expression of it since the pain is now gone.

Holding this distinction clearly in mind we can see that it is possible to apprehend the peculiar appropriateness of the manner in which an emotion is expressed by a work, without falling into any false 'psychologism' about how the artist or the audience must feel. In short, art can be *expressive of* an emotion, *without* being *an expression of* that emotion. A simple illustration of the point is this. Those who write verses for birthday, sympathy and other sorts of cards compose lines which are not an expression of what they themselves are feeling, but which are expressive of the relevant emotion, to be called into use whenever anyone happens to have a use for them.

The question now arises as to whether anything properly called expressivism can survive the drawing of this important distinction. Why is a work's being expressive of emotion something to be valued? Recall Collingwood's explanation of the value of art. In acting imaginatively upon emotion we bring it to consciousness, discover thereby what our consciousness contains and come to self-knowledge. Now if the artist is not expressing emotion, but formulating expressive utterances or representations of it, and if the audience does not need to feel any of these emotions, but only appreciate their imaginative expression, the value of the work cannot consist in self-knowledge on the part of either artist or audience. Since the emotions represented are not *our* emotions, we come to no further knowledge of ourselves by apprehending them. But this still leaves unclear why we should give special attention to the artist's expressive utterances, and why value is to be attached to them.

One response is to say that these are *possible* emotions, with which we may empathize. This is certainly correct, but by implication it divorces audience apprehension from emotion completely because even where the work in question can indeed be said to be expressive of an emotion, it does not matter how the audience *feels* at all, but only what it comes to understand. Collingwood himself seems to make this move in places. He sometimes describes the activity of both artist and audience in the language of cognition rather than feeling. For instance, he imagines a (rightminded) painter declaring, 'One paints a thing in order to see it.' And '[o]nly a person who paints well', he goes on to tell us, 'can see well; and conversely . . . only a person who sees well can paint well'. 'Seeing' here 'refers not to sensation but to awareness. It means noticing what you see. And further: this act of awareness includes the noticing of much that is not visual'

(Collingwood 1938: 303–4). On the face of it, this alternative analysis implies that the value of art lies not in its helping us to come to a proper apprehension of personal (or even communal) feeling but in a greater awareness of the world around us. And this remains the obvious interpretation even where, as in expressive representations, 'the world around us' is the world of emotional experience.

We might put the matter this way. The expressivist theory of art, at least in its commonplace version, holds that where a specific emotion can be assigned to a work of art, the work is an expression of that emotion and appreciation of the work consists in feeling that emotion oneself. If now we say that the work is not *an expression of* but rather is *expressive of* the emotion, appreciating would consist in being brought to a heightened awareness of that emotion. Being brought to a heightened awareness of an emotion does not imply undergoing any element of that emotion. For example, I may to date be unaware of the intensity of your jealousy until one day you hit upon an especially expressive word or gesture. Then I appreciate your jealousy, but I do not share any of it. The expressiveness of your gesture can make me aware of your emotional state without engendering any emotion whatever in me. It is equally possible of course that my being made aware of your feelings gives rise to an emotional response on my part, but any such emotion has only a causal connection with yours; my having the emotion is neither a necessary nor a sufficient condition of being made aware how you feel. Conversely, your gesture may arouse an emotion in me (fear, perhaps) and yet I remain unaware of your true emotional state. What these various possibilities show is that the initially innocent substitution of 'being expressive of' for 'being an expression of' brings about the abandonment of expressivism. If the function of art is to heighten awareness, the special connection between art and emotion that all forms of expressivism try to articulate and maintain is broken. Art can heighten our awareness of many other things in human experience besides emotion.

Collingwood would probably not deny this. His most extended discussion of a work of art is of T. S. Eliot's *The Waste Land*, and what he says about it is instructive, for he sees Eliot as presenting us with a prophetic vision:

> This poem is not in the least amusing. Nor is it in the least magical. The reader who expects it to be satire, or an entertaining description of vices, is as disappointed with it as the reader who expects it to be propaganda, or an exhortation to get up and do something. To the annoyance of both parties, it contains no indictments and no proposals. To the amateurs of literature, brought up on the idea of poetry as a genteel amusement, the thing is an affront. To the little neo-Kiplings who think of poetry as an incitement to political virtue, it is even worse; for it describes an evil where no one and nothing is to blame, an evil not curable by shooting capitalists or destroying

> a social system, a disease which has so eaten into civilization that political remedies are about as useful as poulticing a cancer.
>
> (Collingwood 1938: 335)

In *The Waste Land* Eliot shows 'what poetry can be', for 'the artist must prophesy not in the sense that he foretells things to come but in the sense that he tells his audience, at risk of their displeasure, the secrets of their own hearts' (Collingwood 1938: 336).

What should concern us here is not the justice of Collingwood's estimate of Eliot's achievement but the language he uses to make that estimate. Eliot is said to *describe*, not *feel*, the present evil, and to *tell* the audience, not *express* for it, the secrets of their hearts. This is the language of cognition, not emotion. Collingwood would claim that the world the artist describes and tells his audience about is the world *as charged with emotion* and that talk of 'describing' and 'prophesying' is compatible with expressivism provided we do not confuse consciousness and intellect. It is the intellect, in Collingwood's view, which orders and organizes the data of consciousness and establishes relations between them. But it is art which brings those data to consciousness in the first place by realizing the sensuous impact of experience in a form in which consciousness can grasp it. This is the fundamental function of language in Collingwood's theory, and that is why he regards every linguistic act as a work of art. The works for which the term 'art' is usually reserved exercise this function to perfection or at least to the highest degree. There are thus two kinds of truth: the truth of intellect and the truth of consciousness. Science, broadly understood, is concerned with the former; it is pure thought and has no experiential element. Art on the other hand is concerned with consciousness, because real experience is essential to it. We must actually hear music or see a play in person. It is not enough merely to be told about (or even understand) their structure or content. (Collingwood struggles, it seems to me, with the relation between philosophy and poetry, and in the end appears to conclude that they are the same.) Thus art may indeed be said to describe, to tell, to prophesy, but since its concern is with the truth of consciousness none of this removes it from the world of emotional experience – or so Collingwood contends.

Two observations are pertinent here. First, if one is to speak of truth in art, some such distinction as Collingwood draws is needed, because whatever we learn from artists is not what we learn from the laboratory. This is a subject that will be dealt with more fully in the next chapter on 'Art and understanding'. Second, at the same time, it is only a lingering loyalty to expressivism that causes Collingwood to go on speaking of emotion in the way he does. For 'emotion' at the end of his analysis means nothing more than sensuous experience brought to consciousness. Even this formulation might be misleading, for the term 'sensuous' is not to be understood as feeling or perceiving in any very restricted sense – it includes such things as feelings of anxiety or loneliness, and a sense of mystery or foreboding – and he allows that the bringing of an experience to consciousness (i.e. being made aware of it) is intimately tied to having that experience.

Collingwood is here employing a notion of 'experience' which is to be found in other philosophers in the British Idealist tradition. Now to say that artists give voice to experience, where this is to be contrasted with scientific (or other) abstraction from experience, may well be correct. But to insist that this is *emotional* experience is to extend the idea of emotion until it loses its usefulness. Collingwood says the world of the artist is charged with emotion. He also says that the artist's province is sensuous experience brought to consciousness. He might as easily say that artists are concerned with the imaginative presentation of immediate experience rather than the construction of abstract reflections upon experience. This last formulation leaves out all mention of emotion and the sensuous, and if it does so without significant loss, this is proof that Collingwood's theory of art has been driven beyond expressivism.

That there *is* no significant loss in describing art and the aesthetic in terms of imagination rather than feeling is shown by the following example. Consider this poem:

> I see His blood upon the rose
> And in the stars the glory of His eyes.
> His body gleams amid eternal snows,
> His tears fall from the skies.
>
> All pathways by His feet are trod,
> His strong heart stirs the everbeating sea,
> His crown of thorns is twined with every thorn,
> His Cross is every tree.

These are the first and last stanzas of the poem 'Christ in Creation' by Joseph Plunkett, an Irish nationalist revolutionary executed by the British for his part in the Easter uprising of 1916. A literary critic would no doubt find faults in this poem (though I have omitted the weakest verse), but it is one of the plainest examples I have found of a work which could be said to reveal a *charged* world. Another might be Salvador Dali's picture 'Christ of St John of the Cross', which could be thought of as a pictorial equivalent of Plunkett's poem. But what is either work charged with? The obvious answer is 'charged with religious significance'. In acknowledgement of important differences between science and the arts, we can agree that 'significance' here cannot mean just what it means in the case of an experimental result or a statistical correlation that is said to be 'significant'. To this degree Collingwood is correct in supposing that the contents of mind fall into different kinds. But what does it add if we say 'charged with religious *emotion*'? We could mean by this the kind of experience that leads people to talk in religious ways; either this means no more than 'religious significance' already says, or it refers us to a specific emotional state: Rudolf Otto's *mysterium tremens*, fear of the divine and awe in its presence for instance. If we suppose that the poem is an expression of such a feeling, we face all the objections rehearsed against Tolstoy's expressivism; the poem itself gives us no evidence for supposing that Plunkett was in such an emotional state or that we will (or have to) feel awe or dread in reading and appreciating it.

What we get from the poem, whatever the state of mind in writing it, is an idea of how a Christian belief in the omnipresence of Christ can enter one's experience of the natural world. If this is conveyed, it is not by the transference of an emotional state but by the point-by-point correlation between *traditionally important* features of Christ – his body and blood for instance – and the features of the natural world. (This is why the blood and the rose, the crown and the thorns, the cross and the tree are strong correlations, while the eyes and the stars (and those in the omitted verse) are weak.) To call the world that Plunkett describes 'charged with religious emotion' is harmless enough, provided we understand that this means nothing more than an invocation of the world of religion.

It may be said, of course, that the poem ought to allow us not merely to observe that world, but to enter it imaginatively and thereby in some measure come to understand it. This is correct, but the key words here are imagination and understanding, and the key question is: what kind of understanding is this? If with Collingwood we want to talk about a distinctive truth in art we need to ask not how art stimulates emotion, but how it directs consciousness. This is to ask about art as a source of understanding, and it shows that feeling or emotion, ordinarily understood, has been left behind. So the next topic for us to consider is art as understanding.

Summary

We have now explored three accounts of the value that is to be found in art in simpler and more sophisticated versions. It is true that works of art can give pleasure and can be valued precisely because they give pleasure. To value them solely for this reason, however, is to give art no special status over other sources of pleasure and to rank its importance rather lower on the scale of human values than most writers on art are apt to do. The Kantian aesthetic is an advance on aesthetic hedonism because by taking beauty as its focal point it identifies a pleasurable experience that seems to have some special relation to art, and a more universal character than simple personal desire and satisfaction. Nevertheless, it too has difficulty in explicating the special value of art because it seems to accommodate anything to which 'the aesthetic attitude' can be applied and not just deliberately created artworks. Gadamer's adaptation of the Kantian aesthetic – that art is to be understood as a form of play – overcomes something of this difficulty and not only explains the relation between artist and audience more plausibly but makes possible the distinction between the serious and the lighthearted in art. Its drawback, however, is that it cannot explain the difference between art and play in the literal sense, i.e. sport. Its failure in this respect is chiefly important because there is a striking difference between all sport and some art, namely, that art, unlike sport, can have content. It can *be about* something. Any theory of the value of art that cannot account for this important difference must be regarded to some degree as defective.

The question of content led us on to expressivism – the idea that the content of art is emotion. A number of problems confront this contention. First, it is difficult to locate the expression of emotion in a relevant and plausible account of the relation between artist, work and audience. Second, an emphasis on the artist's emotion robs artistic activity of what would seem to make it special, namely imagination. Third, there is nothing valuable in the expression or arousal of emotion for its own sake. Collingwood offers us a more sophisticated version of expressivism which has the great merit of avoiding what we might call 'psychologism', and which proves as good an explanation of the value of art as one could want. But on closer investigation we saw that these advantages are won through an effective abandonment of the essentials of expressivism. What we end up with, if we follow Collingwood's theory to its logical conclusion, is an account of art as a distinctive way of understanding human experience. And this is the suggestion that is to be investigated in the chapter that follows.

Suggested further reading

Advanced introductory reading

Routledge Companion to Aesthetics (second edition), Chapters 2, 34
Oxford Handbook of Aesthetics, Chapters 11, 24

Classic writings

Aristotle, *Poetics*
Tolstoy, *What is Art?*, especially Chapters XV and XVI
Croce, *Art as Intuition*
Collingwood, *The Principles of Art*

Major contemporary works

Matt Matravers, *Art and Emotion* (1998)
Alan Tormey, *The Concept of Expression* (1971)

4

Art and understanding

The preceding three chapters have shown that while pleasure, beauty and the expression of emotion are all closely connected with art and with our experience of it, none of them can on its own explain the special value of great art. This brings us to another important explanation – that the value of art is neither hedonic, aesthetic nor emotive, but *cognitive*, that is to say, valuable as a source of knowledge and understanding.

Hegel, art and mind

Among the great philosophers, it is Kant's successor G. W. F. Hegel (1770–1831) who is most closely identified with a cognitive theory of art. It is Hegel, too, who was first to see the philosophical importance of distinguishing between the fine arts and giving different accounts of their nature and value. The five fine arts he distinguished are music, painting, sculpture, poetry and architecture, but he also offers us a philosophical account of art in general, and advances the interesting and provocative thesis that art in the modern period is effectively dead.

Hegel is a notoriously difficult thinker. In both the original German texts of his lectures and in their English translation, the prose is obscure and hard to follow. Furthermore, he meant his philosophy to be encyclopaedic, a large interconnected understanding of the human mind and its history that cannot simply be broken up into distinct philosophies dealing with art or science or morality. What Hegel has to say about art is highly original and genuinely insightful, but these insights are easier to appreciate in non-Hegelian language. And despite his encyclopaedic ambitions, the basic ideas at work in Hegel's philosophy of art can be formulated in abstraction from the overall context of Hegel's philosophy. This chapter will explore his general idea that art is a form of knowledge, and the remainder of the book will follow a large part of his philosophical programme by exploring the distinctive nature and value of the different art forms, and raising a question about modern art. But, apart from a short overview in this section, we will not be very much concerned with the details of his philosophy.

Unlike other thinkers, who have viewed philosophy as the intellectual study of a set of universal and timeless problems, Hegel's conception of philosophy is that of a progressive development over time in which the human mind comes to understand itself more adequately. In this development, there are phases which have both temporal and social locations. Human understanding differs in time and place, and later times in different places come to a better, fuller understanding. At the heart of this development is religion, or the life of the spirit, because the essential nature of human beings is subjective not objective. Each human being is a physical object, certainly, but within each such object is a thinking, willing and feeling subject. Human knowledge and understanding is really self-knowledge, because it is knowledge of the animating spirit that constitutes our true nature. Such knowledge makes us free. It frees us from the causal and biological forces by which the physical and animal natures we share with other things in the world are bound.

The course of human development is marked in part by a progressive development from art through religion to philosophy. All three are modes of knowledge and understanding, art no less than philosophy. Whereas philosophy is a conceptual grasp of the truth, art is the presentation and apprehension of truth by means of sensuous images, that is images of sight and sound and touch. But these three modes of understanding are developmentally related such that art is a more primitive mode than religion and religion finds its ultimate expression in philosophy. This pattern of 'art–religion–philosophy' is found not only in the grand sweep of human history as a whole, but within the history of successive cultures. Each has its art, its religion and its philosophy, and in each, one of them is dominant. As Hegel's general picture would lead us to expect, dominance shifts along the same path from art through religion to philosophy. In the ancient world of the Greeks the dominant aspect of culture was art. In medieval Christendom it was religion, and in the 'modern' world (which is to say the world of Hegel himself) it is philosophy. Art, religion and philosophy are found in all three epochs, but with the shifting emphasis from first to third comes a development in art forms. Hegel ranks the five fine arts in a hierarchy of value. At the bottom is architecture, then sculpture, then painting, then music, and finally, at the top, poetry.

This hierarchical estimation is based on the degree to which the various forms of art are to be characterized by a diminishing dependence on the material. Works of architecture such as the Parthenon are huge constructions out of large and heavy materials, and their form has entirely to do with space. Sculpture – Michelangelo's *David*, for example – also uses materials like stone, but it uses them to depict human beings and thus embodies the human spirit. Painting goes a step further and creates its own imaginary space; a medium of two dimensions successfully portrays three. Music abandons space altogether and restricts itself to time. Poetry, finally, is even more 'spiritual' since it realizes itself in a medium that transcends the material altogether. What a poem 'says' is independent even of the natural language in which it is composed, at least in the case of those poems that can be translated without significant loss into other languages.

It is now possible to see why Hegel thought that the modern period would witness 'the end of art'. The development of human understanding consists in a move from art to philosophy. The development of art forms consists in a move from the most material (architecture) to the least (poetry). These two developments lead to a convergence. Poetry completes the movement from the perceptual to the conceptual that is to be found within art; philosophy completes the movement within human understanding to a wholly conceptual form of knowledge; the result is that art is finally sublimated in philosophy. Thus the very process by which human understanding advances in the end leaves art no role; what art had to teach earlier worlds it taught in the forms of architecture, sculpture and painting, but what poetry has to teach the modern world is more clearly stated and more clearly understood through the medium of philosophical thought.

Some commentators interpret Hegel as holding that it is in every era, rather than in history as a whole, that art becomes exhausted, so that what is at issue is not the end of art but the need for its perpetual renewal. The topic of the 'end of art', however, is one we will suspend for the moment and return to in Chapter 10. The principal question here is whether Hegel has laid the foundations for a plausible account of art as knowledge.

Art, science and knowledge

Hegel's philosophy constitutes a remarkable distillation and organization of ideas that were very widely held in his time, but in several respects it is at odds with contemporary ways of thinking. In particular, the belief in progress that underlies it, the pre-eminence he gives to philosophy, and the relative downgrading of art are all likely to be contested or even rejected. Yet we can find counterparts that fit the general picture quite well if we replace philosophy with science. It is widely believed that science is the most successful form of human knowledge, that it has developed progressively (though not uniformly) from its early beginnings in ancient Greece, and that its latest development – evolutionary biology – holds the key to understanding human nature itself. In short, the contemporary world attributes to science the sort of importance Hegel attributed to philosophy, and holds moreover that though art, and especially literature, has things to teach us about human nature, the truth of what it has to say must ultimately be borne out by the sciences of biology and psychology.

In a similar fashion Hegel believed that the knowledge embodied in works of art would have to be vindicated by philosophy. The important point to stress, however, is that he held the value of art to be cognitive (conveying knowledge) rather than hedonic (giving pleasure), or aesthetic (being beautiful) or expressive (communicating feeling). It is this cognitive view of art that this chapter aims to explore. Hegel is not its only exponent. Among twentieth-century philosophers of art the best-known exponent of this belief is the American philosopher Nelson Goodman. In an influential book entitled *Ways of World Making*, he says:

> [a] major thesis of this book is that the arts must be taken no less seriously than the sciences as modes of discovery, creation, and enlargement of knowledge in the broad sense of advancement of the understanding.
>
> (Goodman 1968: 102)

It is easy to assert that art has cognitive value, much harder to explain how. Exactly what do we learn from artworks and how do we learn it? Some answers to these questions are not good enough. For example, while it is true that information of all sorts can be picked up from novels and paintings, this does not show art to be a special or distinctive mode of knowledge because information we pick up in this way is quite coincidental to its being a work of art that contains it; we might as easily pick up the same information from a newspaper or a history book. In other words, the information is not an integral part of the work.

A more integral relationship between artistry and understanding is to be found in works of art (of which there are many) that contain self-conscious statements and elaborations of doctrines and propositions. Artists often have 'messages' that they hope and intend to convey. However, even in this sort of case, we need to distinguish between art and propaganda. The aim of propaganda is to secure belief and assent, and it can do so by the skilful use of the media characteristic of art – words, visual images, film sequences, narrative structures and music. Each of these media can be highly effective in asserting and affirming a message. Good propaganda makes a powerful impact, and its power in this respect is often a function of its artistry.

If art is genuinely to enhance understanding it must do more than merely assert in the way propaganda does. Like the other modes of knowledge and inquiry – history, science, philosophy – it must secure belief through reflective understanding. The interesting version of the claim that we learn from art, then, is not that paintings, poems, plays, and so on, can provide us with information or propagate opinions in attractive ways, but that they advance our understanding by enhancing or enriching it.

To make good this claim about art would increase its importance in most people's estimation. This is because greater status is generally attributed to knowledge and understanding than to entertainment, or even to the expression of emotion. This greater status explains in part the high standing in which science is normally held. This is why Goodman draws the parallel he does and, as we shall see, if art can be construed as a source of understanding, this would explain some of the evaluations that were noted in previous chapters – the discrimination between light and serious art, for example, or the ranking of great artists above successful entertainers.

In the opinion of some philosophers, however, all attempts to lend art cognitive value are to be resisted on the grounds that they sell out 'art proper' to the contemporary obsession with 'science' as the only thing that matters. In an essay entitled 'Must Art Tell the Truth?', first published in 1969 and reprinted several times, Douglas Morgan argues that aesthetic cognitivism forces art into a mould it will not fit, and at the same time grossly overestimates the value of knowledge.

> To the question of the 'cognitive significance of art' I say directly that although many works in many arts can and do give us knowledge of many kinds, nonetheless if this knowledge were the key and limit to the love of art, the world would be even sorrier than it now is.
>
> (Morgan, in Hospers 1969: 231)

In Morgan's view we feel driven to explain the value of art in terms of 'cognitive significance', first because of an 'absurd alternative which offers us only a specious choice between art as a diversion or decoration, on the one hand, or as a peculiar second rate substitute for true-blue empirical knowledge on the other', and second, because of a slavish adulation of science characteristic of contemporary Western thinking but not true of other periods and places.

Morgan rightly alerts us to a real danger – that a preference for explaining the value of art in cognitive terms is no more than a cultural prejudice. He is also right to resist reductionism in art. Any explanation of the value of art must preserve its *distinctive* value and there is a danger that a cognitivist theory of art will lead us to think that the *truths* conveyed are central, while the *art* which conveys them is secondary. To underline this second point Morgan asks, 'Who among us would exchange the Sistine Ceiling for one more monograph, however learned, on Pauline theology?' in confident expectation of what answer any serious theory of art must give.

However, even if the answer to this question *is* plain – no one wants to replace the Sistine Ceiling with a scholarly treatise, and no adequate theory of art can allow such replacements – this does not in fact establish as much as we might think. The Sistine Ceiling cannot be replaced by a theological monograph just as the relevant chapter of a history book cannot replace Shakespeare's *Henry V*. But Shakespeare can still enhance our understanding of English history (perhaps by 'bringing it alive'), and the Sistine Ceiling can reveal something about the theology of Saint Paul.

Morgan bases his criticism on the tacit supposition that 'cognitive significance' must be spelled out in terms of true propositions, that is singular or universal claims about how things are. In fact his central argument against the cognitivist theory relies very heavily upon this idea. The argument that employs it runs as follows: (1) Any truth must be contradictable; (2) One artwork cannot contradict another; (3) Therefore, no artwork can as such be the assertion of a truth. This is a good argument, but only if the cognitive theory of art is expressed in terms of truths. This is not how Goodman expresses it. In the passage quoted at the start of this section he speaks of art in terms of *understanding* rather than truth. While Morgan is right to say that it must be logically possible for any truth-claiming proposition to be contradictable, this is not the case for an understanding or interpretation. An *understanding* of something can be described as defective or inadequate, but it is odd to speak of its being negated.

This is a point that holds as much for science as it does for art. The physical mechanics developed by Sir Isaac Newton, for example, offers a quite different (and as it turned out) more fruitful understanding of the laws of matter in motion than does the physics of Aristotle, which dominated science before Newton. Einstein, in due course, offered an understanding of the same phenomena that overcame the inadequacies of Newton. But it just is not true that Newton *contradicted* Aristotle, or Einstein contradicted Newton in the way that (say) one witness at a trial might contradict another. The difference went deeper than this. If this is true of physics, then the fact that artworks cannot contradict each other does not set art apart from science in the way that Morgan thinks it does.

Morgan follows up his general attack on aesthetic cognitivism by examining its application to specific art forms – music, painting and literature. He thinks it patently absurd that the importance of the 'breathless final moment when you have moved intensively with heart and mind through a quartet of Brahms or Bartok' should be explained by 'what you learned' from the experience.

> Learning, knowledge, and truth are no less valuable because their value is not exclusive. There really are other goods in the world than these, and there really is no need to confect such bogus kinds of truth as poetic or pictorial or musical truth for works of art to wear as certificates of legitimacy.
>
> (*ibid*. p. 232)

The weakness of this line of argument lies in the fact that no one, not even cognitive theorists of art, need deny it. Pleasure – what Morgan dismissively speaks of as 'diversion or decoration' – is certainly *a* value. But as Chapter 1 revealed, a normative philosophy of art that appeals to it as the *principal* value in art cannot explain the significance of art satisfactorily. Pleasure explains the value of *some* art, but not all art, and especially not the greatest art, because degrees of pleasure cannot be correlated with distinctions between the light and the serious in art.

Morgan's objection can be defused by the observation that a cognitive theory of art need not claim that *everything* commonly called a 'work of art' is valuable because of its ability to enhance our understanding. This would obviously be false. Some works are to be treasured because of their beauty, and others are to be valued chiefly for the pleasure they give us. The principal advantage of a cognitive theory is that it can explain what makes major works of art especially important and why the works of great masters are to be described as lasting *achievements*. Its contention is that though these may indeed be pleasurable or beautiful, this is not where their greatest value lies. An adequate estimation of their significance requires us to use terms like 'illuminating', 'insightful' and 'profound', cognitivist terms that aim to convey their contribution to our understanding of experience.

Actually, Morgan has difficulty resisting this contention altogether. No less than others, he wants to speak of art as enriching us, and when he refers to being 'moved intensively with heart and *mind* through a quartet of Brahms or Bartok' (my emphasis), it is difficult not to give this a cognitivist twist: what else could an intense movement of the mind be, if not something to do with greater understanding? It is precisely the inclination to talk in this and many similar ways that lends plausibility to the thesis that we learn from art. And provided we remember always that it is better regarded as a claim about *understanding* than *truth*, nothing said so far shows that we cannot learn from art.

Aesthetic cognitivism, for and against

For all that, cognitivism about art has relatively few supporters among philosophers and artists, and many fewer than expressivism can command. This is partly because it undoubtedly faces several important difficulties that any plausible version must overcome, and in this section we will examine those difficulties. First, though, it is worth reviewing the *advantages* cognitivism enjoys as an explanation of the value and importance of serious art, because these show that there is good reason to persist in trying to solve the problems that it encounters.

First, the thesis that serious art enriches human understanding makes it relatively easy to explain the place of art in our culture. Its role and status in the curricula of schools and universities is immediately intelligible. If the purpose of education is to develop the mind and increase understanding, and if art is one form of this understanding, then the study of art clearly has a proper place in education. That far greater amounts of private time and public resources are devoted to it than to amusement or even sport is no more puzzling than that science is given far more attention than entertainment.

Second, in contrast to the other explanations of the value of art we have considered, cognitivism can make sense of someone's undertaking a lifetime commitment to art, as a painter, poet or composer. In contrast to aesthetic hedonism, which must interpret such commitment as an excessive pursuit of pleasure, or aestheticism which makes it an effete absorption with beautiful objects, or expressivism which must interpret it as an unintelligible wallowing in emotional turbulence, dedication to art, like dedication to science, can be understood as an application to the Delphic ideal – 'Man, know thyself!'

Third, if art truly is a source of understanding, this enables us to explain the way we discriminate between works of art. In just the same way that one experiment or mathematical proof is judged more important than another in the light of its contribution to wider intellectual concerns, so an artwork can intelligibly be said to be more profound if it enhances our understanding, and dismissed as relatively trivial to the extent that it does not.

Fourth, aesthetic cognitivism also enables us to make sense of an important range of critical vocabulary. If art can deepen our understanding, then we can describe a work as the *exploration* of a theme without any conceptual or linguistic oddity. Aesthetic cognitivism makes good sense of the concepts of insight and profundity, superficiality and distortion in art, and makes it appropriate to describe the portrayal of something as convincing or unconvincing, terms that we also apply to arguments and evidence. People often speak of works of art in precisely these ways. If cognitivism (in contrast to hedonism, aestheticism and expressivism) can make sense of them, this is a substantial point in its favour.

So much for cognitivism's advantages. But what of its difficulties? Two of these are crucial. *How* does art advance our understanding, and *of what* does it do this? To appreciate the force of these questions it is instructive to examine in greater detail Goodman's original parallel between art and science. We should understand 'science' here as a general term, not confined to the natural sciences but encompassing a wide variety of intellectual inquiries: history, mathematics, economics and philosophy as well as astronomy, physics, chemistry, biology and so on. In all these disciplines, one way of characterizing inquiry is as a *movement* of thought, from an established basis to a potential conclusion via a logic or set of rules of reasoning. In empirical studies the established base is usually referred to as 'evidence', and the conclusion described as an hypothesis or a theory. In mathematics the equivalents to these are axioms and theorems, in philosophy they are premises and conclusions. While the terminology differs from subject to subject, all these forms of intellectual inquiry share the same basic structure: the aspiration is to demonstrate an incontestable progression from base to terminus. Since an established terminus becomes the base for the next chain of reasoning, successful inquiry moves progressively from terminus to terminus.

There are important differences between disciplines, of course, but the abstract analysis of the structure of intellectual inquiry allows us to pose some important difficulties in the idea of art as a source of understanding. The first of these is this. In a work of art there is no obvious parallel to the distinction between evidence and hypothesis (or premises and conclusion) and no obvious equivalent to the 'logic' of inquiry.

One important reason for this disanalogy is that works of art are works of imagination. This means that, unlike scientific or historical theories, they have no referent outside themselves. For example: Arnold Bennett's novel *Lord Raingo* tells the story of an imaginary British politician in the early years of the twentieth century, and in the spirit of aesthetic cognitivism we might say that it is a study of the interplay of principle and ambition in politics. The same could be said of Stephen Oates's biography of Abraham Lincoln, *With Malice Toward None*. But to speak of both of them as *studies* disguises an important difference between the two. Oates is constrained in what he writes by history, by what actually happened. He presents us with the facts of Lincoln's career, and he leads us by argument and interpretation to take a certain view of his political life. Bennett, by contrast, has no such constraint; he can make the 'facts' of Raingo's career whatever he wishes. Lincoln was assassinated. Oates has no choice about the fact that his life and career ended in this. In Bennett's novel Raingo's career suffers a serious setback. Just when his political fortunes begin to rise again, he contracts an illness that proves fatal. That his life and career should end in this way is a matter wholly of Bennett's choosing. The 'logic' of historical inquiry, the rules by which it proceeds, are in part laid down by the need to present evidence and adhere to the facts. Imaginative storytelling seems to be free from such constraint.

The same point can be made about other forms of art. John Constable's famous picture of Salisbury Cathedral is a wonderful painting, and it is not diminished in any way if as a matter of fact the cathedral cannot be seen from the angle chosen by Constable, and never could have been. A similar misrepresentation in a guidebook would be a serious fault. What seems to follow is this: novelists and painters may indeed direct our thoughts, but they can hardly be said to direct them to reality. Their activity is not the recording of fact but the exercise of imagination.

Aesthetic cognitivism's second major difficulty is this. In history, philosophy or natural science, the evidence, argument and ideas that are employed, the hypotheses advanced and the conclusions defended can almost always be expressed or explained in widely differing ways. There can be better and less good formulations and some explanations are better than others, but for the most part the precise wording of an argument or hypothesis is not essential to its truth and validity. It appears that the contrary is true in art. Every artwork is unique. What it says or shows cannot be said or shown in any other form without significant loss of content. This is a consequence of the unity of form and content in art, long held to be one of its peculiarities. Works of art are 'organic unities', that is entities so integrated that the alteration of a single item within them – a line in a poem, a colour in a painting, a harmonic progression in a piece of music – changes the whole work. This view of art has been current among philosophers since the time of Aristotle, and while it may be an exaggeration to say that not a single feature of an artwork can be altered without altering the whole, it is certainly true that *form* has an importance in art that it does not have in science, history or philosophy.

One consequence of the unity of form and content in art is this: artistic insight and understanding cannot be paraphrased. As soon as we attempt to paraphrase the content of a work, that is, to present it in some other form, we destroy it. Thus the 'truth' in art eludes us every time we try to explain it. Pope's well-known line, 'What oft was thought but ne'er so well express'd', as a description of poetry sounds plausible, but even in the case of poetry can't be right, because the thought or idea in a poem cannot be expressed adequately except in the way the poet has expressed it. In art, the work itself is indispensable, and no paraphrase or summary, however good, can be a substitute for this. I can say to someone, 'Explain Einstein's theory of special relativity to me', and what they go on to say could be said in several different ways. But whatever Shakespeare has to tell me can only be told as Shakespeare told it.

Why does this matter? It matters because it raises a question about how truth in art is to be tested, refined and revised. If I can't state what Shakespeare had to say in any other way than the way he stated it, how can I put it to the test? And if his statement is unique, how could some other statement improve upon it, as a scientific hypothesis might improve upon its forerunners? If such things are impossible, what reason have we for applying the ideas of truth and understanding to art at all? It can certainly be *claimed* that there is a great truth to be learned from art and that art reveals great insight into aspects of human experience. But if it is the sort of truth that cannot be independently stated, and cannot therefore be tested outside the artistic medium, we have no reason to think of it as a truth in the ordinary sense at all.

The appeal to a special sort of 'poetic' truth will not overcome this difficulty. Even if we accept that not all truth is the sort of truth that is established by empirical observation and the experimental method, it is still easy to see that science provides us with a method of arriving at truth and understanding, whether we call it 'scientific' truth or not. The problem for aesthetic cognitivism is not that there is no such thing as 'poetic' truth, but that it is difficult to see what equivalents there are to observation and experiment in art.

A third important difficulty is particularity in art. Cognition, Aristotle tells us, trades in universals. He means that the acquisition of knowledge always involves a measure of abstraction and generalization. We learn not about this or that vine leaf but about vine leaves; we learn not about this person here and now but about the person in general. It is this that allows us to transcend the peculiarities of the particular case and arrive at a greater understanding of a range of cases. Even where it is inappropriate to speak of anything as precise as a theory, there is nonetheless always a measure of abstraction, however modest this may be. Now, though Aristotle himself thought that art deals in universals and thus is something akin to philosophy, this is not a view that is easy to accept. Paintings, plays, sculptures and so on portray, and must portray, particulars. We can say of a face in a painting that it is the face of human distress, but the fact remains that it is *a* face, and how we move from a judgement about this one face to a judgement about humanity seems something of a mystery.

Some philosophers have tried to get around the difficulty by saying that art is concerned with 'concrete universals'. On the face of it, the curious hybrid 'concrete universal' is more a label for the problem than a solution to it. But in any case, universalizing the particular in art does not seem the right sort of solution. For example, Mr Woodhouse in Jane Austen's *Emma* might be said to be a universal image of 'the valetudinarian' (or hypochondriac), but once we regard him as a 'type' with standardized or generalized character traits and patterns of behaviour mirroring those to be found elsewhere, it seems we move away from the 'concrete', the particularity of her imaginative creation. Austen has portrayed a character not a stereotype, and it is in the creation of characters that her genius is correctly thought to lie.

There are then three major difficulties confronting the theory that art is a form of understanding: (1) Artworks are products of the imagination. How then can they direct us to the truth? (2) Unity of form and content is an ideal in art, but if so, this seems to exclude the possibility of putting the understanding it conveys to the test; (3) Art deals in particulars, understanding in universals. How then can art be a source of understanding?

Imagination and experience

Does the fact that works of art are works of imagination really remove them from a concern with reality? In the history of aesthetics a distinction has traditionally been drawn between imagination and fancy. Fancy is completely free, while imagination operates within constraints. A writer who exhibits both is Charles Dickens. Two chapters of the novel *Dombey and Son* – 'The Wedding' and 'Another Wedding' – exemplify this difference. The first is grimly realistic, the second reassuringly romantic, but both are 'made up'. If we are to mark the difference between realism and romance, the relevant distinction must lie within art, not beyond it. And so it does. Imagination is a mode of realistic depiction, but its realism does not lie in 'mimesis', the mere copying or reflection of facts external to the work. It is hard to say exactly where the realism lies, but enough for present purposes to observe that there is a deep and important difference between imagination and fancy. In several of Dickens's novels (*David Copperfield* is a striking example) the ending is 'too good to be true'. What 'truth' means in this context is difficult to pinpoint, but the description is nonetheless apt. Imagination can be distinguished from fancy or whimsy. It is in fact a deliberative act of mind.

Conversely, to come back to the parallel with science, it is a mistake to think of scientists or historians as passively 'tracking' the truth on the basis of empirical data that simply 'present' themselves unbidden. At every stage, intellectual inquiry employs imagination. Hypotheses in science and history have to be checked against the facts, but scientists also 'float' ideas, engage in guesswork, and follow up lines of thought according to their sense of the problem. All these are acts of imagination. Indeed, the 'facts' may need imaginative treatment before they yield much in the way of a test, and often imagination has to be employed in rooting out the facts in the first place.

To assess the merits of aesthetic cognitivism we need to appreciate both the similarities and differences between art and science, and one way of doing so is to compare a map with a photograph. Maps aim faithfully to represent the landscape whose features they record. Because they aim to do nothing more than this, it might be supposed that map making involves the complete suppression of imagination, the soulless recording of fact. However, geographical features are represented on maps by symbols, and the clarity of the representation, and hence the usefulness of the map, depends upon the imagination with which symbols are devised. Old maps often exemplify the truth of this. The difficulty in reading them arises more from the clumsiness than the unfamiliarity of the symbols they use. Nowadays, map making is largely governed by conventional symbols that are universally agreed. Even here, however, the imagination with which these are employed on the map makes a great difference to its utility. One has only to compare maps constructed for special purposes to see that imagination in the devising of symbols is very important. Yet, the use of imagination does not alter the basic purpose of every map – to represent things as they really are.

Now compare a photograph of a landscape with a representation of the same landscape on a map. This comparison reveals the mistake in Morgan's remark about Pauline theology and the Sistine Ceiling, because, though both the map and the photograph give us knowledge of the landscape, no one supposes that either could replace the other. The map provides information in the form of conventional notation; the photograph lets us see the landscape itself. As in the construction of a map, imagination is involved in the taking of the photograph, at a minimum in the choice of a point of view, which then becomes the point of view of those who look at the photograph. However, imagination can enter into the photograph more deeply than it can into the map making. While maps of the same area can differ precisely according to the purposes for which they are drawn – land-use maps and geological maps for instance – the business of the map maker is always to record information in a neutral way. The photographer can do more than this, and select an angle that will give the landscape a particular focus of interest.

The more imaginative a photographer is, the more he or she is likely to select a point of view from which, left to our own devices, we would never have seen the landscape. The photographer's imagination chooses a point of view and the photograph directs our perception to see what we would not otherwise have seen accordingly. This is why it is right to speak of a photograph's revealing new and hitherto unimagined aspects of a landscape, literally and not just metaphorically. This use of imagination in photography is to be contrasted with something quite different – doctoring the photograph. A photograph of a landscape can be highly imaginative, but not in the way that the celebrated 'photographs' of fairies at the bottom of the garden were. In other words, it is *at one and the same time* a work of imagination and concerned with what is really there.

What the comparison between map and photograph shows is that the sharp contrast between reality and imagination on which the first objection to aesthetic cognitivism depends is not to be so clearly drawn. The second difficulty was this. Where is the 'logic' in art, the process of arriving at the truth that we might test? Perhaps imagination is needed in history and science, but there still seems to be this important difference: a work of inquiry has a structure of reasoning by which it moves from premise to conclusion; a work of art does not. To put the same point another way: history and science and philosophy are disciplines, organized systems of knowledge and not merely collections of isolated facts or propositions. A piece of experimental science, an historical narrative, a philosophical argument does not just confront the mind with fact or hypothesis. It *directs* the mind through a progression of thought. This power to direct the mind is what allows us to call these modes *of understanding*. In contrast, it seems, the best that art can do is to present a point of view. Even writers sympathetic to the idea of truth in art have generally supposed that art merely expresses truth, not that it argues for it. If it does not argue for it, however, it cannot be said to *show* anything, and if it cannot show its audience the truth of what it contains, it can at best be a mode of expression or representation, not of understanding.

This sounds convincing, but is it correct? There are undoubtedly important differences between art making and intellectual inquiry, but to contrast them in just this way is misleading. There is more to the life of the human mind than conceptual thought; the activity of the senses is as much mental as that of intellectual reflection. The contents of my mind are made up of the visible, audible and tactile as well as the intelligible. Now sensual experience, as an aspect of mind, is not a matter of passive seeing and hearing but of active looking and listening. When I look and listen my mind is engaged no less than when I think or calculate. It could be true that works of art, even works of literature, do not direct abstract thought (though there is more to be said about this), and it could also be true that they direct the mind, i.e. perceptions, of the audience. The example of the photograph illustrates this possibility. In looking at a photograph we are *given* a point of view. So too in painting, the painter *determines* how we see the objects in the picture, most obviously at the basic level of perspective. Foreground and background are essential elements of our visual experience, and in a picture it is the painter, not the spectator, who determines what is in the foreground and in the background. When I simply look around, *I* determine what I focus on. In a photograph or a painting this is largely (though obviously never wholly) determined for me by the person who took the photograph or painted the painting.

In this sense we can speak of works of art 'directing the mind'. They do not do this by constructing proofs and assembling evidence or even by the presentation of propositional truths, but there are many examples of the other ways in which they do it. Rhythm in poetry, for instance, is more than a linguistic counterpart to music. By determining how we hear the line, and where the emphasis falls, rhythm can determine what the sense is. Composers, conductors and performers all determine how music is heard, which sound predominates over others both acoustically and harmonically. Architects determine the order in which shapes and materials are seen by those who walk through the buildings they construct. And so on.

How, and with what degree of success, these methods of directing the mind can be used to increase or enrich our understanding is a further question yet to be investigated. The answer to it is unlikely to be the same for different types of art, which is why subsequent chapters will treat the major art forms separately. However, enough has been said to establish the possibility of artistic imagination directing the minds of readers, listeners, audiences, etc., and as yet we have seen no obstacle to the idea that this can be done to the advancement of understanding.

There is still the third difficulty to be overcome – that art deals in particulars, while understanding requires universals. For the moment, however, we will leave this to one side, since the solution to it is better presented at a later stage in the argument, near the end of the section 'Art and the world'.

The objects of imagination

Aesthetic cognitivism must answer two questions: how does art enrich our understanding? And what does it enrich our understanding of? The three difficulties we have been concerned with so far relate to the first of these questions. But the second is no less important: what could artistic understanding be about? What is its object? To tackle this question, consider again the parallel of a photograph and a map. Like the map, the photograph can tell us about a landscape, and a good photograph does so by presenting us with imaginative ways of looking at it. Now an implication of this seems to be that there can be *deceptive* photographs, photographs that give rise to mistaken ideas about the object photographed. If so, this possibility counts against the suggestion that photography *as an art* is a source of understanding because, considered as an object of aesthetic interest, the deceptive character of a photograph is of no consequence. In order to decide whether a photograph is worth exhibiting or not, we do not need to inspect the original subject of the photograph. We need not go beyond the photograph; its aesthetic merits and demerits are wholly within the work itself. Precisely the same point can be made about painting. Perhaps in his paintings Canaletto has disguised the grubbiness of the real Venice he knew, but from the point of view of their aesthetic value, the real Venice is irrelevant.

The irrelevance of the independent subject is one consequence of the view that in art the ideal is unity of form and content. In the imagined photograph what matters is not the accuracy of beliefs about the subject that the photograph generates, but the internal harmony between the subject and the way the photograph, deceptively or not, presents it. In other words, the art lies in the harmony of form and content.

In the same way, in a poem or a play what matters is not the truth or falsehood of the sentiment expressed, but the apt or inapt manner of its expression. Macbeth says,

> Life's but a walking shadow, a poor player
> That struts and frets his life upon the stage
> And then is heard no more.
>
> (*Macbeth*, Act V, Sc. 5, ll24–6)

It is irrelevant to assess the merits of Shakespeare by asking whether life *is* a walking shadow. Anyone who said that life is not as bad as Shakespeare here makes it out to be, would rightly be thought to have made a foolishly irrelevant remark. What matters is whether the lines aptly express despair of the sort Macbeth is imagined as undergoing. As with the examples from photography and painting, the content of Macbeth's speech, the 'message' it conveys, is not in itself of any interest from the aesthetic point of view.

What these examples seem to show is that photographers, poets and painters can direct the mind, but the point of their direction does not make reference to anything beyond the work. And it seems it must be so. Collingwood makes this point in connection with portraiture.

> A portrait . . . is a work of representation. What the patron demands is a good likeness; and that is what the painter aims, and successfully, if he is a competent painter, at producing. It is not a difficult thing to do; and we may reasonably assume that in portraits by great painters such as Raphael, Titian, Velazquez, or Rembrandt it has been done. But, however reasonable the assumption may be, it is an assumption and

> nothing more. The sitters are dead and gone, and we cannot check the likeness for ourselves. If, therefore, the only kind of merit a portrait could have were its likeness to the sitter, we could not possibly distinguish, except where the sitter is still alive and unchanged, between a good portrait and a bad.
>
> (Collingwood 1938: 44)

This argument conclusively refutes the idea that what is valuable in portraiture is what philosophers of art often refer to as *mimesis* (imitation), the ability to produce convincing resemblances. (It is important to distinguish the view of 'art as *mimesis*' from 'representationalism'. The difference will be discussed in Chapter 6.) Collingwood assumes, correctly, that we can tell the difference between good and bad portraits even when we do not know what the sitter looked like. It follows that what matters is not faithful copying of the original. This argument can be generalized to other branches of the arts; we can profitably read Tolstoy's *War and Peace* without knowing whether he has accurately represented the history of the Napoleonic Wars; we can watch Eisenstein's *Oktober* without worrying about the actual course of the Russian Revolution.

Though this line of thought is correct so far as it goes, it tends to be misconstrued. It is true that we ought not to think of Macbeth's speech as a short treatise on despair by Shakespeare. Similarly, we ought not to regard a picture like Gainsborough's portrait of Mr and Mrs Andrewes as a faithful record of the appearance of the couple in question, and we ought not to judge *War and Peace* by its historical accuracy. Nevertheless, it does not follow that these works do not point beyond themselves in any way whatever. While not being chiefly concerned with these or those objects, they may still be related to more general aspects of human experience. Consider the example of Macbeth's speech again. It would be wrong for an audience to focus on the content of what is said instead of the fact that it is the character of Macbeth that is saying it. Still, his speaking these lines at that point in the play adds up to an image that has universal reference. The audience would also be wrong to think of the lines as expressing just one man's mood, rather than being expressive of despair itself. Similarly, though we know nothing about what the originals looked like, it is possible to see in Gainsborough's portrait of the Andrewes, something that they themselves may not have been able to see, a visual image of proprietorship. *War and Peace* is wrongly regarded as a record of the impact the Napoleonic Wars had on Russia, but not wrongly regarded as in part an image of the impact of war in general.

There is of course an important question about what exactly makes the image in any of these examples a convincing one. Since the merits of a work of art can only be looked for within the elements of the work itself, they cannot lie in its correspondence with things that lie beyond it, but must be found in the way those elements unify form and content. However, this does not rule out all possible relations between a work of art and an external reality. Indeed the insistence upon unity of form and content as an artistic ideal may work to the advantage of the idea that art has cognitive value. Truth in art is not simple correspondence between artworks and the things they depict, and accordingly such 'correspondence' cannot enable us to establish a work's artistic merits. But this leaves open the possibility that it is only *after* we have grasped the artistic merits of a work that we are in a position to appreciate its relation to the world of human experience.

Art and the world

What then is this relation? The assumption we have just abandoned – that art can only tell us about the world if it stands in some sort of correspondence relation – supposes we have to be able to look independently at reality and then at art in order to see how well the latter has represented or understood the former. This too is a conceptual picture we should abandon. It is far more profitable to view the relation as the other way around. We first look at art and then, in the light of it, look at reality in order to see it afresh. Sometimes, even, it is thanks to art that we become properly aware of some aspect of experience for the first time. The poet Robert Browning expresses this thought in *Fra Lippo Lippi*:

> . . . nature is complete
> Suppose you reproduce her – (which you can't)
> There's no advantage! You must beat her then,
> For, don't you mark, we're made so that we love
> First when we see them painted, things we have passed
> Perhaps a hundred times nor cared to see;
> And so they are better, painted . . .
>
> (lines 297–303)

Browning's point is that mere replication of 'things out there' is worthless since copying can't improve upon the things it copies. But an original painting can make us really see things that, without it, we have passed a hundred times and scarcely noticed. The idea that artistic excellence is found within a work, in a unity of form and content, is not an objection to aesthetic cognitivism, once we have discarded familiar conceptions of truth as correspondence or resemblance, and begun to think instead about viewing the world through art, rather than checking art against the world.

To appreciate the extent of the alteration in thinking about art that this reversal brings about, more needs to be said about the abstract metaphysical notion of 'the world' that this way of speaking employs. 'The world' in this context is to be understood not as a set of objects, like furniture in a room, but as the generalized content of our experience. 'Experience' too is an abstract term, of course. Though philosophers have often used it in a quasi-technical way, for present purposes we can employ it in a more everyday way.

It is common to speak of people having or lacking experience, and classifying them as experienced and inexperienced. Usually when we use the word experience in this way, we have some specific context in mind – military experience, say, or experience of mountain climbing. But as far as the word itself goes, the contexts in which 'experience' may be used are broad. We may talk of experience in specialized contexts (as in the examples just given), or in a more broadly human connection – experience of pain or fear, of love and bereavement for example. Most broadly of all, we refer to 'sense experience'. Some philosophers have thought that in this last use the sense of the word changes, but if, as we saw earlier, the mental life of a human being is comprised of many different kinds of elements, sense experience is simply on a spectrum.

Using 'experience' in this everyday sense, we can say that the life of a human being (as opposed to a mere organism) is in large part a matter of experience. It is not exclusively so, however, because, if the word 'experience' is not to become too general, we must distinguish it from memory, from imagination, from anticipation of the future and from intellectual abstraction. All of these play important parts in the life of a human being, and each of them may inform experience, but they are not identical with it. In paying attention to what is happening around us and to us, it is these other aspects of mind that help us connect up our experience and make it meaningful by linking past events, present experience, hopes for the future and rationally tested beliefs. For present purposes, of these other aspects of mind it is imagination that holds the greatest interest. Human beings have the ability to manipulate their experience imaginatively, and this is one of the ways in which they can bring it more sharply into focus and find greater significance in it.

The preceding three paragraphs have described in abstract terms something with which we are all very familiar. Much of our everyday experience is made up of encounters with the words and actions and gestures of other people. The meaning of these is not always plain; the same words can indicate anger or upset or anxiety. To interpret other people's behaviour adequately we need imagination. Unimaginative people have a hard time understanding others. A complete lack of imagination is rather rare, but we are not all possessed of imagination to the same degree, any more than we all have equally good memories. Some people are much more sensitive to nuances in speech, appearance and gesture than others. It is this variation that creates a significant role for art and artists.

This role is not confined to the imaginative understanding of others, important though that is. What is in view here is human experience in its widest sense – visual, aural and tactile, as well as practical, emotional and intellectual. The version of aesthetic cognitivism elaborated here is the view that works of art are works of imagination, and that the imagination of the artist can transform our experience by enabling us to see, hear, touch, feel and think it more imaginatively, and thus enrich our understanding of it. It is in this sense that art is a source of understanding. Though quite different, art is a form of understanding to 'be taken no less seriously than the sciences' (to quote Goodman 1968 again).

To appreciate this fully, it is essential to see that the process involves moving from art to experience, not from experience to art. This casts in a different light a third difficulty with aesthetic cognitivism identified earlier, and then set aside. This is the problem that art deals in particulars while understanding deals in universals. The images by which we are confronted in art are always images of particulars. In order to illuminate the experience of anyone and everyone, which art must do if it is to be a genuine source of understanding, we need generality. How then can particular images illuminate universal experience?

We are now in a position to resolve this difficulty. To begin with, as Aristotle himself pointed out, images and characters can be *generalized* images and characters. Breughel's celebrated picture of a country wedding, for example, can depict *a* country wedding, without being the picture of any particular country wedding. It will not alter its subject to discover that the faces and objects collected in it were never assembled together at any one time or even that they never existed. The value of a picture lies not in its supplying an accurate record of an event but in the way it enables us to look at the people, circumstances and relationships in our own experience. The question to be asked of such a work is not, 'Is this how it really was?', but rather, 'Does this make us alive to new aspects of this sort of occasion?'

The same point may be made about the example we used earlier to state the problem, Jane Austen's Mr Woodhouse. How can Mr Woodhouse be construed as a generalized 'image of hypochondria' without becoming a stereotype rather than a character? But once we reverse the relation between art and reality, it becomes apparent that what there is to be learned from Jane Austen in this regard is not to be obtained by seeing in Mr Woodhouse bits of real hypochondriacs, but seeing in real hypochondriacs aspects of Mr Woodhouse. Our experience is not summarized in the character, but illuminated, perhaps awakened by it. It is not so much that Mr Woodhouse is 'true to life' but that life is true to Mr Woodhouse, and the genius of Jane Austen is that she brings us to see just how true to Mr Woodhouse life can be.

Understanding as a norm

We have now seen what it means to hold that art, like science, is an important source of understanding. Once this thesis is understood correctly, the problems philosophers have identified in aesthetic cognitivism can be resolved. However, aesthetic cognitivism – the belief that art can illuminate experience by making us more sensitively aware of what it contains – is much more plausible as a normative than a descriptive doctrine. As a *normative* doctrine it says that the arts have the *capacity* to enhance our understanding of experience, not that all and every work of art does this. It also holds that, when artworks do enrich our understanding of experience, this gives us reason to value them more highly than if they simply gave us pleasure or were beautiful to contemplate. It does not hold (or need not) that this is the *only* reason for valuing works of art.

As a descriptive doctrine aesthetic cognitivism seems to be false. There are indefinitely many paintings, sculptures, poems, pieces of music, stories and plays that have nothing much to say about experience, but which are nonetheless widely regarded as works of art. To insist that they should be denied this title is to abandon description for stipulation. But as a stipulation, aesthetic cognitivism is not very plausible either. Morgan is right to insist that there are values other than truth – pleasure and beauty being two obvious examples. Why should we not continue to value works of art that realize these values? It is sheer dogmatism to insist that we should not.

The discipline of philosophical aesthetics since Kant has been marked by repeated attempts to define art, and the principal candidates will be discussed at length in the final chapter of this book. But definitions of art run the constant danger of dogmatism and stipulation. This is why it is best to regard aesthetic cognitivism as a normative theory, an explanation of the potential value of art, rather than an attempt to set out necessary and sufficient conditions for the classification of works as art. But even with respect to its explanation of art's value, something more needs to be said. The belief that the most significant art is to be valued because it enriches human understanding does not imply that an artwork of which this is true is to be valued for this reason only. There is nothing odd or inconsistent in someone's reading a poem, learning from it, being moved by its sheer beauty and deriving great pleasure from it as well.

Art, then, can realize several different values at the same time, and in fact, in so far as its value is restricted, this can be because those who are skilled in language or music or painting have resolved *not* to employ their art for the most serious purposes. Yet they can still produce much that is to be valued. The comic songwriter Michael Flanders once remarked that while the point of satire is to 'strip away the veneer of half-truth and comforting illusion', the point of his songs was to put it back again. The wit and verbal dexterity shown in his lyrics is good enough reason to value them. Why should we insist on more? Similarly, the hugely amusing comic novelist P. G. Wodehouse thought that the writing of great literature was beyond him. He rightly regarded the stories he wrote as of no profundity whatever, and was aptly described by the playwright Sean O'Casey as 'literature's performing flea'.

Yet Wodehouse had a facility with language and a perceptiveness that is highly enviable. While it would have been absurd to describe him as 'our greatest novelist' it was perfectly intelligible for another writer, Richard Gordon, to describe him as 'our greatest writer'.

It is judgements of this sort that incline people to claim and others to deny that the work of people like Flanders or Wodehouse is art. But once all the relevant facts and distinctions have been set out, this is a dispute about labels and nothing very much turns on it. Whether we call the songs or the books art or not, they are to be valued for certain sorts of reasons and not others. They are not deep and serious, but they were not meant to be. There are no great truths to be learned from them, but they can be clever and entertaining, and even astute. Once all this has been said, there is no point in pressing the further question 'But is it art?'

Cognitivism about art explains how it is possible for some creative works of imagination to be more profound than others, and why this matters. 'Depth' and 'profundity' are often taken to imply that more obvious values such as wit, entertainment and enjoyment in art are to be denigrated or discounted. But this is an unwarranted implication. We can welcome the suggestion that there is more to art than the pleasure without denying that pleasure is sometimes one of the things that makes it valuable. A properly normative theory of art, such as the aesthetic cognitivism elaborated here, is not intended to demarcate 'true art' or 'art proper' to the detriment of 'art' that does not or cannot fit this description. It is meant to explain and justify a range of artistic appraisals, a range that is reflected both in judgements about particular works and in the cultural status accorded to art forms.

A normative theory of art does not imply anything about personal taste. Whether one prefers the novels of D. H. Lawrence to those of P. G. Wodehouse, or thinks more highly of the music of Michael Tippett than Scott Joplin, is not to the point. What the theory explains is why (for example) there is reason to include the works of Lawrence and Tippet in an examinable curriculum, why there is something faintly absurd about writing a doctoral thesis on P. G. Wodehouse (as a few people have done) and why Scott Joplin's music was suitable for an entertaining film like *The Sting*.

An adequate normative theory will also explain why such assessments are not the result of mere social or cultural prejudice. If it is true, as aesthetic cognitivism claims, that some works of art can be said to give us a deeper insight into human nature and the human condition, then to rank them more highly than works of entertainment is no more puzzling than the fact that we attribute greater importance to crucial scientific experiments than to amusing or fascinating tricks that exploit a knowledge of optics or magnetism. Science can be entertaining as well as art; it can require very high levels of expertise; it can have practical uses. But the greatest scientific achievements are those that have made fundamental contributions to human understanding.

Aesthetic cognitivism of the sort espoused by Goodman wants to make precisely the same point about art.

Art and human nature

Despite all that has been said, there might appear to be an important disanalogy between science and art. Scientific understanding has an object – the natural world or physical universe. This is what the scientist's theories are about. But we have yet to state clearly what artistic understanding is about. What is its object? The preceding paragraph gave one answer, namely, human nature and the human condition. Great works of art enable us to understand what it is to be a human being not in the way that physiology, psychology or anthropology do, but by providing images through which our experience may be illuminated.

At this point another possible objection arises. Cultural relativists will argue that concepts of human nature and the human condition are not fixed. 'Human nature', their contention goes, is not one thing for all humans at all times; neither is 'the human condition'. Different cultures understand these ideas differently. Consequently, they are concepts that cannot be given universal content, and so they cannot be construed as boundaries or fixed points of reference, common to all members of the species *Homo sapiens*, that we can aim to know or understand better.

Legal systems are culturally relative, and what counts as art has certainly varied from time to time and place to place. It is questionable, however, whether this sort of relativism can be extended to such fundamental concepts as human nature and the human condition. This is because 'the human condition' is made up of elements at least some of which affect all human beings – susceptibility to cold, hunger and disease, the nature of childbirth, the existence of pain, illness, bereavement and mortality – and the concept 'human nature' can be confined to such things as interest in sexual relations, humour, sorrow, anger, pride and so on. All of these provide the recurrent themes of songs, story telling and depiction in every culture.

Besides, even if we were to agree that any treatment of these themes is always shaped by a specific cultural context, this would not undermine the cognitivist theory of art. For the theory to hold, it is enough that concepts of human nature and the human condition are to be found in some cultures. Then, relative or not, they may in those cultures provide us with the subject matter of artistic understanding. Perhaps it is true that the art of one culture cannot illuminate the experience of people from a wholly different culture, despite their common membership of the same species, but this no more implies that no one is illuminated, than the fact that English cannot be used to communicate with everyone implies that English speakers fail to communicate with each other. We can conclude that the cultural relativist's objection, whether sound or unsound, does not undermine the claim that art can be valued for its illumination of human experience.

It is now time to turn from the general to the specific, and from the possible to the actual. Can the claims of cognitivism be made good with respect to all the different art forms, and can it be shown that cognitive enrichment is an actual and not merely a possible value? Literature seems the easiest case. Almost any major Shakespeare play – *Othello*, *King Lear*, *Henry V* – could be interpreted as providing insight and illumination on the themes of human nature and the human condition, as could novels such as George Eliot's *Middlemarch* and Joseph Conrad's *Lord Jim*. But can it be shown that absolute music (music without words) can illuminate human experience? If it can't, is music less important than literature, to be valued only in terms of pleasure and/or the expression of emotion? And what about architecture? Could the building of a temple or a palace be the construction of an image from which we might learn about the human condition? And if so, an image of what? In any case, do we need to give this explanation of its value when it so obviously has another value, namely, usefulness? The visual arts also seem to generate problems for cognitivism – abstract painting, for instance, does not seem to be composed of images at all. So do the performing arts. Could a dance be about human nature?

These are all important questions. They need to be dealt with at length by the normative theory of art as understanding which this chapter has elaborated. This is why the next five chapters of the book leave behind questions about art in general and examine specific forms of art in some detail.

Summary

In this chapter a version of aesthetic cognitivism has been explained and defended. This is the view that art is most valuable when it serves as a source of understanding, which in principle puts art on a par with science, history and philosophy. There are evident differences between all these modes of understanding, but there are good reasons to hold that art contributes significantly to human understanding. In appreciating how it does this, it is essential to see that works of art do not expound theories, or consist in summaries of facts. They take the form of imaginative creations that can be brought to everyday experience as a way of ordering and illuminating it.

Aesthetic cognitivism explains more successfully than other theories why we do and should attribute to great works of art the value we do. Although there is pleasure to be gained from the arts and beauty to be found in them, and though they are often moving, these features alone cannot explain the value of art at its finest. The idea that we come away from art with a better understanding of human experience is able to make sense of this, but it is unclear whether this explanation of value can be applied to all the arts. So we need now to look in more detail at specific art forms – music, the visual, literary, performing arts and architecture.

Suggested further reading

Advanced introductory reading

Routledge Companion to Aesthetics (second edition), Chapters 15, 23, 26, 32, 33
Oxford Handbook of Aesthetics, Chapters 25, 26, 27

Classic writings

Hegel, *Lecture on Aesthetics*
Schopenhauer, *The World as Will and Representation*
For exposition see *Cambridge Companion to Hegel*, Chapter 11

Major contemporary works

Nelson Goodman, *The Languages of Art* (1968)

5

Music and sonic art

Previous chapters examined the three principal ways in which philosophers have tried to explain the value we attach to art. The most successful of them – aesthetic cognitivism – is to be preferred in part because it can accommodate a wider range of valuations, and explain more satisfactorily both the cultural status generally attributed to art as well as the discriminations we make between the serious and the light in art. Philosophy, however, is a critical discipline and cannot take conventional evaluations simply as given. Even the most widely held opinion can turn out to be faulty in some way once it is subjected to philosophical criticism, and this applies to beliefs about art as much as to moral and religious beliefs. So while established beliefs have much greater weight than mere personal opinions, there has to be a dialectical exchange between them and the critical principles of philosophical thought. Sometimes, as we will see in Chapter 10, philosophy raises very substantial doubts about things that are taken for granted.

There are some facts about art, however, that any explanation of its value has to respect. These are the facts about different art *forms*. Music is a different medium from painting, architecture different from drama, and so on. So different are they, that the value of art is an issue that has to be investigated in a more detailed way in relation to each. The discussion up to this point has been concerned with the respective importance of pleasure, beauty and insight in general, but perhaps some forms of art cannot have all of these values. This is why it is appropriate to move to an examination of five principal art forms – music, the visual arts, literature, the performing arts and architecture – and, in the light of the arguments of the previous three chapters, to ascertain what can be said about their value.

Music and pleasure

There are several reasons for beginning with music. Music alone, sometimes called 'absolute music' (as opposed to music with words – songs, arias, chorales and so on), is indisputably one of the arts, and often regarded as art in its purest form. Consequently, any adequate explanation of the value of art must cover music satisfactorily. Second, absolute music very quickly calls into play the arguments of previous chapters. It seems undeniable, for instance, that absolute music can and does give pleasure; it is often valued for this reason. It is also widely regarded as a powerful vehicle for the expression of emotion. Though it is problematic how and whether music can 'say' anything, many composers and musicians have attributed to it a power to reveal something about human life and experience. (In musical analysis, music for which this claim is made is often called 'programme music' in contrast to absolute music in the strictest sense.)

The aim of this chapter is to explore these three dimensions of music, beginning with pleasure. That music can and does give pleasure is not in doubt. The question is whether this is the only or best explanation of the value we attribute to it because many musicians and music lovers claim to find more in music than simple pleasure. For instance, in a once very influential book significantly entitled *The Language of Music*, Deryck Cooke says this:

> to put it in the contemporary way, [the writer on music] is expected to concentrate entirely on the 'form', which is not regarded as 'saying' anything at all. . . . Instead of responding to music as what it is – the expression of man's deepest self – we tend to regard it more and more as a purely decorative art; and by analysing the great works of musical expression purely as pieces of decoration, we misapprehend their true nature, purpose and value. By regarding form as an end in itself, instead of a means of expression, we make evaluations of composers' achievements which are largely irrelevant and worthless.
>
> (Cooke 1957: 5, brackets added)

People have a tendency to objectify their personal preferences, and elevate their likes and dislikes to a higher level. It could be that when musicians and musicologists like Cooke talk in these terms they are simply expressing a preference because this sort of language is rarely applied to jazz or rock music. Certainly, it is relatively rare for people to speak about music in the high-flown language of Cooke. Nonetheless, in identifying what they like or enjoy about music, the range of terms employed quickly moves beyond simple pleasure. Music is described as 'moving', 'exciting', 'haunting', 'thrilling' and so on, more often described in this way than as 'pleasurable'. More importantly, 'pleasant' and 'nice' can be used in ways that make them more negative than positive. To describe a piece of music as 'pleasant' can be to damn it with faint praise. Even when 'pleasant' or 'enjoyable' are used positively, they seem patently inadequate for pieces of music to which we want to give the greatest praise. No one would describe Beethoven's *Quartets* as 'pleasant' or Mozart's *Requiem* as 'enjoyable'.

However, to note that the vocabulary people use about music is wider than pleasure and enjoyment does not show very much. 'Moving', 'exciting', 'haunting', 'thrilling' are all emotional terms. Why should music not be pleasurable precisely because it moves us emotionally? Actually, this is probably the commonest view of music – that it pleases us deeply by expressing and stimulating our most powerful feelings.

The combination of pleasure and emotion in an explanation of the value of music has considerable plausibility. It seems undoubtedly true that we can derive pleasure from the emotional impact that music has upon us. Nevertheless there are important differences between pieces of music that could not be accommodated in this way. One of the most striking is complexity. A major composition such as Beethoven's *Fifth Symphony* has a great deal more to it than a simple melody like *Greensleeves*, and at least part of the difference lies in the complexity of the music. Beethoven's symphonies have a scope and scale far beyond that of the average popular song. This difference in complexity is of considerable importance in assessing the merits of a piece of music. To handle the huge forces of a symphony orchestra satisfactorily, as both composer and conductor, requires a very great mastery of musical materials. Yet from the point of view of pleasurable feeling, there does not seem any reason to prefer or commend this mastery. Complexity in a piece of music does not in and of itself lead to greater pleasure on the part of the listener. On the contrary, since a large-scale piece of music demands a great deal from us in the way of sustained and concentrated attention, simple harmonies with a catchy tune are usually much easier to enjoy.

Complexity is an intrinsic feature of music. By locating the principal value of music in the pleasure it gives, we shift attention away from the music itself and on to the listener. In doing so we naturally come to regard its affective capacity – its ability to move us – as its most important property. But of course music also has a structure. Every piece of music of any sophistication is a construction out of certain variables – melody, harmony, rhythm and form, together with the timbre and texture of sound created by the different sounds of instruments and voices. It is the task of the composer to unite these in interesting and attractive combinations, and great composers do so in ways sufficiently complex to allow both understanding and analysis.

Any assessment of a musical composition must take account of its intrinsic structure as well as its effect upon the listener. A highly sophisticated piece of music such as Elgar's *Cello Concerto* or Brahms's *Violin Concerto* not only is worth listening to but *requires* listening to over and over again. This is not simply because we can enjoy it more than once, but because there is more and more to *discover* in it. It may also be performed again and again in markedly differing ways, because it allows considerable variety of interpretation. A musician can use an instrument or an orchestra to explore a piece of music, and to reveal the results of that exploration to the audience. This is not true of all music. There is a great deal of very pleasant, and even affecting, music that is simple and straightforward. From the point of view of both the listener and the performer, then, some pieces of music are *richer* than others. They contain more of interest than initially more attractive and indeed more pleasurable pieces. Were we to confine ourselves to estimating the value of music in terms of pleasure, even pleasurable feeling, we could not capture the relative structural wealth or poverty that is to be found in different styles and pieces of music, and upon which the judgements of critics and musicologists are based. The songs that Abba produced are genuinely pleasurable in a way that a lot of symphonic music is not. But this does not make them better music. Boccerini's *Minuet* is a very pleasing sound; Beethoven's *Kreutzer Sonata* is not. Nevertheless the second is obviously a superior piece of music. We can only consistently hold both these judgements if we can explain the value of the *Kreutzer* without having, openly or surreptitiously, to appeal to 'deeper' or 'higher' pleasures. The most straightforward way of doing this is to appeal to relative intellectual complexity. Music is not just undifferentiated sound which may or may not please. It has a structure, which lends it interest and consequently value, and great music exploits structural possibilities to a degree that puts it far beyond the level of simple pleasant melodies. It does not merely have an effect upon us, as the melody does, but provides us with material for our minds.

Music and emotion

To counter the simple, perhaps naive view that music is valuable chiefly as a source of pleasure by appealing to structural complexity might be thought to construe music *too* abstractly. It is true that music can sustain intellectual analysis, but it also has affective properties that should not be ignored. To make structure the principal focus of critical attention is to leave out precisely what most people would suppose to be an essential element in music appreciation, namely, the ability to be moved by it. It seems possible that someone could analyse the form and structure of a piece of music and at the same time feel no sympathetic response to it. Such a person might have some understanding of the piece as a composition but could not be said to appreciate it as music, because what is missing from a purely analytic understanding is the very thing that most musicians and music lovers hold to be peculiarly valuable in music, namely, its emotional content.

This argument could be strengthened in the following way. Let us agree to reject the pleasure view on the ground that good music offers us structural complexities that we hope to understand intellectually. But what are these structures for? Complexity for its own sake is not something we have any reason to value. Serial music (invented by Schoenberg) is built around an immensely complex system of composition which is intellectually demanding to master as composer and listener. But it has largely been abandoned because the complexity does not seem to have a good enough 'pay off' in terms of music worth listening to. Atonal music has some enthusiasts still, but has never been satisfactorily incorporated in the repertoire that draws audiences.

Serialism is a subject to be returned to at greater length but, for the moment, its relative failure will serve to show that structural complexity is not to be valued in itself. Indeed music can be criticized precisely for its 'mere' complexity, as serial music has been. The value of structural complexity lies in what it enables a musician to achieve, namely musical effect. No purely formal property has value in music. In fact undue complexity of structure may undermine the very emotional experience aimed at, as arguably it does in some of the music of Telemann.

There is plainly something correct about this line of argument. The idea that mere complexity increases value must be wrong, though whether *mere* complexity is possible in music is debatable. However, even if it is true that complexity in music is only valuable so long as it serves some further end, it does not follow, and is not obvious, that this further end must have something to do with emotion. To be more precise, it is not obvious how emotional effect or content as the end at which musical complexity aims could help us explain the value of great music. This is partly because of the general difficulties about art and emotion rehearsed in Chapter 3. But there is this further great difficulty. Despite the implicit assumption so far, it is hard to see how there could be any connection between emotion and music at all.

People often and easily *say* that music is filled with or expresses or arouses emotion. They do so because it is unquestionably true that we can use emotional terms to describe pieces of music. Indeed some pieces of music are such that it seems impossible to avoid the language of emotion if we are to say much about them. Elgar's *Cello Concerto* is one particularly marked example. Michael Hurd, Elgar's biographer, describes it as 'filled with sadness and regret' and 'shot through with melancholy' and these are descriptions that anyone who has listened to the piece, especially the third movement, will find it hard to resist. Conversely, it seems entirely appropriate to describe the *Rondo* in Mozart's *Fifth Violin Concerto* as irrepressibly happy in tone; there is just no better way of describing it.

The application of emotional terms to musical compositions and performances, together with the established practice among critics and musicologists of doing so, is what inclines people to believe in a special connection between music and emotion. However, there is an important logical gap here. The application of terms is a fact about linguistic behaviour, not a fact about music. Expressivism in music moves from the former to the latter and bases a belief about the nature of music on a fact about the use of language. Is this move justified? Does the ease and regularity with which emotional terms are applied to music imply that music expresses emotion? There are a number of reasons for thinking that it does not.

The first is this. If we try to specify the emotions with which a piece of music can be filled, which it may arouse or which it could express, the list turns out to be surprisingly short. Music is said to be 'sad' or 'happy' (or some variation of these general terms – 'sombre' and 'joyful', for instance). It can also (as we noted) be exciting or haunting. Very few other emotional states or conditions can be ascribed to music without a measure of absurdity creeping into the discussion. *Possibly* it makes sense to say that music can arouse or even express pride as well as sadness, happiness and excitement. But it hardly makes sense to speak of music expressing shame, or embarrassment, or envy or hatred or shyness, or boredom or revulsion, or any of a great many more emotional states that human beings experience. Even love is not something that can have obvious musical expression. Of course there can be love *songs*, but these have words whose power to express all sorts of emotion is not in question. What is in question is the power of music alone – absolute music – to do this. In so far as the language we use to describe it goes, we would have to conclude that at best it can do so only for a severely limited range of emotions.

The second difficulty for musical expressivism is this. Emotional content is supposed to help us avoid pure formalism about music and to explain why complexity is to be valued. This implies that greater complexity of construction facilitates greater emotional expression. But is this true? It seems not. Asked to name the quality of a simple minor chord repeated in common 4/4 time, even very young children will say 'sad', whereas a combination of melody and harmony that has a relatively complicated time signature (Dave Brubeck's *Take Five*, for instance) is not easily identified with the expression or evocation of any emotion at all.

If now we combine these two points – that the range of emotions it is possible for music to express or evoke is extremely limited and that the ability of music to evoke even this limited range of emotions does not seem to have any obvious connection with complexity – and add them to the earlier arguments of Chapter 3 about art and emotion in general, then music will seem of little real value. That is to say, if what is important about music is its ability to express or arouse emotion, and it is this that gives musical complexity its rationale, then music cannot claim to be of much importance.

This is an unwelcome conclusion to arrive at. But in arriving at it we have leapt the same logical gap that expressivism does by assuming that the applicability of emotional terms to music shows music itself to contain emotion. But the mere fact that the same terms are applied to music as are applied to human moods and attitudes does not show that those terms share the same meaning in both contexts. This is a point that Roger Scruton makes: 'The ways of hearing sound that we consider to be ways of hearing music are based on concepts extended by metaphorical transference' (Scruton 1983: 79). 'Metaphorical transference' is sometimes called 'analogical extension' – the extension of language from one context to another by analogy.

It is not just the language of emotion that is extended in this way. A clearer example is the extension of the language of vision to the world of sound. So easily does this take place that it may take an effort to appreciate its oddity. Music is a strictly aural medium, yet somewhat surprisingly it is often described in terms that have their home in strictly visual contexts. The sound of brass is described as 'bright' for example, the stops on an organ are said to give it 'colour', and the tone of a cello or an alto voice referred to as 'dark'. The same sort of analogical transference happens in the opposite direction – colours are commonly described as 'loud' or 'soft'.

This example is especially useful because no one is tempted to leap from these facts about the use of language to conclusions about the nature of sound and vision. To try to measure the volume of a loud colour, for example, would reveal a gross misunderstanding, everyone acknowledges. 'Loud' and 'soft' can be applied to both noises and colours, but we do not infer from this that, despite being wholly different media, sound and vision have common properties. On the contrary, just because they are wholly different, we have reason to think that the same terms have different meanings when applied in such different contexts.

Similarly, though tunes and harmonies are frequently described in emotional terms – sad, happy, and so on – there is nothing *in this fact alone* to support the idea that music has emotional content. On the contrary, since pieces of music and states of mind are so very different, there is reason to think that the use of emotional terms in music is another case of analogical extension. Actually, such extension reaches back into the description of emotional states themselves, for here too terms can be used whose home is some quite other context. The American philosopher Arnold Isenberg once pointed out that we debate about whether 'light-hearted' can be applied literally to a piece of music. But it is no less puzzling what the literal meaning of 'light-hearted' is when applied to human beings. In this particular case the original home was a long-abandoned physiological theory with no modern equivalent, and this shows that at least some of the words we use to describe emotional states are metaphorical extensions without any residual literal meaning at all.

So far we have been thinking of emotion as the *content* of music. An alternative that would not be open to the same objection is to think of music as expressing the emotions of those who compose or play it. Music is never literally sad, but what we call sad music arises from the mind of the composer, which *is* literally sad.

This is a view to which many people are drawn, and it is possible to find examples that it seems to fit especially well. Tchaikovsky's *Sixth Symphony* has four movements rather than the more customary three. The third movement finishes in a cheerful and vigorous style, and then we are plunged into a fourth movement of great sombreness. No one listening to it could fail to agree that 'hauntingly sad' is an accurate description. Commentators have frequently attributed this fourth movement to Tchaikovsky's increasing despondency, and indeed he died shortly after its completion, his death being widely believed to be suicide. This seems a perfect example for the thesis that music expresses the emotion of the composer. However, the example is instructive in a different way. Recent scholarship suggests that Tchaikovsky's despondency was lifting when he wrote his *Sixth Symphony*, and that he may not have committed suicide at all, but died in a typhoid outbreak. The important point to make, however, is this. It does not matter which account of the last days of his life is true; the music remains the same, and the description 'hauntingly sad' continues to be appropriate.

Actually, this is just a particular illustration of a general point made by John Hospers, one that was discussed in Chapter 3. The connection between what caused someone to create an artwork and the character of the artwork they created is a wholly contingent one. We can never legitimately read back from the music to the composer's psychological history. To do so is to compound the all important distinction between 'expressing' and 'being expressive of'. Expression is the communication of a mental state. Expressiveness is an imaginative way of articulating something. What is important about expressiveness in art is that it enhances our awareness. In a sense it is misleading to use the term 'express' at all, since it is not 'things experienced' but 'things imagined' with which expressiveness is concerned. So in emphasizing expressiveness in art we are really leaving behind any direct concern with emotion, and asking whether we can use art to say things. Putting it like this, however, seems to raise a greater difficulty for music than for the other arts. Can absolute music *say* anything?

Music as language

If music can say things, then it must in some sense or other be a kind of language. The title of Deryck Cooke's book, *The Language of Music*, makes this claim quite explicit. The passage quoted earlier continues as follows.

> If man is ever to fulfil the mission he undertook at the very start – when he first began to philosophize, as a Greek, and evolved the slogan 'Know thyself' – he will have to understand his unconscious self; and the most articulate language of the unconscious is music. But we musicians, instead of trying to understand this language, preach the virtues of refusing to consider it a language at all; when we should be attempting, as literary critics do, to expound and interpret the great masterpieces of our art for the benefit of humanity at large, we concern ourselves more and more with parochial matters – technical analyses and musicological minutiae – and pride ourselves on our detached de-humanized approach.
>
> (Cooke 1957: 5)

Neither the justice of Cooke's complaint about fellow musicians nor his view of the language of the unconscious need concern us here. The relevant feature of this quotation is his attempt to establish the importance of music by comparing it with philosophical reflection and literary criticism, both of which are intellectual endeavours to which meaning and meaningfulness are central. Cooke is not alone in making this comparison. Throughout the monumental three-volume work, *Man and His Music*, the English musicologist Wilfred Mellers repeatedly tries to establish the relative importance of composers and their work by appealing to what they have to say, the magnificence of their 'statements' and 'visions'. For example, all Haydn's later music, he tells us, 'reflects the beliefs that had meaning for him – an ethical humanism based upon reason and the love of created nature' (Mellers, Part III *The Sonata Principle* 1962: 606). With equal assurance he asserts that Mozart 'transformed the symphony from rococo entertainment into a personal testament' (*ibid.* 626). (In a similar vein the theologian Karl Barth is recorded as saying that Mozart could cause his listeners to hear 'the whole context of providence'.)

Other musicologists are less confident, and think that Mellers's appeal to this sort of interpretation is excessive. Nevertheless, he is expressing more clearly than most something that has been a constant theme in the writings of musicians and their interpreters. Asked about the significance of his cello concerto, Elgar described it as 'a man's attitude to life', and Beethoven himself evidently held a view of this sort when he declared that 'music is a greater revelation than the whole of philosophy'. Nor is it hard to see just why the thoughts of composers and musicians have moved so easily in this direction. Johann Christian Bach is said to have remarked of his brother C. P. E. Bach, 'My brother lives to compose, I compose to live.' The remark was intended merely to reflect a difference of attitude towards the relative value of music on the part of each of them no doubt, but others have been quick to see in it an explanation of the relative merits of the music that each composed: Carl Phillipe's is of serious interest, Johann Christian's merely light and amusing. To live for the sake of composition, if it is to make sense as a human ideal, requires that what is composed can be properly described in terms such as 'affirmation' and by adjectives such as 'profound'. Even exponents of minimalist music, who might be supposed least likely to think in terms of cognitive content, can be found employing the idea in order to justify evaluative judgements. In a programme note on *Litania*, a piece by the minimalist composer Somei Satoh, the pianist Margaret Lee Teng finds in it a 'dance of the dark soul'.

These examples illustrate that the importance of one type or piece of music over another seems most easily explained by reference to what each has to 'say' to us. This is why composers and performers are often led to think of music in this way. The language of musical criticism seems to confirm the appropriateness of doing so because critics and interpreters often refer to musical 'statements', and re-statements, and to what a particular passage 'signifies' or 'conveys'. They also pass judgements that are difficult to understand unless music can be thought of in this way. For instance, Beethoven's music has sometimes been said to be 'witty rather than funny', Liszt's piano music described as 'structurally clever but thematically banal', and Bruckner has been accused of being 'long-winded and inconsequential'. All these examples show that there is a recurrent tendency for musicians and critics to explain the importance of music in terms of what it communicates. And this implies that music *has* communicative power.

Once again we ought to remember that common and familiar ways of speaking do not settle philosophical questions. The fact that critics and even composers use the language of communication in their descriptions of music does not show that music communicates any more than the use of emotional terms showed that it has emotional content. There is the same possibility here – that these terms used in connection with music are a case of analogical extension. It is certainly plausible to think this in the case of the expression 'musical statement' because often this means nothing more than a relatively plain rendering of the central motif or melody around which the subsequent variations and developments in a musical work are built.

Still, both composers and interpreters have wanted more than this, and applied the language of communication to music with the intention of retaining the cognitive import such language has in other contexts. In other words, they have wanted to say that music *is* a language. Yet, as even Mellers says, music as language raises a fundamental question.

> [I]f music 'conveys' experience as a language does, what kind of language is it? The language of poetry is basically the same as the normal means of communication between human beings. The poet may use words with a precision, a cogency and a range of emotional reference which we do not normally find in a conversation. Yet though the order he achieves from his counters may be more significant than the desultory patterns achieved by Tom, Dick and Harry, at least the counters (words) are the same in both cases. Even with the visual arts there is usually some relationship between the order of forms and colours which the artist achieves and the shapes and colours of the external world. The relation between the formal and the representational elements is extremely complex and not easily susceptible to analysis; but it is at least usually clear that some such relationship exists.
>
> With music, the relationship between the forms of art and the phenomena of the external world is much less readily apprehensible.
>
> (Mellers 1962: vii)

Music and representation

Sometimes the answer to the problem of music's meaning is thought to lie with the ability of music to represent. Up to this point we have used the expression 'absolute music' to mean music alone, without words. But musicologists sometimes draw a contrast between 'absolute' music and 'programme' music, the latter a term coined by the composer Franz Liszt (1811–86) to describe music that conjures up literary or visual images. The idea is that programme music can 'say' things because it can be used to represent to us aspects of nature and human experience. And surely, it might be said, there can be no doubt that music *can* represent – birdsong, battles, storms, armies, royal processions, pastoral countryside – as well as a range of emotions – grief, jollity, excitement and so on.

Certainly music sometimes *seems* to represent. Beethoven's *Pastoral Symphony* is a much quoted example in which we can identify points in the music with specific scenes and events: 'This is the sound of peasants from across the valley', 'This is the storm gathering' and so on. Such apparently clear examples, however, should not distract us from the need to be precise about what such representation amounts to and how far it really does explain the character and value of music.

The first point to be made is this. Some of the things that pass for representation in music are more accurately described as imitation or replication. Replication of the sound of a bell is not a representation of the sound of a bell; it *is* the sound of a bell. If it is to represent something, it has to be something non-aural – a summons or the arrival of a visitor, for example. The distinction is an important one because more sophisticated imitations found in music are often improperly described as representations. Birdsong is an obvious case. A composer may use instruments to imitate the song of a bird and successfully get us to think of birds at that point in the music, but it does not follow that he has represented the bird, still less said anything about it. Indeed this need not be his purpose. The French composer Olivier Messiaen wrote a great deal of music which consisted (he said) in the transcription of sounds made by birds. He did this not for the purpose of representing birds, but because he regarded birdsong as a very pure form of music. Consequently, though Messiaen may rightly be described as imitating or replicating birdsong, he is simply making music. He is not representing anything.

What then is representation proper? We might define it as the use of music, not to replicate the sound of something, but to prompt the idea of that thing in the mind of anyone listening to the music. The example of the bell illustrates the difference. The sound of a triangle might *imitate* or replicate a bell, but thereby *represent* the arrival of a visitor. In a similar way, a trumpet fanfare can represent a royal procession. It is also possible to represent emotional states in music – grief by a slow rhythm in a minor key, fury suggested by violins rushing up a scale, or melancholy by a solo cello. The music is not itself furious or melancholic. Neither is the composer. These are the non-musical things the music represents.

It seems incontestable that composers do use such devices to convey ideas to the minds of their listeners. Many composers have expressly said they do, and their success in doing so is confirmed by the reactions of listeners. No serious listener, for instance, can fail to identify the gathering storm in Rossini's *William Tell Overture*. But we cannot immediately conclude from this that music has the power to communicate, because there is a crucial difference between prompting ideas in the minds of others and communicating thoughts to them in the way that language does.

When I write or speak a natural language such as English or French, I have in my possession a means by which I can do far more than simply cause ideas to come into your mind. I can direct and manipulate those ideas. If you understand the words I utter, you will be compelled to have the thought that I express with them. This is not the same as saying that you are compelled to accept that thought as true, or approve of it in some way. For instance, if I say 'This is a cup of tea', while pointing to a flowerpot, your mind will entertain the thought 'This is a cup of tea', but will not believe it to be true. A natural language is thus a powerful instrument of communication because it allows us to constrain the thoughts of others; it allows us to *make* them think things (though not to make them believe those things) and to do so in a certain way. *Constraining* the thoughts of others contrasts with merely *prompting* thoughts in others. We can prompt ideas in wholly accidental ways. For example, it might be that a chance gesture of mine reminds you of your childhood, or of a play you once attended. I did not communicate these ideas to you; I merely caused you (accidentally) to have them. Nor does intentionality turn this sort of causality into communication. I might know that the gesture in question would cause you to be reminded of an episode in childhood, and I might intentionally make the gesture. But this is no different from causing you pain. If I stick a pin in you, I have caused you pain, and might even cause you to think about pain. But I have not *told* you anything. It would be very odd to describe my action as a form of communication just because you had a thought as a result. In a similar way, merely prompting a thought is not communicating that thought.

Now it is not difficult to imagine this kind of simple 'prompting' being expanded into a system of signs. A group of children, for instance, might invent a 'vocabulary' of gestures which they use to convey information and warnings to each other. Such a system need not be deliberately or consciously learned. Other children might learn it simply in the course of play and thereby become both receptive to messages received in this form and adept at sending them. In such a case we can say there is a form of communication that rests upon widely shared conventions. A similar story might be told for music. Over the years a set of musical conventions has grown up by means of which it is possible for composers to prompt a range of ideas in the minds of listeners, a range that includes both ideas of objects and of feelings. Music has thus become a form of communication in its own right, in the same way that a sign language such as semaphore is a form of communication.

The fact that the music of different parts of the world does not readily transcend the cultures in which it developed, bears out the suggestion that the prime basis of musical communication is conventional. People (somewhat romantically) are inclined to refer to music as a universal language, but it is obvious that (initially at any rate) Chinese, Indian or Arabic music is difficult for those brought up on Western music to understand and appreciate, and vice versa. This is not hard to explain. Take for example a peal of bells used to convey the idea of a wedding or a tolling bell to convey the idea of death. In both cases the sound of the bell gets its 'meaning' from certain social practices at weddings and funerals. These practices are distinctively Western. Mosques do not have peals of bells and accordingly a peal of bells does not have the same associations in Islamic countries with the result that the sound of the bell cannot convey those ideas to Islamic ears.

It would be a mistake to think that the music's ability to convey ideas is entirely conventional. Some of the conventions build on natural associations between sounds and rhythms; it is no accident that the ringing of bells at weddings takes the form of a peal – loud and jangling – whereas that for funerals takes the form of a toll – slow and solitary – and each seems 'naturally' fitting to the occasion. And there are non-conventional associations that rely on isomorphic relationships. A rapidly rising sequence of notes is naturally associated with upward physical movement, and it seems to have an equally natural association with excitement. Thus almost every setting of the Christian Mass makes the music of the line '*Et resurrexit tertiam die*' ('And on the third day he rose again') move vigorously upwards. And there appear to be other natural associations that composers can exploit. Talk of musical 'jokes' is often rather strained, but there is no doubt that some musical sequences do make people laugh, just as there are musical sequences which make them pensive.

There are then a number of devices – some conventional, some natural – that composers can use to convey ideas in their music. Together they add up to a reasonably complex and sophisticated set of devices for the stimulation and/or provocation of feelings and ideas. But is this enough to allow us to declare music to be a language? Do these devices give music the power (and hence the value) that Cooke, Mellers and others attribute to it?

Musical vocabulary and musical grammar

We now need to return to the distinction between a means of signalling or prompting ideas and a form of communication in the fullest sense. Consider again the case in which some chance gesture of mine awakens in you a memory of childhood. I have caused you to think of your childhood, but on its own that does not amount to my having conveyed the idea to you. Nor would the difference be made up if my gesture was one of a complex sequence that causes a corresponding sequence of images or thoughts. Why not? The answer is that mere causality of this kind does not rely upon your understanding anything. It simply exploits certain contingent connections between my gestures and your early childhood experience. I have no more communicated an idea to you than has a dog whose barking reminds you to lock the door at night, or the alarm clock that 'tells' you it's time to get up. In both cases, you have merely been caused to have the idea.

Something of the same sort might now be said about the representational use of music. I might use the sound of a triangle to prompt in you the thought 'A visitor', but if I succeed, this is not because you have, in any proper sense, *understood* the sound, as you might a word, but that you have come to associate the sound of a bell with the arrival of visitors. What is missing is the idea that my music has *constrained* your thoughts. In a famous experiment the Russian physiologist Ivan Pavlov (1849–1936) conditioned dogs to salivate at the sound of a bell. It may be correct to say that the sound of the bell prompted the idea 'meat' in them. But it would be entirely fanciful to suppose that they understood the bell to be saying 'dinner time'.

This idea of *constraining* thought has a parallel in painting. A painter might arrange abstract colours and shapes on his canvas in a way that, as it happens, causes you to think of a tree that once grew in front of the house in which you lived. Or a painter might paint the house and tree with which you were familiar, but paint them so that you are *obliged* to see them the wrong way round – the tree behind the house. This illustrates the ability of painting to use perspective not merely to *prompt* but to *constrain* perception, and it is what makes painting a form of communication. The question is: is there a parallel to perspective in music?

We have already noted that music has considerable representational resources in a wide range of natural and conventional associations. However, once we introduce the distinction between a means of communicating thoughts to others (best exemplified in a natural language) and a means of prompting ideas in others (which we will call a representational system), it becomes apparent that there can be representational systems of considerable complexity which nevertheless fall far short of being a 'natural language'. Their deficiency might be expressed thus: they have a vocabulary but no grammar. They can point to single ideas or sets of ideas, but they cannot say anything about them.

Music can be interpreted as having a vocabulary. It is easy to find examples in which a musical phrase can plausibly be said to indicate or represent some object, emotion or event. In this sense, objects and ideas can be represented in music. It is hard, though, to identify any way in which music directs or guides our thoughts about what is represented. Consider once more the simple case of the bell. The sound of a triangle imitates a bell and thereby represents the arrival of a visitor. But what are we to think? Thus far described, 'O good! Here is a visitor' is as apt an interpretation of the music as 'O no! Not a visitor.' Precisely the same point can be made about far more sophisticated cases. In *The Language of Music* Deryck Cooke interprets 'the descending minor 5–3–1 progression' as the expression of a 'falling away from the joy of life' (Cooke 1957: 137). This is a more controversial example of representation in music than the bell, of course. But even if we accept that music can represent such high-level states of mind and feeling, the same point about ambiguity arises. The progression could mean 'It is time to fall away from the joy of life' or it could mean 'Never allow yourself to fall away from the joy of life.' Since these are contradictory injunctions, the music cannot be considered an effective means of communication at all. It prompts ideas and thoughts, but since it cannot constrain them in any particular direction, it cannot use them to say anything.

Ambiguities and uncertainties in music can be resolved when the music has some linguistic accompaniment, most obviously words (libretto) but even a dedication or a title. One of the best-known pieces of programme music is Mussorgsky's composition *Pictures at an Exhibition*. Originally ten piano pieces, now generally performed in an orchestral arrangement by Ravel, Mussorgsky was inspired to write it by an exhibition of paintings in St Petersburg. Knowing this, and knowing something of the pictures that the music is supposed to represent, we can see why Mussorgsky composed what he did. But someone who did not know the title of the work or the individual movements could not identify the objects in the various pictures just by listening to the music. Linguistic identification is essential. Similarly in Prokofiev's *Peter and the Wolf* or Saint-Saën's *Carnival of the Animals*, although the instruments and tunes that represent the different animals are appropriate in a general way – the cello for the gliding swan, the double bass for the elephant, and so on – different instruments could equally well serve for a number of different animals. We only know precisely what animals are represented because we are *told*, in words; the music itself is not enough.

This is not to say that the words do all the work. A musical setting can embellish, illustrate and illuminate words, and on occasion transform them almost from banality to the sublime (Benjamin Britten's *Saint Nicholas* might be an example). It can conversely reduce them to farce (to my ears, this is the effect of the section 'Fling wide the Gates' in Stainer's *Crucifixion*). A composer can take a familiar text and by setting it to music revitalize it, or give it a definitive interpretation (Handel's *Messiah* is a very clear example of this). In all these ways music has powerful effects of its own to add. Nevertheless, the relationship between words and music is asymmetrical. Words resolve ambiguities in the 'meaning' of the music, but should the words themselves be ambiguous, the music cannot resolve the matter. In short, the music always follows and never leads the words; it lacks the ability to impart a meaning of its own.

This deficiency and its importance are both illustrated in a well-known example. Against the theme of the finale of his last string quartet Beethoven wrote '*Muss es sein? Es muss sein*' (Must it be? It must). Most commentators have taken these words as indicative of the meaning of the music and have thus understood the music to be expressing a hard-won mystical or religious acceptance of the human condition that Beethoven achieved only towards the end of his life. However, a (possibly apocryphal) story goes that Beethoven claimed the words recorded an exchange between him and his housekeeper who was asking for more money. Let us suppose the story is true. Perhaps this interpretation was a joke on his part, and the words really express resignation. Or perhaps it was not a joke and he wrote these down as a reminder that the music he himself regarded as the finest he had ever written arose from the mundane need for money (an interpretation that does nothing to diminish the value of the music). All of these are plausible, and the philosophical point the example makes is this. Neither listening to nor analysing the music will settle the matter in favour of one interpretation, because the music itself is consonant with all of them. If the music really did *communicate* the metaphysical or religious ideas that some have found in it, there should be no doubt that Beethoven was joking or the story is apocryphal. Since there *is* a doubt here, it follows that the music by itself cannot direct our thoughts in one way rather than another.

This particular example is especially telling. Beethoven's late quartets are often cited as examples of the most serious and profound music ever written. If true, this is music we have reason to value more than any other. It is common to hear this profundity explained in terms of the ideas about human life and experience that the quartets express. Yet as we have seen, the music itself cannot confirm this explanation. Even if we agree that these quartets prompt us to have certain moods and ideas, they cannot tell us what to think about them. If the same thing were true of a work of philosophy or science, we would declare it a failure. Philosophers and scientists could merely state or assert ideas, and thus prompt us to have those ideas in our heads. But this would not add to our understanding of human experience. The point of a philosophical or scientific argument is to *bring* us to a conclusion, just as the painting imagined earlier *places* the tree in front of the house.

In short, even if we make large concessions to those who believe that music can be said to have content other than harmonious sound, and allow that music may be used systematically for the suggestion of ideas and feelings, we still cannot conclude that music constitutes a true form of communication. Communicative power, therefore, cannot be the explanation of its importance and value.

Résumé

The argument so far has shown that if we value music solely because of the pleasure it gives us, we cannot explain why we should value greater complexity and sophistication of structure. At the same time, to attribute the difference in value solely to complexity seems to leave out what most people think important about music – its emotional content. But the relation between music and emotion is not easy to isolate. Partly because of quite general reasons, and partly because of factors having to do with music in particular, it seems that a familiar and attractive account of music and its value has to be abandoned. We cannot make sense of the idea that music itself contains emotion, and we have no grounds for thinking that music described in emotional terms must have had its origins in the emotional life of the composer. The application of emotional terms to music is unobjectionable, but they take their meaning by analogical extension from the context of real emotion which was their original home.

An alternative attempt to explain the difference between 'serious' and 'light' in music is to be found in the suggestion that music is a form of communication by means of which beliefs and ideas about human experience can be conveyed. Careful examination shows, however, that while music can indeed represent things, it can do so only to a very limited extent. Furthermore, the form of this representation falls far short of communication in the fullest sense. Beethoven was right if he thought that his music should be held in the highest regard, but not because (as he claimed) it was a greater source of revelation than philosophy. Music has elements that can be thought of as a vocabulary, but it has nothing equivalent to a grammar. The result is that it can operate something like a system of signs that stand for things in the way that non-linguistic road signs do. A road sign tells us that we are approaching a junction, but it cannot tell us whether to turn right or left. In a similar fashion, a fanfare of trumpets 'says' royalty, but without words to guide us, it does not tell us whether to hope or fear, admire or despise. We can call music a language if we will, but it is a 'language' that does not allow us to say anything of any sophistication.

Where then *does* the value of music lie?

The uniqueness of music

Many musicians find the conclusion that music is not a language deeply disappointing, since they think this devalues it with regard to the other arts, as well as science and philosophy. Yet the more we think about music, the easier it becomes to see that its value has to lie in its uniqueness. There is an old joke among opera goers that Wagner's music is better than it sounds, while Puccini's music sounds better than it is. There may be a point the joke is making, but its humour arises from the absurdity of the idea that music can be judged independently of how it sounds, because music just *is* sound. Consequently attempting to explain the merits of Wagner or demerits of Puccini in terms other than how their music sounds is attempting the impossible.

The general lesson is that we should be on our guard against any explanation of the nature and value of music that makes hearing the music itself redundant. Curiously, though the ideas about emotion and representation that we have been considering find great favour amongst both musicians and musicologists, this is precisely what both of them do – render music redundant. For example, Mellers, one of the most enthusiastic proponents of the idea that music is a language, suggests that Beethoven's late quartets say in music what the poet T. S. Eliot's *Four Quartets* say. But if this really were true, Beethoven's music would in a sense be redundant; we could read Eliot's poems instead.

It seems right, then, to insist on the irreplacability of music. No other medium can do what it does. All attempts to explicate the character or meaning of music in non-musical terms – emotions and ideas are the two we have considered at length – are doomed from the outset. This is because what we are seeking to explain – music – is unique. Music differs from other art forms in this respect. It is neither unintelligible nor silly to think that photography could replace painting. This is why painting has been challenged to assert its distinctiveness since the invention of photography. Similarly the value of theatre is threatened somewhat by the advent of film and television. Even literature can be threatened in this way by the adaptation of novels for the screen. Painting, literature and the theatre may indeed have values that these other media cannot replicate, but it seems obvious that they offer the same sort of thing as photography and film, namely the visual and the narrative.

But what could possibly take the place of music? In a later section we will consider the recent emergence of other 'sonic arts' but in so far as such things are possible they are non-musical. Music truly is unique. It is a mistake, however, to suppose that the uniqueness of music means its value cannot be spelled out in any way whatever. What is needed is a way of saying something about the value of music that does not attempt to explicate it in non-musical terms, but does allow us to consider critically the claims that can be made on its behalf.

Music and beauty

The uniqueness of music is worth exploring further. It is sometimes suggested, even by composers, that music is a refinement of things found in nature – the wind in the grass, the song of the birds, the sound of rushing water and so on. Now it could be the case that the invention of some instruments came about in this way; the early origins of music are too remote for us to know. But what is not true is that these natural sounds are themselves a kind of music. Birds chattering, wind blowing and water splashing have nothing remotely resembling the resonance, the structure or the organization of the simplest composition for the smallest orchestra. The only thing in nature that is properly described as musical is the singing human voice, and of course singing is itself a form of music.

Music then is not just unique, it is uniquely human (ignoring for present purposes the possibility of *angelic* voices). Music is something that human beings *make*, and their ability to make it has developed over a very long period of time. This is true even of singing. To hum or sing a series of notes is a spontaneous activity in human beings, perhaps, but to turn this series into an extended and developed melody with organized keys and scales is not. Singing even a popular song takes us far beyond the ability and inclination of the baby in the pram to make resonant noises.

The point of stressing the non-natural character of music is this: music is not obtainable anywhere else than in the music-making activities of human beings. Why does this matter? If music is unique, then only in music can some values be realized. Nowhere else can we encounter values whose realization requires intentionally organized aural experience. One such value would be beauty in sound. Beautiful things are to be valued, and if it is only in music that beautiful sounds are to be found, then music is uniquely valuable as our only source of one kind of beauty.

This is a plausible line of argument. No one can doubt that beauty is something to value, and that music is frequently beautiful. What can be doubted is whether this constitutes the final or most satisfactory explanation of its value. To begin with, the claim that beautiful sound is to be found only in music is too sweeping. While it is misleading to describe natural sounds like birdsong or the low moan of the wind as music, it is quite plausible to describe some of them as beautiful. The cry of a bird has no melody and is in no key, but some birds make an ugly noise, others a beautiful one. There is an unmistakable difference between speaking and singing. The second is music, the first is not, but I can properly describe someone as having a beautiful speaking voice. What such examples show is that there can be beautiful but non-musical sounds, for which it follows that music is not uniquely valuable by being a source of beautiful sounds.

Besides, beauty does not correlate very satisfactorily with creative accomplishment in music. A large-scale and complex symphony is no more (and probably less) beautiful to listen to than a simple melody for a single violin. We might usefully contrast here Beethoven's and Bruch's violin concertos. Bruch's, it seems to me, is the more beautiful but Beethoven's the greater work. Certainly melodies and harmonies can be extremely beautiful, but there is no reason to think that beauty and harshness exhaust the possibilities for assessing harmonic patterns or explaining what makes them worth hearing. Beethoven's harmonic structures are more frequently interesting than beautiful but nonetheless valuable for that. In short, music may be our most familiar source of beautiful sound, but it is not our only source, nor is its being such a source an adequate explanation of the value we attach to it.

Nevertheless there is something right about this general line of thought. Music is the sole source of *organized* sound. One end to which it can be used is the exemplification of beauty, but there are others. The philosopher Malcolm Budd identifies several of these when he writes:

> One general value exemplified by many fine musical works is the unification of diverse material . . . so-called 'unity in diversity' or 'organic unity'. . . . Other values that can be exemplified in music include beauty, gracefulness, wit, imagination and mastery. Unblemished musical works that exemplify these values are paradigms of perfection, appreciated as such.
>
> (Budd 1995: 171)

This seems correct. Music exemplifies imagination and mastery, neither of which is exemplified in natural sounds, however beautiful, and it exemplifies these in a unique medium. Nowhere else do we find exercises of imagination that create structures out of sonic materials. Is this, then, the final explanation of the value of music, and is it sufficient? Budd obviously thinks so since he concludes by asking 'How could anything more be demanded of music as an abstract art?' But there is at least one further feature we can add. When we listen to music we are presented with not only evidence of the composer's imagination and mastery, but an exploration of one aspect of human experience – aural experience.

Music as the exploration of sound

Music is for listening to as nothing else is. When I listen to you speaking, or listen for the door bell, or the sound of a taxi arriving to collect me, I am listening for the meanings of these sounds – what you are saying, not how you are saying it, what the door bell signifies, not how it sounds. But music presents us with occasions for *pure* listening. This is why it is important *not* to attribute to it emotional content or representative meaning because both of these would lead us *past* the music, in the way that listening out for information on the radio, say, leads us past the distinctive sound that radio voices make.

In this way, music is the direct and immediate exploration of aural experience, and what is interesting about it is the richness it can have. So accustomed are we to listen past the sounds we hear, and thus to regard them as mere media, it may come as a surprise that sound itself can have such a remarkably complex nature, so complex in fact that it can sustain a rich descriptive vocabulary drawn by extension from the worlds of emotion, vision, engineering, narrative. What is striking about music that is described as bright or sorrowful or architectonic, or work comprising a theme and its development, is not that they in some odd way are connected with lights or emotions or buildings or stories, but that sound – pure sound – can have properties so much more sophisticated than simple loud/soft, fast/slow.

Once we understand the centrality of aural experience to music, we can see how there can be intelligible and demonstrable differences between the creations and explorations of different composers. A composer invites us to discover new qualities of sound, qualities that we have to describe in metaphorical or analogical language. It is not analyses of their 'meaning' by musicologists, or the observation of moods induced in listeners, in which these qualities are demonstrated by the performer *in the music*, and we apprehend them not by reading the score or the programme notes, but by listening. Borrowing an expression from literary theory, we could say that music is the 'foregrounding' of sound. In music, noise-making ceases to be a mere means of expression or communication, and ceases, indeed, to be mere noise. Aural experience becomes the focus of interest in its own right. Reflection and analysis can help us discover the properties of a piece of music, certainly, and where the music is of a highly developed sort we may need the vocabulary of technical analysis to isolate and describe the structures of sound to be found within it. Nevertheless, if we are to know that *these* sounds have *that* property, listening is inescapable. If we locate the value of music in its unique ability to extend and explore *aural* experience, we cannot have that experience non-aurally, and thus the activity of actually listening to music cannot be eliminated. The theory of music as aural foregrounding avoids the danger of making music redundant which, as we saw earlier, is the principal defect in theories that locate its value in pleasure, emotion or representation.

It has this further advantage. We saw earlier in the chapter that any propositional meanings we are inclined to attach to pieces of absolute music are invariably ambiguous, because there is nothing about the music that directs (as opposed to prompts) our thoughts. But now we can see that, as the painter directs our visual perceptions, so the composer and performer direct our aural perceptions. Listening to music is not just a matter of sound pouring into a receptor, but of the mind being directed through a series of perceptions. We are, so to speak, guided through our experience. It is as though the composer were saying 'It must be heard *this* way' by actually making us hear it that way. An analogy might be this. We enter a series of underground caverns where our journey can take alternative routes through spaces of differing shape, dimension and atmosphere, lighted by different means. Each composer is the guide who decides upon the lighting and directs us through the caverns. The shapes and dimensions of the caves are 'there for all to see' of course but they can be seen only this way or that. The way we see them and the ways that are especially worth seeing, are matters for which we rely upon our guides.

If the final answer to the question 'What is the value of music?' is that music provides us with a means of exploring the dimensions of aural experience, someone might then ask, 'What is so important about exploring aural experience?' To this question, the only answer would appear to be that aural experience is part of a distinctly *human* experience. We have every reason to think that other animals equipped with auditory powers can *hear* music; but only human beings can *listen* to it. It is by enlarging and exploring this dimension of experience that music assists us in understanding better what it is to be a human being. Aesthetic cognitivism can to this extent be applied to music. Compositions are objects of understanding in their own right. To understand the structure of a piece of music and apprehend the full range of its tonal, rhythmic and harmonic properties is an achievement, just as understanding a mathematical proof is an achievement. Its composition is also an achievement, an act of thought and imagination that is also comparable to the creative mind of the mathematician. Music is thus a source of understanding, but contrary to the implied suggestion in Beethoven's claim about revelation, it does not offer us any understanding of the non-musical. Nevertheless, the aural is a world of experience and music offers us an understanding of that world. In this way the value of great music may be explained as the value of great art.

Sonic art and digital technology

This explanation of the value of music rests heavily on music giving us unique access to the world of sound by foregrounding it. Is it really true that *only* music can do this? Until the early decades of the twentieth century the answer would have seemed obvious. There is nothing to compare with music and nothing to substitute for it. But three important developments can be seen to introduce new possibilities.

The first of these developments was the experimental music that originated with the Viennese composer Arnold Schoenberg (1874–1951). Having come to believe the normal resources of tonal music in the European tradition were close to exhaustion, Schoenberg became the advocate of 'atonalism' and then the inventor of 'serialism'. Serialism is a method of composing that abandons traditional harmonic structures in favour of a composition that arranges 12 tones in accordance with quasi-mathematical rules. Composing in this way results in a radically different sound, since it has nothing in it that strikes the ear as melody or harmony, and although the basic materials out of which such compositions are built are tones, this strangeness is described as 'atonal'.

Schoenberg's serialism was taken up with great enthusiasm by other composers, notably Anton Webern (1883–1945) and Alban Berg (1885–1935), but serialism proved too constricting (even Schoenberg broke his own rules) and atonal music proved to have difficulty in attracting and retaining audiences. Schoenberg's significance, however, lies not so much in the method he invented as the great wave of experimentalism in music that he inaugurated. Subsequent composers – Pierre Boulez (b. 1925) and Karlheinz Stockhausen (b. 1928) and especially Edgar Varese (1883–1965) – went much further and began to incorporate in their compositions a quite different range of sounds and devices – vacuum cleaners, bat and ball, and gun shots, passages of screaming and shouting as well as singing, and a 'prepared' piano with nuts and bolts or other items inserted into it, the keyboard of which the pianist does not merely play with fingers, but thumps with arms and elbows as well.

Several of these experimentalists began to capitalize upon a second important development – the invention of sound recording. Stockhausen used electrically generated tones, and Varese employed recording devices extensively. The ability to record sound and then manipulate it meant that, for the first time, non-musical sounds could be combined in structured ways. Early attempts to do so sound primitive now, but that is because they were wholly experimental. What emerged was a new type of composition. One of its most successful exponents is the American composer Steve Reich (b. 1936). Reich composes tonal music in which recording devices are used to combine both instruments and singers in highly repetitive, mesmeric patterns of sound. But he has also created compositions out of the speaking voice. This is atonalism properly so called, because its basic materials are not tones at all, but simply sounds. Schoenberg's atonalism was highly experimental, but it was with composers like Varese and Reich that the possibility of non-musical composition came about.

It is a possibility that was hugely extended with the third major development, the invention of digital technology. Digital technology has not merely made computers and the internet part of everyday life, it has also transformed some of the media important to the arts. Electronic instruments and digital cameras are obvious examples, but the real significance of digital technology lies in the vast power of detailed manipulation, both of images and sounds, that it has made possible. Following in the wake of ground breaking musical experiments, such as those of Schoenberg and others, the combination of recording equipment and digital technology has finally brought about a completely new way of foregrounding sound and hence exploring the world of aural experience.

What is this new medium to be called? The names it is actually given – electro-acoustic music, sound art, sonic art – vary chiefly with respect to their differing connotations. The first signals a belief on the part of many new composers that this form of composition is continuous with music. It also constitutes their claim to the status of music. The second is the name generally given to aural presentations in art galleries, and for this reason implies a move away from the music of the concert hall and a closer alliance with the plastic arts of painting and sculpture. But there is reason to prefer the third because it signals, correctly, that this new style of composition uses sound but not music as an art material. Of course musical composition also uses sound, so that 'sonic art' could serve as an umbrella term for both musical and electro-acoustic composition.

Is electro-acoustic composition music? This is a question that has been quite widely discussed and yet it does not seem to be of very much consequence. The important point is that a completely different way of foregrounding sound has come into existence, and what is interesting is not what we should call it, but whether it matches or even rivals the sonic art – traditional music – that came before it.

Conventional music is a structured exploration of tonal sounds deploying certain recognized variables – harmony, rhythm, timbre, form and texture, chiefly. Natural sounds such as birdsong and waterfalls do not have this tonal quality. That is why it is misleading to call them music. But it does not follow that they have no *aural interest*. If they are not especially worth listening to in and for themselves, that is because they lack any structure. As Arnold Isenberg once pointed out, Rimsky-Korsakov's *Flight of the Bumble Bee* is worth listening to precisely because it does not replicate the monotony of an actual bee in flight. But now digital technology has provided us with the means whereby the aural interest that there is in the sound of the bee can be isolated, captured and manipulated into a form that does have structure. In other words, thanks to digital technology, natural (and other non-musical) sounds can not just be foregrounded; they can be turned into structures that make them worth listening to.

Digital composition need not of course renounce musical sound, but it is not restricted to it. With digital technology singing can *become* the noise of screaming which in turn can be *transformed* into the sound of the wind, or for that matter into sounds whose novelty is such that we cannot easily name them in this way. Echoes and reverberations that are not possible in standard kinds of music can be manipulated into structured forms, as theme and variation with recapitulation, coda and so on. And all such constructions can be more or less imaginative, more or less compelling to listen to.

We can call this 'music' if we wish, but to do so is to disguise its radical novelty. That is why I shall use the term 'electro-acoustic art'. But the important point is not whether we decide to call it music or something else, but whether compared to conventional music, electro-sonic art is an enrichment or an impoverishment.

In part this is a question that cannot yet be decided. We have seen at several points in this chapter that music can sustain the use of a very important and wide range of descriptive terms. The ease and naturalness with which, for instance, the language of emotion is applied to music leads to the errors of expressivism, which mistakes analogical extension for literal meaning. But the use of this language is still in place. Music can be happy, solemn, sombre, exciting, etc. Can these terms, and the full range of terms normally applied to music, also be applied to the composition of electro-sonic art? It is too early to say because not enough composition of this kind has entered the general consciousness. When it does, we will discover how people who are neither composers nor advocates naturally describe it, just as we will discover whether they enthusiastically attend recitals.

But a more important issue is this. Are such recitals performances? Electro-acoustic composition of this kind is inextricably connected with the technology that makes it possible. In some of the experimental music previously referred to, composers who wanted to incorporate non-musical sounds into their compositions devised new systems of notation that would instruct the instrumentalists in how to produce sounds other than tones. The Polish composer Witold Lutoslawski (1913–94) was well known for this. But in composition that uses digital technology to produce new sounds, there is no need to do this. In fact, there is no *place* for it, because the composition and its realization are one and the same. In other words, there is no gap, either temporal or conceptual, between composition and performance, the sort of gap that there is between a musical score and its realization. What this implies, however, is that this new music is indeed radically new: it has eliminated something which hitherto has been an essential feature of music, namely performance.

Electro-acoustic composers tend to deny this implication and assert that performance has not been eliminated, so much as changed its character. No less important than the sounds that comprise an electro-acoustic composition is the way it is listened to. That is why they devote considerable attention to the positioning of speakers in relation to the audience, and to the order in which the recorded sound is relayed through those speakers. Since the positioning of speakers and the order in which they are used can differ from occasion to occasion, it seems to make sense to refer to different 'performances' of the same electro-acoustic composition. But are these really performances, rather than recitals? We can say that there is scope here for something we might call interpretation, though in the normal case the interpreter will be the composer. But it does not seem that there is any artistic space for a *performer*, still less for a whole group of performers.

Why does this matter? It matters partly because interpretation in performance is, for both the performer and the audience, a significant further avenue for the exploration of sound. It is commonly said in programme notes and reviews that great performers have the ability to 'get inside' a piece of music and 'reveal' its true character. These may be metaphorical ways of speaking but they do capture a real and important dimension of music making, and its value. It is precisely because of this that we can speak meaningfully of 'definitive' performances. Conventional music, in other words, provides for a collaborative exploration of sound by composer and performer (and arranger, sometimes). In digital composition, by contrast, it seems that in principle the composer does everything.

But more importantly, *if* it is true that electro-acoustic composition does not admit of performance, this makes it radically different from music, since music is one of the performing arts. Sonic art without performance is the equivalent in sound to visual art – painting, engraving and so on – a construction presented by the composer to an audience. By excluding performance, electro-acoustic art is not merely a radical innovation in the long tradition of music; it is departure from its essential character. But to see what this means and why it matters, we will have to wait until Chapter 8 and the examination of performing art in general.

Summary

It is evident that music gives many people great pleasure; also true is that it is widely believed to be expressive of some of the deepest human emotions. Neither fact properly explains its value, however. Pleasure does not explain the distinction between light and profound in music and may even give us reason to prefer less profound music. Although music can properly be described in emotional terms, these terms have an analogical or metaphorical meaning when extended to music and this makes it questionable whether music can be said to express emotion in its ordinary human sense. Several important writers on music have attributed to music both a power to represent and the properties of a language. Upon examination, however, it can be shown that the power of music to represent is limited and dependent upon conventional associations. At best the analogy with language shows that music has a vocabulary but no grammatical structures. This means that though it may be used to prompt thoughts and impressions, it does not have the capacity of a genuine form of communication.

Nevertheless a connection may be made between music and the cognitivist theory of art. Music is special among art forms. While in theory photography could replace painting or cinema replace theatre, nothing could replace the experience of hearing music. Music is unique in providing us with extended structures of organized sound by means of which we may explore human experience, and in conventional musical sound this richness is increased by the possibility of interpretative performance. However, the aspect of human experience we explore with the assistance of great music is not that of the emotional or intellectual life, but the experience of hearing itself. To claim this as the distinguishing feature of music as an art is not to diminish its importance, because active listening, by contrast with passive hearing, is one aspect of the self-consciousness that makes human existence what it is.

Over the last 100 years or so, experimental music, sound recording and digital technology have combined to present new possibilities which challenge the uniqueness of music. Whether we call these innovations 'music' or not, they are radically different since they depart entirely from tonality. But they may also differ in another important respect – that unlike conventional music, they remove the exploration of sound from the realms of performing art.

Suggested further reading

Advanced introductory reading

Routledge Companion to Aesthetics (second edition), Chapter 51
Oxford Handbook of Aesthetics, Chapter 28

Classic writings

Hanslick, *On the Musically Beautiful*
Nietzsche, *The Birth of Tragedy*
Schopenhauer, *The World as Will and Representation*

Major contemporary works

Peter Kivy, *Music Alone* (1990)
Jerrold Levinson, *Music, Art and Metaphysics* (1990)
Roger Scruton, *The Aesthetics of Music* (1997)

6

The visual arts

The previous chapter, the first on a specific art form, was devoted to music since this has often been thought to be art at its purest. But it is a notable fact that the word 'art' is most naturally associated with the visual arts and painting in particular. E. H. Gombrich's *The Story of Art*, which has sold millions of copies and gone into 16 editions, is really the story of *painting*, with some references to sculpture and architecture. Neither music nor poetry makes any appearance in it.

This tendency to identify art in general with the visual arts both arises from, and lends support to, a very ancient view of art as *mimesis* (Greek for 'copying' or imitation). Art on this view is the replication of things in nature that are especially beautiful or in some other way worth contemplating. Such a conception, as we saw in the previous chapter, has a difficulty over music, where the idea of representation is problematic. But it fits the visual arts very easily and it is for this reason that representationalism – the view that representation is one of the chief functions of art – is so often applied to painting. In its commonest version, representationalism is a *normative* view – a view about good and bad in art. It leads people to place a high value on very lifelike portraits such as those by the great masters – Michelangelo, Rubens, Velásquez and so on – and to raise questions about the value of 'modern' art – the cubist distortions of Picasso, the surrealist figures of Jan Miro, the abstracts of Kandinsky or the 'action' paintings of Jackson Pollock.

Though twentieth-century art has become familiar to a large proportion of the general public, the belief persists that there is some important connection between lifelike representation and artistic value. This is partly because the historical development of painting was closely identified with gradual mastery of better and better methods of representation, but representationalism is also a view that some of the great artists themselves have endorsed. The important French sculptor and graphic artist Auguste Rodin (1840–1917), famous for the statue *The Thinker*, is recorded as saying 'The only principle in art is to copy what you see. Dealers in aesthetics to the contrary, every other method is fatal' (Goldwater and Treves 1976:

325). Representationalism has also found support among philosophers of art. Aristotle makes the activity of representing things the distinguishing character of what we now call 'the arts'. Plato decried art precisely because he thought it did no more than reproduce the appearance of things.

Representationalism, then, is a widespread view with a long history and important credentials in both art and philosophy. Yet as we shall see, representationalism is false as a descriptive theory even in the case of the visual arts, and while representation is clearly important in painting, it does not adequately explain its value. At the same time, it is a view well worth examining, because it is only once we have seen the errors in representationalism that we will fully appreciate the sort of value visual art can have.

What is representation?

Ideas about good and bad painting are often uncertain because of a tendency to confuse representation with copying. While people praise and admire lifelike portraiture and landscape painting, they also suppose that artists should not merely copy what they see but add an element of personal 'interpretation'. It is in this 'interpretation' that many people think the art lies and which raises it above simple copying. This is partly why they often wonder whether photography, which merely reproduces what is 'there' by causal means, can really be an art.

Yet whether photography is an art or not, it does not produce copies of the appearance of things. We never see in sepia or monochrome. When I look at a black and white photograph of a group of people one of whom has red hair, that person is represented in the picture, but not by a copy of her appearance. Even in a full-colour photograph, the redness of her hair can be enhanced by filter, exposure or lighting. Besides, every photograph has an angle from which it is taken. Since there is no neutral position that we can think of as the 'true' angle from which a person or an object has to be seen, the angle is the choice of the photographer. 'Copying' suggests passivity, but perfect passivity in photography is impossible. It is this fact and other similar facts upon which the art of the photographer is built.

The same is true of painting. We are inclined to think of representation as copying partly because the dominant convention in painting has long been to represent *via* strict resemblance. But this need not be so. Figures in ancient Egyptian art often appear peculiar and somewhat primitive to us, as though the artists were incapable of better. Part of the reason for this, however, is a different convention in representation. Ancient Egyptian art operated with the principle that each part of the human anatomy should be represented from the angle at which it is best seen. Thus while the face was depicted in profile, the torso was depicted from the front, and legs and feet from the side. Taken as a whole the end result was a body unlike any that has ever been seen. But it would be a mistake to conclude that there was some failure of representation. There was merely a different *convention* of representation. Ours may seem to us more 'natural', as perhaps it is, but its naturalness should not deceive us into thinking that it is more representational.

Foreshortening, perspective, the use of light and shade, which contribute so significantly to representation in Western art, were all important discoveries that greatly increased the power of the painter. But the power they give to the painter is not to reproduce what is 'there' but to create a convincing *impression* that we are seeing the thing represented. The consequence is that even the most lifelike representations cannot be thought of as mere copies. Their creators follow conventions determining how things are to be represented and employ techniques which oblige us to look at things in certain ways. John Constable (1776–1837), that most 'natural' of painters, whose painting *The Haywain* is one of the best-known and best-loved pictures in existence, uses blues and greens that are never actually found in sky or foliage. In *Gimcrack*, George Stubbs (1724–1806) represents the speed of a racing horse very effectively, but movie stills reveal that horses do not actually gallop that way. (All the paintings referred to in this chapter can be found in E. H. Gombrich's *The Story of Art* (1995).) Any depiction of nature that tries just to copy must fail, partly because every 'copy' of nature must involve seeing selectively, and partly because the work must reflect the representational resources available to the painter.

The divorce between representation and copying is complete when we turn to a popular area of visual art – cartoons. No mouse ever looked like Mickey Mouse and no ancient Gaul ever looked like Asterix, yet it is obvious even to small children what they are. Many famous woodcuts, drawings and engravings could be cited to sustain the same point. It is simply a mistake to think of representation in the visual arts as a simple attempt to 'copy' what is 'seen'.

Representation and artistic value

'Resembling', 'copying' and 'representing' are easily confused, but they are quite different. Cartoons can represent without resembling, and pictures can resemble the things they represent without being copies of them. Under the influence of naive representationalism people sometimes complain that the faces and figures in so-called 'modern' art do not look anything like the real thing. This is probably not a complaint peculiar to the modern period. It seems likely that those brought up on the highly realistic pictures of Dürer (1471–1528) and Holbein (1497/8–1543) thought something of the same about the rather more extravagant paintings by El Greco (1541–1614). But the important point is that if representation and resemblance are different, the visual arts can abandon resemblance without ceasing to be representational. Might they then go further, and abandon representation without ceasing to be art?

One reason for thinking so is the fact that some outstanding artists whose skill at representation is unquestionable have abandoned strictly representational painting. In *The Story of Art* Gombrich invites us to compare Picasso's *A Hen with Chickens* with his slightly earlier picture *A Cockerel*. The first of these is a charming illustration for Buffon's *Natural History*, the second a rather grotesque caricature. Gombrich makes the point that the first of these pictures amply demonstrates Picasso's ability to make lifelike representations. Consequently, when we note that the second drawing looks 'nothing like' a cockerel, instead of dismissing it we should ask what Picasso is trying to do with it. According to Gombrich, 'Picasso was not content with giving a mere rendering of the bird's appearance. He wanted to bring out its aggressiveness, its cheek and its stupidity' (Gombrich 1987: 9). L. S. Lowry (1887–1976) is another artist illustrative of the same point. In his most famous pictures people are generally drawn with a childish simplicity, 'stick' figures in fact, but his early drawings of male nudes show that this manner of depiction was a matter of choice, and we will only appreciate the pictures properly if we look into the reason for that choice.

Gombrich's interpretation of the Picasso cartoon brings out an important distinction that representationalism tends to overlook. There is a difference between representing something and giving a rendering of something's appearance. Those who favour representational art usually mean to favour painting that gives a good rendering of the appearance of things. As we have seen, 'giving a good rendering' is not a matter of 'copying' the appearance of things but creating something that resembles and thereby gives the viewer a convincing impression of having seen the object. Now what the example of Picasso's cockerel shows is that the creation of a resemblance is only one purpose for representation. The cartoon does not look like a bird we might see, but it is still representational. What it represents is not the bird's appearance, but its character. This shows that representation can serve purposes other than creating a resemblance, and in turn this opens up the possibility that these other purposes can be served by means other than representation.

Consider some further examples of representation. Almost all the painting from the European Middle Ages is religious in inspiration and purpose. The aim of much of it was to provide the illiterate faithful with instruction in Bible stories, Christian doctrine and the history of the Church, especially the history of its saints and martyrs. It did not aim at *mere* instruction, however, since it sought also to be inspirational, to prompt in those who looked at it an attitude of mind that would be receptive of divine grace. One interesting example of this is Dürer's engraving *The Nativity* (Dürer is a particularly good choice here because his pictures give such obviously excellent 'renderings of the appearance of things'). The engraving shows a dilapidated farmyard in which Joseph, depicted as an elderly peasant, is drawing water at the well, while in the front left-hand corner Mary bends over the infant Jesus. Much less prominently portrayed (looking through a rear doorway in fact) is a kneeling shepherd, accompanied by ox and ass. In the very distant sky there is a single angel. The difference in scale of these traditional nativity figures, relative to the house and farm buildings, is striking. But it is also a little misleading; the picture is not any the less a nativity scene than those in which shepherds and angels are more prominent. What Dürer has done, by a magnificently detailed representation of a common Northern European farmhouse, is to convey very immediately the compelling atmosphere of Holy Night with the purpose, we may suppose, of inducing a deeper sense of the mystery of the incarnation in the sort of people for whom the picture was intended.

Compare Dürer's engraving with *No. 1* by Jackson Pollock (1912–56). This painting is a result of Pollock's celebrated 'technique', later known as 'action painting', in which the canvas is placed on the floor and commercial enamels and metallic paints are dripped and splashed on it spontaneously. The outcome is an interesting and unusual pattern which the advocates of action painting thought revealed something of the artist's unconscious. But whether it does or not, the painting itself does not resemble anything.

At first sight, these two paintings could hardly be more different. Pollock's was intentionally the product of spontaneity and made with some speed, Dürer's the result of hours of painstaking work. Dürer's is representational to an unusually high degree, Pollock's wholly non-representational. Yet despite these striking differences, it is not implausible to say that both works share something of the same purpose. Pollock's *No. 1* is an example of 'abstract expressionism', and much of the painting that falls under this label was influenced by Eastern mysticism. Both the spontaneity of production and the random patterns it brings about were thought valuable because they shake ordered preconceptions. We are forced to see visual chaos rather than visual pattern and thus to see the uncertain, even unreal, nature of the world of appearance. Using the visual to create impressions of unreality is similar to the way in which some versions of Buddhism try to shake our preconceptions as a means of spiritual enlightenment. The paintings of abstract expressionism might be thought of as visual equivalents of Zen *koans*, the questions which the novice is made to contemplate, such as 'What is the sound of one hand clapping?' (Of course the creation and contemplation of *zenga*, or Zen pictures, for the most part abstract works of calligraphy, are an important part of Zen Buddhist practice also.)

Interpreted in this way, both Dürer's and Pollock's paintings, despite their striking differences, share the same purpose – to make people aware of spiritual realities behind everyday experience. It is not crucially important here whether the spiritual purpose so described fits either case. These two pictures illustrate the point that, in intention at any rate, representational and non-representational styles of painting, despite their radical differences, are both means that can be employed to the same artistic purpose.

What this shows is that we should not think of representation as the sole or even chief *end* of visual art, but only as one, admittedly very prominent, *means*. To see this is to reject representation as the criterion by which visual art is to be judged, since a means is only as valuable as the end it serves. It remains the case, of course, that representation is the stock in trade of visual artists, and nothing in the foregoing argument involves denying this. Even the Surrealists, a school of which Salvador Dali (1904–89) is perhaps the best-known member, who rejected the idea of 'renderings of the appearance of things' still made extensive use of representation. One of its greatest exponents, Rene Magritte (1898–1967), is a brilliant representational artist, but the things he represents are fantasies that could not possibly be how actual things appear.

We should infer from this, not that most painting is visual representation, but that representation is a highly valuable technique in visual art. Importantly, it is not the only one; there are other techniques to be explored. But to understand the value of visual art, we must go beyond both representation and these other techniques, and seek the ultimate purpose they serve. This brings us back to our central question. What is the most valuable end that art can serve? Preceding chapters concluded that neither pleasure, nor beauty nor the expression of emotion can adequately fill this role. The answer aesthetic cognitivism gives is, 'Enriching human understanding.' Can painting do this and, if so, how?

Art and the visual

Constable, commenting upon a new attraction on view in London, denied that it was art since it involved visual deception, and 'art pleases by reminding, not by deceiving' (quoted in E. H. Gombrich *Art and Illusion* (1977)). What this remark reveals is the assumption that the purpose of art is to please; the only question in Constable's mind is in the manner in which it does this, by reminding or by deceiving the eye. This assumption is probably widely shared. Yet as we saw in Chapter 1 it sits ill with everyday social practice; works of imagination are not ranked according to the pleasure they give. The clearest possible examples of drawings, paintings, photographs and films that are intended to give pleasure, and frequently do, are pornographic ones. It is hardly these, however, that will be held up to be the principal products of the art world. Of course it will be said, correctly, that there are pleasures other than sexual titillation. But this is not to the point. The arguments in Chapter 1 showed that there is no way of distinguishing between pleasures that will allow us to hold both that the value of art lies in the pleasure we get from it, and that there is an evaluative difference between serious and light art. We need not rehearse those arguments to see that they apply with equal force to a particular branch of art, in this case painting.

Someone persuaded by the arguments made in Chapter 1 might nevertheless be reluctant to abandon the idea that the value of visual art (or part of it) is the pleasure it gives, and may maintain that, at least in one respect, the greater the art, the greater the pleasure. This respect is the skill displayed by the artist. The history of Western art from c. 1400 to 1900 is a story of the discovery of a wide range of techniques in the use of perspective, composition and colour, and of the achievements these made possible. Both the skills of the great painters and the effects they achieved in their paintings are truly astonishing. They are, we might say, a delight to behold, and whether or not we call our delight in them 'pleasure', the fact remains that it is partly for the pleasure that we value them.

Still, even if this is true, it tells only half the story. Human beings have mastered many astonishing techniques, but the question of the value we should attach to those techniques remains unsettled until we know what they can be used to achieve. The *Guinness Book of Records* lists a large number of achievements made possible only through the mastery of skills which, though rarely mastered because of their difficulty, accomplish largely trivial ends. Some painters have shown a remarkable ability to bestow tactile values on visual images, to convey visually a sense of how objects feel. This is impressive, but so too is making bird noises while smoking cigars (a *Guinness Book of Records* example), and we must therefore ask whether the painter's skill serves any non-trivial end.

Representation is part of the answer. The skill of the painter increases representative power and, especially before the days of photography, lots of purposes are served by the ability to represent – commemoration and decoration being among the most obvious. In general we assume that representative painting has a serious purpose, partly because it requires a skill that it is natural to admire. Why expend time and effort on the mastering of such a skill if not for a serious purpose? (Though the challenge presented by the example of cigars and bird noises remains.) But which of the many serious purposes representation can serve is distinctively artistic, and what is valuable about it? It is the task of a normative theory of art to answer this question.

In the history of visual art (and the arts more widely perhaps) the importance of this question has only come to be recognized relatively recently. Throughout most of its development, painting has so clearly had a social function – the decoration of churches, stately homes and civic buildings, the painting of portraits, the recording of momentous events and so on – that the question of any further *raison d'être* for the visual arts has hardly arisen. As Gombrich says, in the 'good old days'

> no artist need ask himself why he had come into the world at all. In some ways his work had been as well defined as that of any other calling. There were always altar-paintings to be done, portraits to be painted; people wanted to buy pictures for their best parlours, or commissioned murals for their villas. In all these jobs he could work on more or less pre-established lines. He delivered the goods which the patron expected. True, he could produce indifferent work, or do it so superlatively well that the job in hand was no more than an occasion for a transcendent masterpiece. But his position in life was more or less secure. It was just this feeling of security that artists lost in the nineteenth century.
>
> (Gombrich 1977: 397)

Gombrich identifies several historical causes, including the invention of photography, for the rift between the artist and the public. This rift brought into question the justification of painting as an occupation (and a similar question arose about sculpture). An appreciation of these historical developments is important for understanding the relation between the value of art and the forms of art prevalent at any one time, but the question we are concerned with here is not itself a historical one. It could be asked in any historical period why and to what extent skill at painting is to be valued. Charting historically the changing perceptions of the role of art may illuminate the answers we give, but of itself it cannot supply them because there may have been periods when this ability was overestimated or underestimated.

Previous chapters concluded that art enhances the understanding of human experience. We may ask here, therefore, whether this is something the visual arts can do. One obvious way is through heightened experience of the visual itself. This suggestion may seem to make art superficial – literally – a reduction of painting to the level of mere coloured patterns. This is a charge sometimes laid against 'modern' art, especially so-called 'abstract art' – that it has set aside centuries of achievement in the art of representation for the construction of mere pattern, and sometimes not even this. For example, the paintings of Marc Rothko (1903–70), which many art critics have regarded highly, are simply large patches of colour. At the same time, presentation and exploration of the strictly visual has long been a quest in the history of art. Perhaps this quest has only come to full self-consciousness of late, but we should not conclude from this that it was ever wholly absent.

Besides, whatever reservations we might have about modern art, there are good reasons to regard the exploration of the strictly visual as an achievement. In the preceding chapter it was argued that music is a foregrounding of the aural, and that this is one of its valuable characteristics. Similarly, a special accomplishment of painting could be the foregrounding of the visual. We saw in the first part of this chapter that it is a mistake to think of representation as mere copying. Painters do not merely imitate. They cannot be thought of as presenting the 'raw' visual data which the spectator then 'observes'. Painters have to choose from all the things that can be seen. Often what they present are hints and suggestions of what is seen. The mind of the spectator then supplies what is missing to form an image. This is how it is possible for painters such as Constable to use unnatural colours and yet give us a convincing impression that we are seeing the thing he has chosen to paint. In this way prior knowledge enters our perception of a painting.

This prior knowledge can also be a distortion of the visual, however, especially if it is the painter's knowledge as well as the spectator's. This is what is happening in the Egyptian figures referred to at the beginning of this chapter. The painter knows what arms and legs and profiles look like from different angles, and then combines different perspectives in a single representation that does not resemble the normal thing at all. To appreciate the end result, we need to suspend our visual preconceptions. This is not an easy business, but once a move in this direction is made, we may find that true representational likeness recedes as well. Exponents of the school of art known as Impressionism were keenly aware of the fact that we do not give most of the things we see close attention and only receive a fleeting impression of their appearance. They knew that bright light and deep shadow eliminate visual features so they tried to capture something of this phenomenon in their paintings, one consequence of which was a loss of 'realism' as detailed features were suppressed. A particularly good example of this is Monet's *Gare St-Lazare*, in which the objects we would expect to find in a picture of a railway station are dominated and almost eliminated by the visual impact of sunlight, smoke and steam. *Gare St-Lazare* can be understood as an attempt to strip the act of perception of all preconceptions, and thus encapsulate the purely visual.

Foregrounding the visual is not incompatible with representational art, however. Whistler's famous painting entitled *Arrangement in Grey and Black* is a highly representational portrait of the artist's mother. The title reveals that we are invited to see the seated woman from a purely visual standpoint. This is why the work lacks a certain three-dimensional depth. So, if the prime purpose of a work of art is to foreground the visual and make abstract all preconception of how things are to be seen, then representational faithfulness is of secondary importance. A desire to heighten awareness of colour, or draw attention to incipient patterns, as in many of the paintings of Vincent Van Gogh (1853–90) and Paul Gauguin (1848–1903), may call for representational freedom. Only if, without reason, we insist upon the primacy of representation in art can these be called distortions.

More than this, once we see that a painter can be concerned with experience and yet not primarily interested in representation, we admit the possibility of paintings supplying us with wholly novel visual experience. This is what happens to some degree in Cubism and Surrealism. Picasso's well-known picture *Violin and Grapes* provides us with something we could not see without the artist's intervention, namely, the different aspects of a violin from several different angles and all at once. Many of Dali's paintings (whatever the theory behind them) exaggerate and hence draw attention to visual 'ambiguities' – the shadow of a swan or the outline of an elephant, for instance, in *Swans into Elephants*.

The Dali example introduces again some of the themes of Chapter 4, where it was argued that we ought not to think of the relationship between art and reality as one of correspondence in which art reflects reality. Rather, art enhances our understanding by providing us with images and perspectives through which everyday experience may be seen afresh. This accords with the conclusions of this chapter that representation in the visual arts is not to be thought of as copying. The painter gets us to attend directly to our visual experience rather than seeing past it for the sake of the information it provides. Thus, Monet's painting of the Gare St-Lazare is in one sense a picture of what is actually seen, but in another it is not, because normally our minds would supply details that are cloaked by the steam and the sunlight. Monet's achievement is to get us to focus on one aspect of our experience that is usually neglected. Dali's surrealist paintings, by contrast, can hardly be said to depict real experiences. Yet the visual ambiguities in his pictures are merely exaggerations of real features of our visual experience. Dali creates an alternative experience rather than capturing the visual in our normal experience, and at the same time his creations can be seen to be explorations of that experience. The same can be said for the engravings of M. C. Escher, many of which are now famous for just this reason. These explore perspective. The eye is drawn around, for instance, a waterfall. Each level seems lower than the one before, yet somehow as the eye moves round we reach the top of the waterfall again. These engravings are not merely technical puzzles; they show how the mind and thus experience may be manipulated in the perception of the visual.

To construe visual art as a medium for the enhancement and exploration of visual experience does not trivialize it. It allows us to make sense of certain important developments in the history of contemporary painting. But if this were all that could be said for visual art as a form of understanding human experience, we would have failed to explain the importance of representation within an adequate theory of art. On the face of it, there is no special role for representation in 'the foregrounding of the visual'. This means that as an explanation of the value of the visual arts, foregrounding skews our view of painting in the direction of modern developments. It gives little or no account of most of the great achievements of the past which all had *subjects*. Additionally, though painting might in these ways reveal interesting aspects of our strictly visual experience, the strictly visual is a small item in our experience as a whole. If painting cannot move beyond the visual, it is inevitably of limited value and interest.

Visual art and the non-visual

Can the non-visual be portrayed by visual means? There is an abstract painting by Piet Mondrian (1872–1944) entitled *Broadway Boogie-Woogie*. As the title suggests, the picture aims in some sense to present in a purely visual medium a dimension of the same thing that is found in 'boogie-woogie' sound. This move across the senses is sometimes called 'synesthesia' and Gombrich has argued that, once we have understood it properly, Mondrian's picture is a good, if limited, example of it (Gombrich 1987: 367–9). Now while it would be difficult to deny that, as a matter of brute experience, seeing a colour, say, can cause someone to feel tingling in the spine, it is debatable that synesthesia in the pure sense of the word is ever realized. It is certainly remarkable how successfully painters have managed to portray visually the sensual richness of fabrics and so on, such that we might almost speak of their having pictured how these things feel to the touch. Nevertheless, there are strong arguments that these and similar ways of talking about the senses must be regarded as less than literal. Some of the same points arise here as arose in the discussion of music in the previous chapter. Language that appears to bridge gaps between the different senses may be a matter of analogical extension. Let us suppose, then, that the strictly visual is limited in just the way that absolute music is. Even so, there is an important difference between the two, and it is just here that representation becomes of consequence. Painting unmistakably has a power to represent that music lacks, and this power to represent is in fact a means of going beyond the strictly visual.

Consider a simple case. Thoughts are not visual; we can hear and understand them but not see them. Yet a cartoon character can be represented as thinking by a simple and well-understood graphic device – a little sequence of bubbles coming from the head. It might be said that this is not a good case of the visual representation of the non-visual, since the thought within the final bubble is usually conveyed by linguistic rather than visual means. But in fact the thought can be just as easily represented by a picture. Even small children readily understand a purely graphical representation of 'He's thinking of his cat'. Clearly then the visual *can* portray the non-visual. Included in the non-visual it can portray are states of emotion. The child will just as easily interpret the cartoon as saying 'He's *missing* his cat' even when there are no verbal clues. Now this identification is made possible by a process of highly selective representation on the part of the cartoonist. It is a remarkable fact that a few simple lines can portray a disconsolate face, and the same fact makes it possible for the cartoonist to ensure that what strikes us about the face is its disconsolateness.

The cartoon is a simple example. In the history of art there are many more sophisticated ones, often portraits that speak volumes about mind and temperament – Holbein's *Sir Richard Southwell* or Goya's *King Ferdinand*

VII of Spain, for example. Yet these representations are not significant for what they tell us about what their sitters looked like – who knows whether Ferdinand really looked as stupid, arrogant and smug as Goya's portrait? Whether he did or not does not matter. The aesthetic value and significance of great portraits does not lie in their faithfulness to the sitter, even if most of them are in fact faithful in this respect. Rather, to contemporary viewers who are unfamiliar with the appearance of the original subject, such paintings present visual images of a state of mind and character which, in a similar way to a poetic image, can alter our everyday experience, including emotional experience. By making us more aware of what that experience contains, the representative power of the visual arts enhances our understanding in precisely the way aesthetic cognitivism requires.

Representation is one way in which visual art enhances our understanding of life. The idea behind the expressionist school of painting was that emotional states could also be portrayed by the more strictly visual. Thus Van Gogh wanted his picture of *The Artist's Room in Arles* to portray restfulness, and expected to accomplish this largely through the use of colour. There are difficulties about sustaining Van Gogh's view of emotion in painting, but it is sufficient for the general argument about the value of visual art to see that it has the power to portray mental and emotional states, whether this is accomplished solely through representation or by other means as well.

How far can this representational power go? Might it have something to offer in the way of intellectual apprehension of experience as well? Such a claim is made implicitly in a lecture to the British Academy on a cycle of frescoes by Ambrogio Lorenzetti of Sienna. Quentin Skinner claims that it was Lorenzetti, and not the most eminent philosophers of the thirteenth and fourteenth centuries, who 'made the most memorable contribution to the debate' about the ideals and methods of republican self-government. This suggests that Lorenzetti's frescoes can be thought of as structured forms of argument, a suggestion confirmed by the subtitle of the lecture 'The Artist as Political Philosopher'. In fact, upon examination, Skinner means to claim only that an 'ideal of social and political life is being held up for our admiration' in a 'dramatic way', and in his detailed analysis of the frescoes, he refers to such features as the placing of the various figures as an 'apt illustration' of a political theory. Almost nothing is said about how the frescoes might bear out the theory or sustain it as the truth.

Perhaps it is fanciful to suppose that they could. The artist qua artist cannot be a political philosopher. Nevertheless, if visual art is to be more than the dramatic or memorable illustration of truths arrived at elsewhere, if it is to be itself a source of human understanding, there must be some fashion in which it *directs* the mind to the apprehension of truth and reality.

We have in fact already encountered two ways in which visual art can do this. First, by forcing our attention to pure visual experience, it may lead us to explore that experience. Second, by providing us with visual images of emotion and character, painting and sculpture may heighten our awareness (not merely our consciousness) of those states in ourselves and in others. But third, if it cannot supply us with any 'philosophy', it may nevertheless broaden the horizons of our understanding by imagining possibilities and giving form to things whose substance is in doubt.

Consider this case. Saint Theresa of Avila is one of the most famous Christian mystics. It is clear from her own account that she underwent some very intense experience. What is less clear is just how this experience is to be understood. In the descriptions she herself gives, the language used is so closely associated with sexual experience that it raises a doubt about whether her mysticism may have had its origins more in sexual fantasy than in an encounter with the divine. But it is only a doubt because if her experience was a mystical one of peculiar intensity, perhaps the language of sexual excitement is the best available substitute, though a poor one. If we are to rely on her record alone, then, there must be some uncertainty about the nature and reality of her experience.

We might try to settle the question in another way, by denying, for instance, that there is any such thing as mystical experience. If so, Saint Theresa can only have been engaged in sexual fantasy. But this implication and hence the claim upon which it rests is acceptable only if there is no distinguishable difference between the two. It is here that we might make appeal to imagination in the visual arts. The celebrated sculpture of Saint Theresa by Bernini (1598–1680), in Santa Maria della Vittoria in Rome, portrays her in a state of ecstasy, and about to be pierced by the angel with his golden arrow. There are many interesting things about this work, especially given its place in the historical development of art. But a further question is this: has Bernini succeeded in imagining a specifically religious state of mind? Is this a convincing representative image of a state of ecstasy other than sexual excitement? We do not have to be in a position to answer these questions to see its relevance in the present context. If he has succeeded, then nothing has been proved about Saint Theresa. But what has been shown is that those who want to collapse religious ecstasy into sexual fantasy have overlooked important phenomenological differences of which, in this case, the work of art has made us aware.

Bernini's sculpture may or may not be a well chosen example, but at the very least it points us towards a real possibility: that visual art should contribute to the consideration of questions about the possibilities of human experience wider than those which arise within the confines of our own immediate experience.

If this is true, we have now seen three interesting ways in which visual art may be said to enlarge and enhance our understanding. It is important to record and underline these because only then can we give a satisfactory explanation of relative value in the visual arts. Nothing that has been said is intended to deny that one valuable feature of art is the development of skilful ways of creating beautiful objects. But the same may be said of the art of the jeweller. Many great works in the visual arts are indeed very beautiful and are to be valued as such. Not all are, however, and even among those that are, beauty does not encompass the whole of their value. What we now need to ask is whether this other (and I should say deeper) capacity – the ability of the visual arts to enhance our understanding – also has its limits.

One obvious limit is this. The images with which we are presented in painting and in sculpture are essentially static. This is not to say that movement cannot be represented in painting – many of Turner's paintings show just how successfully this can be done (*Steamer in a Snowstorm* is an especially good example). But painting cannot present us with a developing point of view. While it can underscore the significance of a particular event within a known story, no painting can itself tell the story. This is a limitation, as countless paintings of the Nativity reveal. Of course an artist can paint a series of pictures, like the cycle of frescoes by Lorenzetti already referred to. But he must take a chance as to the order in which the spectator chooses to look at the frescoes, and indeed as to whether those who look at his work continue to see the paintings as importantly related in sequence. If sequential viewing is *not* to be left to chance, but determined by the artist, we must turn from painting and sculpture to another visual art, namely, film. As the name 'the movies' makes explicit, film can transcend the limitations of the static image.

Film as art

The dynamic character of film has been regarded as one of its most important attributes, by both film theorists and the makers of film. The French film critic and theorist André Bazin says 'photography is a feeble technique in the sense its instanteity compels it to capture time only piecemeal. The cinema [by contrast] makes a molding of the object as it exists in time and, furthermore, makes an imprint of the duration of the object' (Bazin 1967: 97, brackets added).

In a similar spirit, the great Russian director Sergei Eisenstein identifies the peculiar strength of montage in the succession of filmic images.

> The spectator is compelled to travel along the selfsame creative road that the artist travelled in creating the image. The spectator not only sees the represented elements of the finished work, but also experiences the dynamic process of the emergence and assembly of the image just as it was experienced by the author . . . every spectator . . . creates an image in accordance with the representational guidance suggested by

> the author, leading him to understanding and experience of the author's theme.
>
> (Eisenstein 1943: 34)

Eisenstein's view is common (though not universal) among those who have written about film. In order to understand his view in its proper context, we need to begin by looking at a more sceptical question. The claim that film may be a more powerful visual art form than painting makes the assumption that film is indeed an art form. This has been doubted and continues to be doubted in some quarters. The basis for this doubt usually arises from the fact that photography is a mechanical art and the corresponding belief that it employs a purely causal process into which artistry cannot enter.

This doubt about photography has already been addressed in the course of the discussion, and we need not now rehearse the arguments. It seems to me evident (1) that choice and deliberation enter into photography in ways that clearly correspond to all the other arts, and (2) that causality in art is not restricted to photography. As Noël Carroll remarks, 'When I write a novelistic description of a room and my fingers touch the keyboard of my IBM typewriter, the process of printing the words is automatic. Is the mechanical process between me and the final text any less automatic with the typewriter than with the camera?' (Carroll 1988: 155). It is worth adding that arguments against photography as an art form could not in any case be applied without amendment to cinema, for although it is true that most contemporary cinema is photography based, its origins lie in the development of moving pictures and projection, not photography, and to this day some animation continues to exploit the development of cinema without recourse to photography.

Despite these rather obvious facts, from time to time the charge continues to be levelled at film that there is nothing more to it than *mimesis* in the sense of copying – we point the camera and mechanically record what is in front of it. This recurrent doubt is partly explained by the attitudes of those who first used photographic film as a medium. At its inception, film plainly had striking advantages as a method of recording real people and historical events, and was largely valued as such. Second, early use of film for artistic purposes did indeed take the form of recording artistic performances. The camera was placed in a fixed position before a stage on which a drama was performed, and the aim of the filmmaker was largely to provide an opportunity for those who were unable to attend the live performance, to see the drama nonetheless. In addition to its historical genesis, the view that photography and hence film is mere copying gathered further support from the undeniable facts that the objects in a photograph must 'be there', and the photograph does indeed reproduce them, whereas the objects in a painting or a drawing need not 'be there', and may on occasions be wholly the products of artistic imagination.

Montage vs long shot

The responses of film theorists to this sceptical view can be divided broadly into two groups. First there are those, of whom Eisenstein and Rudolph Arnheim are among the best known, who claim that film has the ability to escape the limitation of what might be called 'inevitable attachment to reality'. Thus, commenting upon the idea that the audience is merely the 'fourth wall' of a stage (the other three being the backdrop and wings), Leon Moussinac says on the contrary 'in film the fourth wall of the room in which the action takes place is not simply left out, but . . . the camera is brought into the actual room and takes part in the story'.

Arnheim, quoting Moussinac on this point, elaborates upon the idea by remarking that film becomes an art form when the mere urge to record certain actual events is abandoned in favour of 'the aim to represent objects by special means exclusive to film'.

> These means obtrude themselves, show themselves able to do more than simply reproduce the required object; they sharpen it, impose a style upon it, point out special features, make it vivid and decorative. Art begins where mechanical reproduction leaves off.
>
> (Arnheim 1958: 55)

Arnheim's answer to the sceptic, then, is to insist that film can leave 'mechanical production' behind, and in this way film becomes an art form. A contrary view is to be found in the voluminous writings of André Bazin. Bazin thinks that it is precisely the ability to copy what is 'there' that gives film its special role as an art form.

> The aesthetic qualities of photography are to be sought in its power to lay bare the realities. . . . Only the impassive lens, stripping its object of all those ways of seeing it, those piled up preconceptions, that spiritual dust and grime with which my eyes have covered it, is able to present it in all its virginal purity to my attention.
>
> (Bazin 1967: 15)

These two lines of thought are in large part reflections of different styles of filmmaking. But they are normative as well as descriptive theories and may thus be seen to recommend different techniques of direction. Thus Arnheim's view is both a description and a commendation of films such as Eisenstein's. In these the device of montage, a rapid series of short shots, is used extensively to focus the spectators' attention sharply and drive it through a selection of specific images. Montage departs from how things 'really are', since we do not see the world as a series of discrete visual episodes, and since in Arnheim's view the art in film depends upon such departures from reality, montage is to be commended in the construction of film. Bazin's theory, on the other hand, reflects the style of filmmaking dominant in America in the 1950s, in which much use was made of medium and long shots, which present a wide and continuous visual field, and this is just the sort of 'realistic' filmmaking Bazin commends.

To appreciate the contrast at work in these two views, consider the following simple episode. A family is having a picnic by a river. Unnoticed by her parents, the little girl is stumbling perilously near the water. The family dog barks and runs to the child. The parents are alerted and bring her out of danger. In a long shot of this episode, the camera and the scene would be so arranged that all the actors would be visible all the time. The camera might focus more clearly on one or the other from time to time, but at no point would anything be out of view. To treat the same episode in montage, there would be separate shots of the family, the child, the parents, the dog, the rescue.

One obvious difference between the two techniques is that montage focuses the spectator's attention in a way that long shots do not. Those like Eisenstein and Arnheim who favour montage, do so because it enables the filmmaker to select and emphasize what they want the spectator to see. 'It is essential', Arnheim says, 'that the spectator's attention should be guided' (Arnheim 1958: 44). In the episode just imagined, montage makes clear the role of the dog's barking. By contrast Bazin and others favour long shot over montage chiefly because (they allege) this is how we actually see things. We do not see events in separate snapshots. While in montage selected shots are artificially collated, in a long shot the camera follows the actors just as our eyes would, and this is why it is more 'realistic'. More importantly perhaps, they reject deliberate selection on the part of the filmmaker, believing it desirable to preserve a measure of uncertainty in order to preserve the spectator's freedom of interpretation. In the passage omitted from the quotation above, Bazin says, 'It is not for me to separate off, in the complex fabric of the objective world, here a reflection on a damp sidewalk, there a gesture of a child.' Spectators must be left to make such selections for themselves.

There is, however, something of a tension in Bazin's view. On the one hand he commends 'realistic' film because it 'lays bare realities', while at the same time wanting to preserve 'ambiguity'. But if viewers are to have reality forced upon their attention, this necessarily eliminates at least some of the ambiguity. It is not hard to see that at the level which matters, the dispute between montage and long shot is based upon a false dichotomy. Many of the differences between montage and long shot are matters of degree rather than kind, and the exclusive merits of each need not be in competition. The length of a shot is to be understood as merely the time given to the spectator, and this can obviously be longer or shorter. In montage it is less, in long shot more, but there is no radical difference between the two. If the collation of short shots serves some purposes and the presentation of long shot others, a director is free to employ both at different points in the film.

Bazin thinks that the ability of film to 'copy' gives it the means to direct our attention to reality. He would of course be wrong to draw the implication that the director is in any sense passive. The plot, direction, angle and focus of every long shot still has to be worked out. The point to stress is, whatever else they may disagree on, the 'realists' as represented by Bazin share the view of the 'creationists' as represented by Arnheim: the value and interest in film are in its revelatory properties and these properties derive in large part from artistic use of the camera. In other words, both schools of thought in classical film theory aim to demonstrate that film is an art, one by showing how far the use of the camera enables us to depart from mere reproduction, the other how the peculiar power of photographic reproduction gives film an artistic advantage that other art forms cannot enjoy.

The interesting question for our purposes, then, is not whether film can be an art, but whether these theorists have succeeded in isolating features of film that will give it distinctive value. On this of course they differ, and not only between a preference for montage as opposed to long shot. They differ in fact over whether film is strengthened or weakened as an art by the introduction of sound, which brings us back to the issue with which this section began. Is film a more powerful visual art than painting, or does it gain this additional power precisely in so far as it ceases to be a purely visual art?

'Talkies'

Arnheim believed that with the introduction of sound, the art of film had effectively been destroyed just when its truly artistic purposes had begun to be realized. His principal reason for thinking this was his belief partly that black and white film without stereoscopic vision can provide unique visual experiences, and partly because film offers us a way of exploring the visual dimension of experiences that are not purely visual in reality. He gives the following example of the first:

> in Jacques Feyder's *Les Nouveaux Messieurs* [t]wo lovers . . . are seen in conversation, with their heads close together. Then a close-up is shown in which half the picture is covered by the dark silhouette of the back of the man's head (the camera being placed behind him) and this head partially conceals the woman's full face, of which the remainder is seen in bright light.
>
> . . . The reduction of depth serves . . . to emphasize the perspective superposition of objects. In a strongly stereoscopic picture the manner in which these various objects are placed relative to one another does not impose itself any more than it does in real life. The concealing of certain parts of the various objects by others that come in front seems chance and unimportant. Indeed, the position of the camera in a stereoscopic picture seems itself to be a matter of indifference

> inasmuch as it is obvious that there is a three dimensional space which may just as easily, and at the next moment probably will, be looked at from another point of view. If however, the effect of depth is almost negligible, the perspective is conspicuous and compelling. . . . There is no leeway between the objects: they are like flat surfaces stuck over one another, and seem almost to lie on the same plane.
>
> Thus the lack of depth brings a very welcome element of unreality into the film picture. Formal qualities, such as the compositional and evocative significance of particular superimpositions, acquire the power to force themselves on the attention of the spectator. A shot like that described above where half of the girl's face is cut off by the dark silhouette of the man's head, would possess only a fraction of its effectiveness if there were a strong feeling of space.
>
> (Arnheim 1958: 54–7)

One of the examples Arnheim gives of the second special effect of film, namely, to draw attention to non-visual phenomena in visual terms, is now well known.

> [A] revolver shot might occur as the central point of a silent film; a clever director could afford to dispense with the actual noise of the shot. . . . In Josef von Sternberg's *The Docks of New York* a shot is very cleverly made visible by the sudden rising of a flock of scared birds.
>
> (37)

What Arnheim is chiefly concerned with (and spends a long time detailing) is the peculiar power of film as a *visual* art. In his view, technical advances in filmmaking, especially colour and sound, threatened this status precisely because they allowed greater naturalism. To the 'realists', by contrast, they promised greater representative power. With the benefit of hindsight we can see that there is no need for exclusiveness on either side. Those features that impressed Arnheim are still available to the modern filmmaker; a revolver shot can still be 'made visible' in the way he describes, and perhaps to even greater effect just because sound as a normal accompaniment is the order of the day. So too with colour. Steven Spielberg's film *Schindler's List* is shot in sepia, which allows him to use red in just one scene to give special prominence and significance to a young Jewish girl. A similar point can be made about the technical preferences of Bazin and others. A film that uses montage or close-up extensively can also use long shots in which the camera follows the action continuously. Nor need we share Bazin's anxieties over montage's curtailing the interpretative freedom of the spectator; interpretative freedom (if it is indeed properly thought of in this way) merely enters at a higher level in understanding the significance rather than the content of the images in montage.

Nevertheless, there is a point of some consequence here. Film has advanced beyond the silent screen. Arnheim regarded the arrival of sound as a misfortune because it removed film from the sphere of the purely visual, and this he thought to be an impoverishment. Others have regarded the same development as an enrichment, since it supplies us with a medium of greater power for aesthetic purposes. But both views concur with the fact that modern film cannot be regarded as a purely visual art.

Does this matter? In one sense, contrary to Arnheim, it does not. He thinks that artistry in filmmaking requires that we 'consciously stress the peculiarities' of the medium. But he gives no reason for this, and his examples and explanation of artistry in filmmaking aim to show only that films can go beyond mere recording to accomplish artistic purposes. He appears to conflate the idea that film has distinctive ways of achieving such purposes with the idea that it is only through these distinctive methods that film can achieve them. But this is obviously wrong. We can agree that montage is a method unique to film and at the same time hold that an accompanying soundtrack can make a film sequence still more arresting. To appreciate film as an art we certainly need to stress its distinctive powers, but this does not warrant the sort of purism Arnheim seems to think it does.

On the other hand, it is true that modern film has gone beyond the purely visual. While the techniques of close-up, montage, special lighting, and so on are important, acting, dialogue and soundtrack are no longer mere additions, but integral parts of filmmaking. It is odd that Arnheim should have regretted the introduction of sound since the soundtrack of a film is no more 'mere recording' than is the photography, and can be used in many of the ways that Arnheim thinks important. Aural 'montage' is a familiar and useful technique. Loud noises can be used to much the same effect as the looming shapes he discusses.

Arguably such additions are not to be regretted but welcomed as ways in which we can both exploit visual experience and transcend its limitations. It has sometimes been claimed that in film almost all artistic limitations are overcome. Filmic representation can explore formal visual properties; it can contain dramatic action as in a play, while nevertheless retaining the greater control over spectator attention that directed photography allows; it provides the fullest possible context in which dialogue is made significant; it employs sound effects; it adds music to visual images, thereby intensifying their evocative power. In short film is the super-medium, the sort of thing that Wagnerian opera aimed (but arguably failed) to be. Viewed in this way, Arnheim's anxieties about departing from an original purity are unfounded and misplaced. Every technical advance is gain.

The 'auteur' in film

Yet, if film truly is the super-medium this line of argument suggests, should it not have come to outclass other art forms? Should the major works of modern art not be films? Film has *not* come to dominate the art world in this way. What then explains this gap between potential and actuality? Some of the explanation is socio-historical. Film may have the making of a super-art, but it is also an outstanding form of entertainment. The result is that the money for moviemaking has come largely from the entertainment industry. Accordingly, most of the effort that has gone into filmmaking has been devoted to this end, and to its commercial success. It is as if the primary efforts of painters had been devoted to wallpaper design. The contingent associations that this fact has given rise to have further circumscribed film's actual use as an artistic medium. 'Hollywood' does not have the same cultural resonance as 'Bayreuth', 'The Tate' or even 'Broadway'. The result is that among the countless films that have been made, relatively little of lasting artistic significance has emerged.

Commercial potential and cultural context have been important in the reception of film, but there is something in the nature of film itself which helps to explain its relatively modest contribution to art. The move to a super-medium is not *all* gain. There can also be loss. Where music accompanies film, for instance, it is possible for one to vie with the other for our attention, with the result that the impact of each, far from being heightened, is diminished. It is sometimes the case that the score for a film, or part of it, becomes a recognized piece of music in its own right, something that is worth listening to and better listened to on its own. (Some of Shostakovich's music is a good example.) Given modern conditions for the commissioning of music this may be an important way in which new compositions emerge, but taken by itself it is a mark of failure. The desirability of 'liberating' the music from the film demonstrates the existence of fragmentation where there ought to have been organic unity.

The potential scope for such fragmentation in filmmaking is immense. A film comprises the following elements: plot, dialogue, action, direction, screenplay, camera work, editing, score and special effects. When academy awards are made, frequently a film scores highly in only a few, sometimes only one, of these respects. Superb camera work can record a poor plot, brilliant special effects may follow ham acting, memorable music may accompany a trivial story, and so on. Of course, paintings, novels and musical composition can also be analysed by distinct elements which may differ in quality or even conflict with one another – colour *versus* subject, characters *versus* dialogue, harmony *versus* melody, for example. But there is still an important difference; in all these cases it is just such tensions that ought to be resolved by the creative imagination of a single mind – the painter, the author, the composer – whose greatness is measured in part by the degree of imaginative unity achieved. A film on the other hand has no single author.

Or so it can be argued. Another important point of discussion in the philosophy of film has been *auteur* theory. For some theorists, the concept of 'auteur' in film is applicable only to a body of cinematographic work. A director becomes an author not by making a single film but by developing an identifiable style exhibited through a body of film work – Hitchcock and Ford are authors by virtue of their distinctive visions. More everyday directors are not.

In a similar spirit it might be claimed that the writer of a single book, even if it is very well regarded (Harper Lee and *To Kill a Mockingbird* would be a good example), can hardly be described as an author in a broader sense when compared to a writer like, say, Joseph Conrad whose style is extended over many works. But even if we were to agree that this is so, there is a striking disanalogy between the two cases. While there is no doubt about the identity of the artist with respect to one book or many, there can be different accounts of who is to be regarded as the author of a film, the *auteur* in a narrower sense.

The fact that this is a matter of dispute is a point of difference not just between movies and books, but between film and most of the other arts. It is also a fact to which sufficient attention is not always paid. The existence of any artwork requires more than one party – books have to be read, music played and listened to, pictures looked at – the assigning of books to their authors ('Tolstoy's *War and Peace*'), pieces of music to their composers ('Beethoven's *Fifth*') and pictures to painters ('Picasso's *Guernica*') is unproblematic. In the case of films this is not so. The most natural candidate for the role of *auteur* (in the narrow sense) is the director. *Citizen Kane* is regularly and repeatedly listed as one of the greatest films ever made and universally regarded as the work of Orson Welles. But though there are some instances such as this one where there is no practical uncertainty about authorship, this is not generally true. Perhaps in many, even most, films the director is the principal influence on the final form of the film. Even so, the role of the director is properly thought of as one of choosing rather than creating. Directors do not construct the plot, write the screenplay, work the cameras, build the sets or compose the score. They do not always cast the parts, only occasionally appear in the film themselves, and usually oversee the final cut rather than directly editing it themselves. What this means is that the relation of the director to all these collaborators cannot be compared to that between the author of a play and those who perform it. This is demonstrated by the fact that whereas a good play can be performed badly, bad performance in a film makes it to that extent a poor film. Directors of films do not stand to the outcome of their efforts as playwrights do to theirs.

It is not a *necessary* truth about film that it has no single mind at work to control it. One can imagine one person superhumanly performing all these roles, and it is true that in some of the best films one person fills many roles. Perhaps it is not an accident that *Citizen Kane* is an outstanding film, because Orson Welles not only directed but took the lead role and wrote the screenplay. Yet, despite a few striking examples like this, it is an important fact about film as a medium that it has to combine the technical skill and artistic imagination of a great many people. Modern film is a multimedia art form that makes a single *auteur* practically impossible. Accordingly its power to transcend the limits of any one medium – the purely visual for example – and to work with dynamic and not merely static images, is offset by its liability to fragmentation. The greater the power, we might say, the harder it is to control. If the greatest works of art are those that direct the attention of the audience to and through an imagined experience which in turn illuminates real experience, this is somewhat paradoxically less likely in film than in other arts, despite the powers at its disposal.

Thus Arnheim's purism and his anxiety about the introduction of elements other than the visual, though unwarranted on the basis of the reasons he gives, is not without some foundation. Interestingly Eisenstein, several of whose films are among those most fitted to Arnheim's analysis, went to extraordinary lengths to retain control over every aspect of the finished result. He was famous for the large number of immensely detailed drawings, diagrams and instructions he produced for the guidance of actors, cameramen and setbuilders. And where he used music he required it to 'be composed to a completely finished editing of the pictorial element' (Eisenstein 1943: 136).

This analysis of the inherent weakness in film as an art appeals to the principle that 'the greater the power, the harder it is to control'. The same principle does not work in reverse. It is not the case that 'the harder to control, the greater the power'. While it is true that the multifaceted character of film makes it a more powerful medium potentially, while at the same time increasing the tendency to fragmentation, it is a mistake to think that such power is possible only through multimedia. In fact, there is a medium that can completely transcend the limits of the visual, the aural, the static, the tangible and so on. This is the medium of language. Language allows us to create imaginative images of the visual, the aural, the narrative, the emotional, etc. These images are apprehended intellectually rather than sensually. Language has the power of film, we might say, without the disadvantages. Both the powers and the problems of the literary arts are the topic of the next chapter. But so far as the visual arts are concerned, the arguments of this chapter give us good reason to conclude that the ability of film to transcend the limitations of static visual images brings a further different limitation in its wake.

Summary

The word 'art' is often used to refer exclusively to visual art, and painting in particular. This tends to give prominence to the idea that representation is especially important in art. While it is true that much visual art is representational, representationalism or the belief that representational accuracy is of greater importance or value is mistaken, even in painting. Representation is a means and not an end in art. The ends it serves may be served in other ways, and can in fact be satisfied by wholly abstract painting. What matters is the value or importance of these ends. One of these is simply that of bringing visual experience itself to prominence. However, the visual arts can pass beyond the purely visual. Somewhat surprisingly perhaps, they can supply us with images which capture and illuminate the non-visual – states of emotion and character for instance. What painting cannot do is depict the dynamic of a narrative or developing sequence. It is in this respect that film, while also a visual art, succeeds where painting fails. Film has the resources to construct and display dynamic visual images and may thus transcend the limitations of the static visual image. Its own weakness arises from the fact that it is a multimedia art, and this means that it is almost impossible for a film to be the result of a single directing mind. Films thus tend towards fragmentation. The sort of transcendence that film makes possible, but which remains in the control of a single author, seems to be available in literature. This is the next art form to consider in our discussion.

Suggested further reading

Advanced introductory reading

Routledge Companion to Aesthetics (second edition), Chapters 30, 46, 47, 48, 49

Oxford Handbook of Aesthetics, Chapters 10, 29, 32, 36, 37

Classic writings

E. H. Gombrich, *Art and Illusion*

Richard Wollheim, *Painting as an Art*

Major contemporary works

Noël Carroll, *Philosophical Problems of Classical Film Theory* (1988)

Dominic Lopes, *Understanding Pictures* (1996)

7

The literary arts

We have seen reason to think that art at its best significantly enriches human understanding. This is why, despite all the evident differences, amongst human achievements it is to be ranked alongside science and philosophy rather than sport and entertainment. In the preceding two chapters we have been exploring the problems that arise for this understanding of art when we try to apply it to music and to the visual arts. The exploration showed that both are importantly limited from this point of view. Music is confined to enriching our understanding of the world of aural experience, and while the visual arts can reach beyond the merely visual, they reach beyond the static only at the risk of fragmentation. Once we turn to the literary arts, however, *all* limitations appear to vanish. Since language is the medium par excellence for inquiring, learning and understanding, it would seem to follow that the literary arts are ideally suited to the task of contributing to human understanding.

Yet this very fact raises a doubt. If language is a medium common both to the literary arts and to other forms of human understanding such as history, philosophy and the sciences (as well as practical, everyday understanding), why should we need or value literary *artistry*? To put the matter simply, though a little misleadingly, why do we need poetry as well as prose?

Poetry and prose

The eighteenth-century English poet Alexander Pope was author of a couplet which has subsequently become very familiar as a description of literary or poetic 'style'.

> True wit is nature to advantage dressed,
> What oft was thought, but ne'er so well expressed.

What this couplet identifies as the poetic is not what the words say, but how they say it. This implies that the 'thought' in a poem is independent of the words expressing it, and so may be identified independently of the way the poet or writer has expressed it. If so, then what the poem has to 'say' can be said in other ways, and we can then ask where the value or advantage of saying it in a poetic way lies. What is said is worth saying, let us agree, but why say it in the form of poetry?

Pope's view of poetry was common in the eighteenth century. The great literary critic and conversationalist Dr Samuel Johnson, for instance, believed that the purpose of poetry was to delight and instruct. The instruction lay in the content, the delight in the form. But he differed from Pope in that he further held that the delight that we get from poetry is of limited significance and value. This is why in matters of real import poetry is to be abandoned. To employ poetic devices in the service of religion for instance, so Johnson thought, is to set the serious around with frippery. 'Repentance trembling in the presence of the Judge', he says,

> is not at leisure for cadences and epithets. . . . Poetry loses its lustre and its power because it is applied to the decoration of something more excellent than itself. All that pious verse can do is to help the memory, and delight the ear, and for these purposes it may be very useful; but it supplies nothing to the mind.
>
> (Johnson 1906: Vol. 1, 212)

These remarks are directly concerned with religious verse, but the same view can be extended to any 'serious' poetry – that poetry itself (in Johnson's useful phrase) 'supplies nothing to the mind'.

This does not necessarily mean that poetry is in every sense redundant. Johnson offers two explanations of its value – memorability and musicality – and we could add some more – beauty, comic value or originality perhaps. But any such explanation of the value of poetry, because it employs a distinction between the form and the content of a poem, cannot say that poetry *as* poetry enhances the *understanding*; anything that a poem has to say, its 'content', can as satisfactorily, if not as strikingly or as memorably, be said in a prose paraphrase. If this is true, however, from the point of view of any increase in understanding we might hope to gain, the existence of a paraphrase renders the poetry itself superfluous, essentially a matter of decoration. This has the unhappy implication that the art form which would appear to transcend the limitations of music, painting and film cannot after all be accorded the kind of power and importance aesthetic cognitivism attributes to the greatest artworks.

Pope's own poetry provides many examples that precisely seem to illustrate the point. Here is one:

> A little learning is a dang'rous thing;
> Drink deep, or taste not the Pierian spring:
> There shallow draughts intoxicate the brain,
> And drinking largely sobers us again.

The first of these lines is so convenient a summary of one fact about human experience that it has taken on the status of a proverb. Probably most people nowadays think it *is* an authorless proverb in fact. It provides a striking and memorable way of saying something people often have reason to say. But it is a simple matter to say the same thing in other words: 'People who know only a little about a subject are often strongly inclined to believe themselves to be expert.' Pope's comparison between learning and drinking in the last two lines is (or was) novel, but once more the thought behind it is easily expressed without the poetry: 'The more we know about a subject the more sober a view we are likely to take of it.' As far as the *content* of these lines goes, then, paraphrase will do just as well. The value of the poetic version has to lie elsewhere.

Pope's poetry is not unique. There are many instances in which the meaning of the poem and the manner of its expression can be independently identified. In these cases the poem can be paraphrased without loss of significant content, and since there is no reason to think that these are not perfectly good poems, it follows that poetry cannot be said to *require* a unity of form and content. Consequently, the value of poetry *as such* cannot lie in the contribution it makes to our understanding. This is not because poetry cannot have meaning or a 'message', but because, so long as the meaning can be conveyed independently in a paraphrase, the 'message' is not shown or revealed by the poetry; it is merely asserted in a poetic manner of expression. Poetic form in itself then, as Johnson claims, supplies nothing to the mind.

If this is true of all poetry, we have to say that the reason to write and read a poem must lie not in its intrinsic character but in its contingent usefulness, as an aide-memoire, say, or because of the pleasure we derive from it. Such a view, however, has odd implications. It would mean, for example, that the importance of what the magnificent poetry in Shakespeare's plays has to teach and tell us is not intrinsic to it. Even if no one happens to have said the same things, or if Shakespeare said them first, what is insightful and profound in some of the greatest poetry in the English language could as well be stated in other ways. But in this case the language of the plays only provides us with a source of entertainment and a storehouse of memorable lines, expressing the sort of thoughts and sentiments people commonly have.

Now there is no doubt that poetry can be a pleasure to read and listen to, and that poetic devices can be employed and exploited for the purposes of delight and amusement, but the clearest examples of this – the poems of Lewis Carroll (1832–98) in *Alice in Wonderland*, or nonsense verses by Edward Lear (1812–88), for instance – are clearly examples of poetry that neither is nor is meant to be serious. Lear's poem 'The Owl and the Pussycat', for instance, does not aim to 'say' anything.

> The owl and the pussycat put to sea
> In a beautiful pea-green boat

They took some honey, and plenty of money
Wrapped up in a five pound note.

Indeed at the extreme, such poems do not even *mean* anything. Take the first verse of Lewis Carroll's 'Jabberwocky':

'Twas brillig, and the slithy toves
Did gyre and gimble in the wabe:
All mimsy were the borogroves,
And the mome raths outgrabe.

Both poems are fun to read and listen to, and they show that both Lear and Carroll had genuine poetic gifts. But they are clearly to be distinguished from *serious* poetry. The 'metaphysical' poetry of Donne and Herbert, for example, is the work of gifted writers, and 'delights the ear'. However, it also aims to be, and is generally regarded as being, concerned to capture and illuminate some aspect of human experience, to give us insight as well as pleasure. What then is the crucial difference between the two types of poetry?

The unity of form and content

Some writers have thought that the attempt to paraphrase a poem is *always* a mistake. Cleanth Brooks, in a chapter of *The Well Wrought Urn* entitled 'The Heresy of Paraphrase', writes as follows:

> We can very properly use paraphrases as pointers and as shorthand references provided that we know what we are doing. But it is highly important that we know what we are doing and that we see plainly that the paraphrase is not the real core of meaning which constitutes the essence of the poem.
>
> (Brooks 1947: 180)

Contrary to the generality of Brooks's assertion, it seems that there are good poems in which the content and the form are easy to separate. But what he says is true of *some* poems, poems in which the interconnectedness of image and utterance is so marked that it is difficult to differentiate the two. A verse, in which the poet John Donne (1572–1631) offers us a summation of Christian doctrine, begins like this:

We hold that Paradise and Calvary,
Christ's Cross and Adam's tree, stood in one place;
(*Hymn to God my God, in my Sickness,* fifth stanza)

The verse comes in the middle of an extended geographical metaphor and it is difficult to see how Donne's conception of the theological relation between pre-Fallen Man and the Crucifixion could be otherwise expressed.

Any attempt at paraphrase which departed from the geographical idiom would lose not just the form but the essential *idea* at work in the poem. The thought and the manner of expression are in this way inseparable. Nor is this close association between thought and image a peculiarity of the metaphysical poets or even of poetry with metaphysical or theological aspirations. In *Portrait of a Lady*, T. S. Eliot has this compelling description:

> We have been, let us say, to hear the latest Pole
> Transmit the *Preludes*, through his hair and finger-tips.

The phrase 'transmit the *Preludes* through his hair and fingertips' captures not only a certain style of piano playing, but also an attitude to musicianship of that kind, *and* a further view of that attitude. This complexity can be pointed out, but it would be impossible to say the same thing to the same effect in a paraphrase. This is because the lines do not merely record a scene or episode; they get us to apprehend or imagine it in a certain way. It may be wrong to say that the same idea cannot be conveyed in *any* other way – a picture might do it for instance – but it is clear that the extended elaboration and explanation characteristic of paraphrase would destroy the very thing that makes the poetic expression arresting, namely the inner complexity of the lines.

There are indefinitely many other examples we could cite, but even these two are sufficient to show that in some poetry, for practical purposes content and expression are inseparable and paraphrase in the ordinary sense impossible. We can often, perhaps always, give a short summary of the general import of a poem, but where content and expression are intimately connected as they are in these examples from Donne and Eliot, a prose paraphrase, even if it is useful for other purposes, will always bring with it significant loss of meaning.

All the examples we have considered so far are good poems by gifted poets. Yet there are obviously important differences between them. Lear and Carroll are examples of wordplay. Pope is more than wordplay, since the poetic form has serious content. But in Donne and Eliot, the content and the form are inextricable. Poetic form, then, is sometimes empty of content and sometimes largely decorative of the content it has. But it can plausibly be held that not all poetry is of equal value, and further that the degree to which poetry cannot be paraphrased is an indication of its worth. In other words, we might take inseparability of form and content in a poem as a mark of its value. To do so is to believe that the harder to paraphrase, the greater the poetry. What reasons are there for believing this?

We saw at several points in previous chapters that to be cognitively significant, art must *direct* the mind and not merely supply it. Mere assertion or presentation is not enough. In music, we are not simply presented with a cacophony of noises, but with a way of hearing them. In painting, the painter uses colour, perspective and similar devices to get us to see things in certain ways. The account of Pope's famous couplet conceives of poetry as a form of presentation. By contrast, in poems where form and content are inseparable, the apprehension of the content is only possible through the poetic devices embedded in the form. This is why it makes sense to say that 'the harder to paraphrase, the greater the poem', but only in so far as it really is true that mental direction is sometimes accomplished by the devices of poetry itself – rhythm, rhyme, alliteration, assonance and such, and above all imagery. If this *can* be shown, then we will have demonstrated that poetic form can be essential to what a poem says, and not merely an agreeable or delightful wrapping.

Figures of speech

Showing that the devices of poetry can contribute directly to our understanding encounters an important obstacle. There is a longstanding belief among philosophers, not only that poetic devices are merely ornamental, but that their use actually *diminishes* the prospect of arriving at a proper understanding of reality. One of the best-known and most uncompromising expressions of this view is to be found in the work of the seventeenth-century English philosopher John Locke (1632–1704). Locke's *Essay Concerning Human Understanding* (1690) was a highly influential work in the history of philosophy, and in it he says this:

> [I]n discourses where we seek rather pleasure than information and improvement, such ornaments [as metaphors, similes and the like] . . . can scarce pass for faults. But yet if we would speak of things as they are, we must allow that all the art of rhetoric, besides order and clearness; all the artificial and figurative application of words eloquence hath invented, are for nothing else but to insinuate wrong ideas, move the passions, and thereby mislead the judgement; and so indeed are perfect cheats: and therefore, however laudable or allowable oratory may render them in harangues and popular addresses, they are certainly, in all discourses that pretend to inform or instruct, wholly to be avoided.
>
> (Locke 1896: II, 146)

What lies at the back of Locke's view as expounded in this passage is the idea that language can be plain and fact stating, or it can be embroidered and embellished. Embroidery and embellishment is what oratory and poetry go in for, but if we are to grasp clearly and plainly truths about the world and human experience, then we should relinquish them. Figures of speech 'can scarce pass for faults' in flowery and poetical language, but in the pursuit of 'human understanding' they cloud and distort things.

Accordingly, the devices of poetry, however much pleasure they give rise to and whatever other values they serve, must be abandoned if what we are concerned with is increasing our understanding.

Locke's influence has been so great that this is a familiar view in the history of philosophy. Yet it is relatively easy to show it to be mistaken, because it is impossible for *any* use of language to be purged completely of any figurative element. There is no such thing as the *plain* speech that Locke imagines, which is to say speech stripped of literary devices. Even a brief consideration of the most mundane uses of language shows this. Simple attempts to understand and explain are replete with metaphor, simile, analogy, synecdoche, and so on. Take the common expressions 'I *see* what you mean', 'I *follow* your argument' or 'I *get* your point'. These are all metaphors. I do not *literally* see meanings or follow arguments. It does not take much imagination to spot metaphors in prosaic reports of simple episodes and instructions about everyday matters – 'I *caught* the bus', 'She *spun* me quite a story', 'Let the wine *breathe* before you pour it', etc. If we were to try to expunge such expressions from factual conversation, what could we put in their place? And without a replacement, we should not have unembroidered speech, but silence.

What is true for ordinary language is also true for more specialized uses. It is just as impossible to engage in science, history, sociology or philosophy without figures of speech. We say that electricity *flows* in a *current*, magnetic *forces* arrange themselves in *fields*, electoral *campaigns* are *fought* and that social *pressures mount*. Even Locke, contrary to the philosophical thesis he is defending, employs metaphor in expounding it when he describes literary devices as 'perfect cheats'. Every variety of natural, human and social science makes use of every type of literary device, and the purpose is to describe and explain objective reality. The question whether 'poetic' utterance (meaning the use of metaphor, simile, and so on) can direct the mind has to be answered in the affirmative. The important question is not whether it does this, which it obviously does, but to what end it may be done and what counts as doing it well.

There is no one answer to the first of these questions. Figures of speech are common to many different uses of language. As well as having an important role in scientific and historical investigation, they are to be found in advertising, speech making and religious practice as well as the literary arts. It follows from this that while figurative language is an important feature of poetry and works of literature, this cannot be their distinguishing feature. We will not have understood the nature and value of imaginative literature until we have isolated the special use to which poets and novelists put such devices in literature.

Expressive language

Imaginative and clever use of language can entertain and delight us. Everyday puns are straightforward instances of this, and more sophisticated 'literary' examples are easy to find – in the writings of Oscar Wilde, for instance, whose wit has a very marked linguistic component. In short the use of language itself can be amusing. But a properly literary use of language goes beyond the amusing. It can supply us with heightened and more effective means of expression, for instance. The commonest cases of this are to be found in proverbs (such as the saying originating with Pope) where a specific image or a memorable phrase expresses our own attitude better than we could ourselves.

One of the commonest occasions for this use of poetic language in the history of English literature has been expression of religious feeling and sentiment, and there is a good deal we can learn about poetry and literature by thinking about hymns, psalms and set forms of prayer. The Anglican *Book of Common Prayer*, written for the most part by Thomas Cranmer (1489–1556), and the Christian hymns of Isaac Watts (1674–1748) and Charles Wesley (1707–88), are very fine examples of literary writing that is valuable from an expressive point of view. All three authors have provided generations of English-speaking Christians with the means of giving expression to religious feeling, as well as expressive phrases that have crept into the use of English more broadly. Their hymns and prayers also underline the importance of the distinction between 'being an expression of' and 'being expressive of' that was discussed in Chapter 3. This is a distinction that specially needs to be borne in mind if the distinctive value of the literary arts is to be understood properly.

Obviously the beautiful and affective language of hymns and set prayers can express the religious emotions that are actually felt by the people who use them. It is doubtful, however, whether this is often their real function, because ordinary people only rarely feel the elevated and refined emotion that religious poetry typically expresses. Most hymn singers are not themselves mystics or even especially devout. Consequently it is only on rare occasions that the hymns they sing express what they are actually feeling. More usually religious poetry is 'expressive of' religious emotion rather than an 'expression of' it. The literary critic Helen Gardner makes this point:

> A complaint is often made that . . . it is absurd for a congregation of ordinary wayfaring Christians to be expected to sing sentiments that even saints can hardly be expected to feel habitually. There is a well-known joke about the Duchess singing in a warm tremolo 'Were the whole realm of nature mine, That were an offering far too small' while she hunted in her purse for a sixpence to put on the plate. But the joke is misconceived. A hymn is not intended to express the personal

> warmth of feeling of an individual singer, but a common ideal of Christian feeling and sentiment which the Christian congregation acknowledges as an ideal.
>
> (Gardner 1983: 156)

Gardner's point is that the sublime expression of feeling may serve purposes other than actually expressing feelings. A hymn that is truly 'expressive of' feeling enables ordinary worshippers to apprehend and understand something of the nature of Christian devotion, whether or not they experience these feelings of devotion within themselves on any particular occasion that the hymn is sung. An expressive hymn may at some point allow worshippers to come to have such feelings, but whether it does or not, it can still provide a measure of insight and understanding in regard to those feelings. In other words the imaginative expression of religious feeling and sentiment *can* 'supply something to the mind'.

This is not something peculiar to hymns or to religion. The same point may be made about other forms of expressive poetry. Much of John Donne's love poetry has an intensity which cannot be the standard for the much more mundane romances that most of us have known. To say 'When thou sigh'st thou sigh'st not winde but sigh'st my soule away' would be affectation for most of us. Yet even if we never feel such intense sentiments towards anyone, we can nonetheless acknowledge them as comprising *a* state of the human mind, and from the powerful expressiveness of such a love poem be led to a better understanding of that state. Similarly, First World War poetry, which includes both Rupert Brooke's patriotic fervour and Wilfred Owen's hatred of war, arose from an historical episode of great intensity which none of the poetry's contemporary readers have experienced. It is a mistake to think of this poetry as an expression of that experience, because not having been through the war ourselves we could not tell whether it is an adequate expression or not. Indeed even if we had been in the war, it would be impossible to tell if the poetry is an adequate description of *their* experience. But if instead we think of it as *expressive* of attitudes and emotions, these problems disappear; its value can be seen to lie in and be assessed according to its power to reveal and make intelligible the experience of war. In short, we learn from expressive poetry, precisely because it does not express anything we have ever felt.

Poetic devices

The question now arises: how do the devices that expressive (or lyric) poetry employs succeed in enlightening us in this way? How do they direct the mind? In formulating an answer to these questions it is useful to recall the parallel between art and logic that was considered in Chapter 4. Arguments, which are governed by logic, direct the mind by steering our thoughts through patterns of validity, and the task of logicians is to devise generalized accounts of these patterns. It is, however, a mistake to think of the principles of logic as providing us with an *a priori* checklist of valid and invalid moves. In reality arguments, even in philosophy (where factual evidence plays a very small part), are complex. They do not follow simple forms, and need to be considered case by case as free-standing pieces of thought. The devising and application of logically valid formulae may sometimes assist in producing greater clarity of argumentative structure, but they do not provide us with a general and semi-automatic method of testing for validity. Moreover, they have little to say about the loose inductive reasoning we most usually employ. In other words, the discipline of logic is not especially useful when it comes to deciding upon the cogency of actual arguments. Similarly, the ways in which poetic devices – rhythm and rhyme, metaphor, assonance, alliteration, onomatopoeia, and so on – direct our attention and work together to weave a composite image upon which a poem focuses our minds can only be formulated and generalized about to a degree. As in the case of philosophical arguments, each poem must be examined in its own right, and this is the business of literary criticism rather than art theory.

Still, if we are to conclude that poetry does indeed direct the mind, some indication needs to be given of the ways in which literary devices can serve this end, and so the next task is to indicate and illustrate a few poetic devices and how they work.

The first and most obvious of these is the use of sound and stress. Indeed in the absence of any better definition, poetry can best be characterized as the deliberate use of sound and stress in language, although of course it is not only this. Just where the sense or meaning of a sentence lies, is a very large philosophical topic. Using a distinction of the German philosopher Gottlob Frege we may say that the meaning of an utterance combines sense and force, and it is not hard to see that the force of an utterance (and possibly the sense as well) depends in part upon stress and inflexion. The simple sentence 'He was there' is an assertion or a query depending upon whether I raise or lower my intonation on the last word. Poetry works upon facts like these and uses patterns of sound and stress to oblige us to read and to hear a line in one particular way. A simple example of this is to be found in Keats's sonnet *On First Looking into Chapman's Homer*.

> Oft of one wide expanse had I been told
> That deep brow'd Homer ruled as his demesne
> Yet did I never breathe its pure serene
> Till I heard Chapman speak out loud and bold:
> Then felt I like some watcher of the skies
> When a new planet swims into his ken;
> (lines 5–10)

The first four lines here prepare us for the momentous discovery of Homer through the good offices of Chapman, and the placing of 'Then' at the beginning of the fifth line forces us to focus upon the culmination. To see this, compare 'I felt then . . .'. The effect is quite different. There are in fact two devices at work here, stress and word order, but the sound of words themselves can also be used to create special effects, the reinforcement of an image, for instance. The fourth stanza of Gerard Manley Hopkins's *Wreck of the Deutschland* reads:

> I am soft sift
> In an hourglass – at the wall
> Fast, but mined with a motion, a drift,

It is impossible to say 'soft sift' without an audible reminder of the image employed. Hopkins combines the use of sound and stress in fact. The emphasis appropriately falls on 'Fast' only to be eroded by the alliteration of 'mined' and 'motion' which audibly emphasizes the idea of slow but inevitable movement.

A second poetic method is what we might call 'wordplay', the distortion of language and syntactic structure. There are poems where this is done for fun – Lewis Carroll's 'Jabberwocky' which was quoted earlier for instance – but it is not hard to find examples of the same thing serving more serious purposes, manipulating a reader's previous knowledge in new directions. The opening line of *The Calls*, an unfinished poem by Wilfred Owen, runs 'A dismal fog-hoarse siren howls at dawn'. This line is so constructed that to the very last moment we expect (and are expected to expect) the familiar word 'foghorn'. We only register in retrospect the occurrence of something different and unfamiliar. The principal effect of this is to draw out the element of 'fog' in the word 'foghorn' even though this word is unused and thus to emphasize an element which both ordinary and metaphorical uses of this common word have largely suppressed. 'Fog-hoarse' is an invented portmanteau word which captures elements of two familiar words. This juxtaposition of the familiar and the unfamiliar forces us to hear and to consider afresh things to which we would otherwise pay little attention. 'Playing' with words in this fashion is chiefly effective as a device for disturbing expectation. It is given notably extensive use in the poetry of Hopkins. Hopkins does not merely combine existing elements in unusual ways. He makes one part of speech into another, constructs sentences and phrases whose grammar sounds nearly correct and, largely by the use of sound and stress patterns which the ear has to follow, shakes up the expected order. For example:

> As kingfishers catch fire, dragonflies draw flame;
> As tumbled over rim in roundy wells
> Stones ring; each tucked string tells, each hung bell's
> Bow swung finds tongue to fling out broad its name;

Each mortal thing does one thing and the same:
Deals out that being indoors each one dwells;
Selves – goes itself; *myself* it speaks and spells,
Crying *Whát I dó is me: for that I came.*

These lines, from 'As Kingfishers Catch Fire', are quite hard to say (even harder is Hopkins' poem *Harry Ploughman*). It is almost impossible to stress them in ways other than those intended, and the distorted grammatical constructions force our attention on what is being said. Both sound and structure lead to the invented verb 'Selves' which is of course a summation of the thought of the poem.

Grammatical distortion may also be used to enliven an image or mental picture. Here is Donne in *The Progresse of the Soule*, describing the movements of the mandrake as it stirs from its 'darke and foggie plot'.

And as a slumberer stretching on his bed
This way he this, and that way scattered
His other legge.

(Stanza XV)

'This way he this' is not grammatically correct but for that very reason highly effective in creating before our minds a striking picture of the first stirrings of the mandrake.

Donne also provides us with an example of a third poetic device, which may work to similar ends, namely the accumulation of imagery. A poem can draw out or suppress the normal associations we make, not by wordplay or grammatical distortion, but by the systematic assemblage of unusual figures of speech. Consider *The Sunne Rising*. In common thinking the sun has, so to speak, a good reputation. It is easily associated with positive ideas – light, life, warmth, and so on. To draw attention to a quite different attitude generated by contexts and occasions when the sun is unwelcome requires a special effort, and Donne uses a sustained sequence of unlikely images to accomplish this.

Busie old foole, unruly Sunne
Why dost thou thus,
Through windowes, and through curtaines call on us?
Must to thy motions lovers seasons run?
Sawcy pedantique wretch, go chide
Late schoole boyes, and sowre prentices,
Go tell Court-huntsmen, that the King will ride,
Call country ants to harvest offices;
Love, all alike, no season knowes, nor clyme,
Nor houres, dayes, months, which are the rags of time.

The opening words of the stanza set the tone. Donne piles contemptible references one upon the other (including the reference to King James I and VI's addiction to hunting), and the rhythm contributes to this effect by driving us through all these references to 'rags' in the last line as their culmination. The effect of this is that he is able to retain the generally favourable associations of the sun, which a few images will hardly destroy, while at the same time comparing it unfavourably with the relative value of his lover. So he continues:

> Thy beames, so reverend, and so strong
> Why shouldst thou thinke?
> I could eclipse and cloud them with a winke,
> But that I would not lose her sight so long.

One final example of poetic method is often referred to as dramatic irony, but it is more instructive to call it multilayered representation. A multilayered poem trades on another familiar feature of language: ambiguity and the possibility of multiple interpretation. By the systematic exploitation of differing shades of meaning, a set of utterances and images may be made to present us simultaneously with more than one perspective. Something of this sort is to be found in the lines quoted from Eliot's *Portrait of a Lady*, but a more sustained example is Robert Browning's *My Last Duchess*. This poem takes the form of a monologue by the duke as he shows an unnamed visitor a portrait of his now dead wife. What he reveals unintentionally, as the monologue proceeds, is an attitude and a history which he would be at great pains to deny. In fact, he has had her murdered out of a peculiar sort of jealousy and finds the inanimate portrait more suited to his purposes than the living woman whose portrait it is.

> She had
> A heart . . . how shall I say? . . . too soon made glad,
> Too easily impressed; she liked whate'er
> She looked on, and her looks went everywhere.
> . . . . She thanked men – good; but thanked
> Somehow . . . I know not how . . . as if she ranked
> My gift of a nine-hundred-years-old name
> With anybody's gift . . .
> . . . . she smiled, no doubt,
> Whene'er I passed her; but who passed without
> Much the same smile? This grew; I gave commands;
> Then all smiles stopped together. There she stands
> As if alive.

In the course of the poem Browning manages to represent the duke's thought in language which reveals an external perspective on the duke's attitude and conduct from which his motivation is mad. At the same time the duke gives us access to the internal mindset from which his own mad jealousy seems eminently reasonable. The deliberate employment of multilayered language is doubly revealing of the duke's mentality and in this way provides us with a more rounded understanding of a certain sort of mentality; we see both how it is and how it feels.

The use of sound and stress, word order, the distortion of grammar, accumulation of imagery and construction of multilayered language are all devices by which poetry may be said to reveal or show things, analogous to forms of reasoning by which an argument might show or an experiment uncover something. There are of course important differences, but it does not seem misleading to describe the devices identified here as means by which the mind is directed. To speak of poetry in this way is not to assume that what is revealed or demonstrated is incontestable, any more than a belief in the power of dialectic to lead us to the truth implies that every argument must supply a conclusive demonstration of the thesis it means to support. We can be led in many different and competing directions by arguments and experiments which all claim validity, and so too we may expect poetic revelation to throw up a variety of images for our consideration. But enough has been said to establish the claim that poetic form is not just an agreeably ornamental way of saying things whose truth or substance is to be established in some other way. The relation between what is said in poetry and how it is said can be more intimate than that.

However, even if it is accepted that poetry as a form of understanding does not yield to paraphrase without significant loss there is a further question for this chapter to address: can the same be said of the other literary arts? The poetic forms described and discussed so far are closely connected with 'poetry' narrowly understood. Other literary arts have other forms, and it needs to be shown that these are also ways of directing the mind to a better apprehension of some aspect of human experience. Can storytelling, whose form is narrative, be used in this way?

Narrative and fiction

The device of multilayered representation is to be found in novels as well as in poetry. A striking counterpart in this respect to Browning's *My Last Duchess* is Kazuo Ishiguro's novel *The Remains of the Day*, subsequently made into a highly successful film. Ishiguro's story is set in the England of the 1950s. The principal character is a butler, Stevens, who takes a few days' holiday motoring across the countryside with the ultimate purpose of seeking out a former colleague. The journey provides the occasion and the context for extended reminiscences of previous, rather more glorious periods of service. The story is told in the first person from the butler's point of view and, to a degree, Stevens reminisces in order to construct an *apologia*, a self-justification of his past actions and attitudes. Nevertheless, in the telling, the reader is led to see the butler's life from several different points of view. As in Browning's poem, Ishiguro uses his story to draw our attention to the contrast and complementarity of 'how it is' with 'how it feels'. One of the most notable instances of this is the butler's recollection of the night his father died, also the night of a major social event in the household. What emerges is, on the one hand, a powerful sense of sheer absurdity – that Stevens should believe the trivial requirements of social grandees sufficient to generate reasons strong enough to call him away from the deathbed of a parent – and on the other an 'internal' perspective from which his doing so has a certain moral substance to it. Objectively (how it is), death is the supreme master before which nearly every other consideration pales. Subjectively (how it feels), true professionalism requires a commitment that is willing to set aside the preferences of personal life.

Some of the other devices which typify poetry can be found at work in novels. But here the devices take on a special role in contributing to the business of storytelling. There is something comparable to Donne's accumulation of imagery in the opening pages of Dickens's *Bleak House*. As is well known, the plot of *Bleak House* revolves around a law case of great complexity that seems to have been lost permanently in the labyrinthine structures of the English legal system of the nineteenth century. The result is that none of the parties or their lawyers understand any longer what the legal point at issue is. The novel's second paragraph begins:

> Fog everywhere. Fog up the river, where it flows among green aits and meadows; fog down the river, where it rolls defiled among the tiers of shipping and the waterside pollutions of a great (and dirty) city. Fog on the Essex marshes, fog on the Kentish heights. Fog creeping into the cabooses of collier-brigs; fog lying out on the yards and hovering in the rigging of great ships; fog drooping on the gunwales of the barges and small boats. Fog in the eyes and throats of ancient Greenwich pensioners, wheezing by the firesides of their wards; fog in the stem and bowl of the afternoon pipe of the wrathful skipper down in his close cabin; fog cruelly pinching the toes and fingers of his shivering little 'prentice boy on deck. Chance people on the bridges peeping over the parapets into a nether sky of fog, with fog all around them.

Dickens pursues this compelling description of the physical condition of the river into the surrounding streets to Lincoln's Inn Hall and finally into the courtroom. As he does so he converts, almost imperceptibly, the literal fog of the river into the metaphorical fog of the court case.

> Never can there come fog too thick, never can there come mud and mire too deep, to assort with the groping and floundering condition [of] this High Court of Chancery.

The fog, both literal and metaphorical, occupies several pages during which a single master image of enveloping obscurity is created before we reach the first spoken words in the story, from the Lord High Chancellor who sits 'in the midst of the mud and the heart of the fog'; thus Dickens obliges us to take a certain view of the venerable legal persons and procedures with which he is concerned.

The example from *Bleak House* shows that imagery in narrative can be used in a fashion similar to ways in which poetically constructed lines can. This is not surprising. One of narrative's distinguishing features is that it presents material in an order – beginning, middle and end. Accordingly, just as a poet may use sound and stress to get us to hear and understand words in a certain way, so an author can construct a story that obliges us to attribute a special significance to the events related. Moreover, this can be done in ways peculiar to narrative that have no obvious poetic counterpart (ignoring the complications introduced by the hybrid, epic or narrative poetry). For example, an author can choose to keep the reader in ignorance for a time and thus let the relative importance of events emerge in a striking manner. The denouement of a story can cause us to reinterpret earlier episodes, to see in them a significance we did not see on first encounter. In this way our understanding is positively directed by the structure of the story. All sorts of devices of this nature are available to the storyteller. For example, an author might systematically suggest, without explicitly stating, as Katherine Mansfield does in her short story, *The Woman at the Store*, that the first person narrator of the story is male. When it is revealed that she is female, the ambiguity of previous actions and attitudes are both emphasized and resolved in the mind of the reader.

Devices of this sort can be used to various ends. Storytelling is probably the oldest and most persistent form of entertainment. It is striking how easily and at what an early age children can have their interest arrested by stories. The special features of narrative construction seem to be a natural form of entertainment. The method of revealing the significance of earlier events in the denouement is a notable feature of mystery stories, often most marked in the most hackneyed kind. Agatha Christie, whose stories have no other evident literary value, used this device again and again to entertain the reader, by having Hercule Poirot or Miss Marple reveal all.

This is not to deny that there can be good stories whose sole purpose is entertainment. A more subtle form of narrative construction, in which earlier events are only properly understood later, is to be found in the spy stories of John Le Carré (especially in *The Honourable Schoolboy*) where a large number of fragmentary episodes are related and whose significance is revealed through slow accumulation, a method of construction which has now been copied rather tediously by a large number of less gifted writers.

Stories can be moving and deeply captivating as well as entertaining – Tolkien's *Lord of the Rings* is a striking example – and the peculiar devices of narrative may be used to these ends also. But narrative can do more than this. Because it has the structure of beginning, middle and end and is a work of imagination, it can create a unity out of actions and events that the flow of real historical events never has. When did the French Revolution begin and end? This is a foolish question from a historical point of view even though there will be some wrong answers, because a historian may find significant historical connections before and after any dates we arbitrarily designate. But a novel has a beginning and an end (though not always an ending; some stories are open-ended); there is no 'earlier' or 'later' into which it might be extended. Similarly, there are no 'facts' about the characters or events other than those the author chooses to invent. The world of the novel, unlike that of the history book, does not go beyond that which it contains.

Occasionally, people have thought that the contrast between history and fiction tells against fiction, but this betrays a misunderstanding of the possible significance of imaginative literature. Compare hindsight and denouement. When we apprehend the significance of events in retrospect they are, so to speak, brought fully into the story. They are no longer merely interesting fragments, but integral parts of the whole. The difference between history and fiction is this. While the historian, with the benefit of hindsight, *discovers* events to be significantly related and assembles evidence to persuade us of this conclusion, the novelist with imagination *makes* the events relevant, and uses denouement to direct the mind of the reader into seeing a significant relation between them.

In a parallel fashion, the historian selects out of pre-existing material to make a coherent narrative. It is always possible for the narrative to be amended or corrected by a demonstration of the relevance of some of the material omitted. But nothing of this sort can happen with a novel. However flawed it might be, we cannot correct a novel because there are no events and characters external to it out of which its story is made. Of course a novel can be badly written, its plot inconsistent, and its characters unconvincing. But these are not faults of misrepresentation or omission but of construction – it does not 'hang together' and does not therefore impress upon our minds a single image or set of interrelated images.

If this way of thinking about novels is correct, it may prompt yet another doubt about whether works of fiction can enhance our understanding of human life. If, unlike a historical narrative, a novel is not a selection from a multiplicity of facts but a free-floating creation of the imagination, how can it have the necessary reference to human experience? The answer to this question has already been surveyed in an earlier chapter. We must think of works of art as being *brought to* experience rather than being *drawn from* it. This is not meant to imply that the author works in a vacuum. It is obvious that in realistic as opposed to fantastical stories, constraints operate that reflect the way life is. Nevertheless, a novel is not to be thought of as providing us with a faithful reflection of experience or a skilful summary of it, but as obliging us to view some aspect of experience through an image which allows us to attain an illuminating perspective upon it.

A simple illustration of this point is to be found in Malcolm Bradbury's novel *The History Man*. One of the best-known episodes in this novel is the departmental staff meeting. Some commentators have said both that Bradbury has described academic staff meetings with deadly accuracy and others that it is a gross distortion. Neither remark is pertinent, however, to the novel as imaginative literature. We should not think of the novelist's purpose as that of recording reality, as a newspaper report might, and thus liable for praise or blame according to the accuracy or inaccuracy of the report. Rather the novelist is engaged in imagining things, and what an episode of this sort offers is an image of a staff meeting; it bears upon real staff meetings just in so far as we can view them afresh in its light, see *both* how close they come to farce, *as well as* how far short they fall of it. In brief a good literary image does not distil or summarize experience; it casts it in a new light.

The History Man arguably is essentially a lightweight work. But something similar can be said of much greater works of literature. Take, for instance, Anthony Trollope's *Lady Anna*, which Trollope himself thought the best of his novels. Lady Anna is the daughter of Countess Lovell, the course of whose unhappy life has been determined by doubts about the legality of her marriage to the Earl of Lovell. She has spent countless years in trying to secure her rights and title, assisted only by a constant friendship of a Keswick tailor and his son. When the novel opens a law case is underway over the proper beneficiary of the Earl's will, but it soon becomes clear that the Countess's claims are to be vindicated and that her only daughter will accede to a title and great wealth. It then emerges that Lady Anna, in the days of their penury, has engaged herself to the tailor's son.

The larger part of the novel is concerned both with the pressures that operate upon her to break her engagement and with the moral rights and wrongs of her doing so. However, the story is not simply an occasion for airing views about the individual in a class-structured society, though there is plainly an element of social comment, if only in the fact that Trollope represents Anna's disregard of social sentiment and convention sympathetically (a fact which partly explains the poor reception *Lady Anna* received on publication). But more than this, the novel presents us with contrasting images of fidelity – the faithfulness of the old Countess to the cause for which she has given so much and the faithfulness of Anna to her childhood lover. The first dehumanizes the Countess; the second attests to the true humanity of Anna. Almost everything that happens or is said in the novel contributes to the fashioning of these images, for unlike many Trollope novels, there is virtually nothing in the way of subplot. Through these images we can come to see something of the close connection between faithfulness on the one hand and fanaticism on the other, between faithfulness to a cause beyond oneself, and a faithfulness that amounts to moral self-indulgence.

These are important and illuminating images, but there is more at work than this, and a still deeper theme. Throughout the larger part of the novel, Anna has a choice to make. At the same time the final result is never in doubt. What determines this second fact is the conception of womanhood operating in this as in many of Trollope's other novels. At one level Anna can be said to stand out against the norms of her society, can even be said to reject them (though that society, in true English fashion, accommodates itself to her and the tailor in the end), while at another level her behaviour is determined, as she herself may be formed, by social norms.

There is not the space here to expand upon or defend a claim about this particular novel. Nor is it necessary. The example is intended only as an illustration of the way in which imaginative literature can create images through which the realities of our own experience are illuminated. The episode from *The History Man* may not only amuse but throw interesting light on the experience of those few people who have attended academic staff meetings. *Lady Anna*, on the other hand, enables us as human beings to look again at steadfastness and to see expressed in moral character a conception of half the human race, namely women.

Literature and understanding

The arguments and examples of the last two sections have been intended to show that the literary devices of poetry and the novel can be used to create images which oblige us to view our experience in certain ways and thus illuminate aspects of it. It is this possibility (perhaps relatively rarely realized) that allows us to describe imaginative literature as a source of understanding and which entitles us to attribute considerable importance to it. This claim can be misinterpreted, so it needs to be emphasized that what we have been discussing are possibilities. It is not the purpose of a normative theory of art to discover the definitive characteristic that makes all 'art' art. Its purpose is to identify the different ways in which art can be of value, and assess the relative importance that we should attach to its various manifestations. As a normative theory applied to the literary arts, aesthetic cognitivism should not be taken to imply that all imaginative literature must enrich human understanding, or that it is commonly valued on these grounds. Probably the majority of poems and stories are valued because they are amusing, delightful, absorbing or interesting.

These are important values. A life devoid of delight and amusement is an impoverished one. At the same time, a life that never rises much above delightful and amusing experiences is limited. It is the fact that the works of Shakespeare, Donne, Austen, Dickens, Racine, Goethe, Cervantes, Tolstoy, and so on offer us more than this that both explains and justifies us in regarding them as we do. For in the most celebrated imaginative literature, the devices of poetry, story and drama are harnessed, not just to please and entertain, but to create images – character, scenes, events, ideas – through which the reader's apprehension of human nature and the human condition is enhanced. Literature at its best gives us a deeper understanding of what it is to have a life, and it is the fact that it can play this role (though it need not and does not always) that gives us reason to value it so highly.

But the greatest literary masterpieces, along with the masterpieces of the other arts, can go beyond enabling us to reflect upon our social and moral experience. They actually create the world of that experience for us by fashioning master images that become paradigms for thought and conduct. One such paradigm is that of Shakespeare's *Othello*. Othello is *the* image of destructive jealousy. Another is Herman Melville's *Billy Budd* – with Budd himself a paradigm of fatally vulnerable innocence.

Other arts also provide even more striking instances of the master image as paradigm. Here is one example from film. The Russian Revolution is an event which played an important part in the conduct of Soviet life and in its relations with the rest of the world for almost seventy years. Yet the 'Russian Revolution' that played this role is not the event historians investigate and its political significance is only loosely based on historical realities. What influenced subsequent history through the minds of its participants was an *image* of the Russian Revolution, the most powerful version of which is to be found in Eisenstein's film *Battleship Potemkin*. In a famous scene the proletarian crowd storms the Winter Palace in St Petersburg. The crowd confronts enormous, ornate doors, symbols of power and wealth, and finally manages to force them open as a mighty act of combined strength. Their solidarity has made them invincible.

As far as history goes, no such event ever took place. This is not how the past actually *was*, but how it *had to be* in order to sustain the idea of a world-shattering revolution with all the political significance that it had. In creating this fine film, Eisenstein was not engaged in servile propaganda. No doubt he created his image in ignorance of the real history of events (an ignorance no greater than most people at the time, it should be said). His gift was to know the mentality of the times, but to do more than this as well. He supplied the times with a lasting image. Henceforth 'The October Revolution' out of which the Soviet Union was born, and to the defence of which future policy was supposed to be directed, was not the history of 1917 about which the leaders and people of the former Soviet Union knew relatively little, but this image from *Battleship Potemkin*.

'The people overwhelming the best defences of Tsarist Russia' is an artistic image that did not merely reflect, but *structured*, the world of political experience. Art can have the same sort of relation to moral and social experience. A useful distinction to draw upon here is that between *stereotypes* and *archetypes*. The master images of the greatest artists are not to be understood as distillations or summations of the variety in experience (stereotypes) but imaginary paradigms against which we measure that variety (archetypes). And in certain contexts these archetypes may be said to constitute the only reality that there is. Such things as 'a lover' or 'a gentleman' or 'the perfect marriage' or 'a consuming passion' or 'innocence' do not await our discovery in the way that black swans or seams of gold do. They are patterns which structure our approach to the social and moral world in which our lives have to be lived and determine our attitudes to the behaviour of ourselves and others. Works of art that come to have a common currency contribute to the formation of these patterns, and in the case of the greatest works they have been definitive. Art thus contributes to social and moral experience and, for this reason, may be said to provide us with the possibility not only of understanding but of *self*-understanding.

Take for example the relationship between two people who might be or become lovers. How are they to think of the relationship it would be good to form and the sort of human pitfalls that lie in their way? Every relationship has an external and an internal aspect and the internal is rarely on view. In the works of imaginative artists this division is surmountable. Fiction and poetry put both mind and action equally on view; characters and events can be seen entire. Novels and poems supply patterns of human relationship, its fulfilment, destruction or corruption, and these can enter directly into the moral experience of those who are reflecting upon how best to live, because the devices of art reveal to us the internal 'how it feels' as well as the external 'how it is'.

In fulfilling this function, literature is especially important because it is especially powerful. Music, as we saw in Chapter 5, can structure our aural experience. Visual art can do the same for visual experience and, as I argued in the previous chapter, can to some extent go beyond the purely visual. A painting or a sculpture can certainly reveal something of the personality as well as the appearance of a figure represented – see for instance the mentalities revealed by the faces in Caravaggio's *Beheading of John the Baptist*. But literature can create and explore inner lives to a far greater extent. It is in literature – poems, novels, plays – that our self-images are fashioned with the greatest complexity and where exploration of the constitutive images of moral and social life is most obvious. This is one of literature's peculiar powers and gives it, in this respect, pre-eminence among the arts.

Summary

This chapter has addressed the difficulties that lie in the way of applying the theory of aesthetic cognitivism to imaginative literature. These difficulties arise chiefly because it is natural to think that any cognitive element in poetry or novels – what there is to be learned from them – is in *what* they say and not in the *form* in which they say it. Yet if the form of a poem or a novel is not central to its assessment as an artistic achievement, it would appear to follow that literary art cannot amount to more than 'embroidery and embellishment' (to use John Locke's terms), and that paraphrase can replace poetry without significant loss of meaning. However, closer examination has shown that form and content in literature are often impossible to disentangle and that a variety of poetic and literary devices can be integrally employed in the creation of imaginative literature which prompts us to see and think about our experience of life differently. It is this power that gives literature its cognitive value.

It is not obviously true that such a power is possessed by all art forms. In addition to those already examined there is another for which the case seems especially hard to make, namely architecture. This requires a chapter to itself. But before that we should consider the performing arts in which the musical, the visual and the literary all combine.

Suggested further reading

Advanced introductory reading

Routledge Companion to Aesthetics (second edition), Chapters 27, 28, 44
Oxford Handbook of Aesthetics, Chapters 21, 22, 30, 35

Classic writings

Cleanth Brooks, 'The Heresy of Paraphrase' in *The Well Wrought Urn*

Major contemporary works

Peter Lamarque and Stein Haugon Olsen, *Truth, Fiction and Literature* (1994)
Martha Nussbaum, *Love's Knowledge: essays on philosophy and literature* (1990)

8

The performing arts

In Chapter 5 we explored the nature of music, and ended the chapter by noting that no special account had been taken of the fact that music is a performing art. In this chapter that omission is to be remedied, but since music is only one of the performing arts, the best way to do so is to consider the performing arts in general, and re-examine music alongside dance and drama.

Artist, audience and performer

Why do the performing arts need a chapter to themselves? What is so special about them? Are they not just other sources of pleasure, beauty and imaginative insight? The answer seems to be obvious: yes they are. Yet we can note an important difference straight away. The plastic and literary arts involve a two-place relationship between artist and audience. On the one side is the painter, sculptor, novelist or poet and on the other the viewer, spectator or reader. As far as aesthetic engagement is concerned, artist and audience exhaust the possibilities; we are either one or the other. But the performing arts involve a *three*-place relationship. Works of music, dance and theatre may begin with the ideas and imagination of a composer, a choreographer or a playwright, and the resulting work – the composition, the choreography, the drama – is generally intended for an audience. But it can only reach that audience by means of a third party – the player, the dancer, the actor. These performers are vital to realizing the work of art – literally 'making it exist' – because without them the music would remain nothing more than the black marks on the score, the choreograph a set of instructions about movement and the script a collection of unspoken sentences.

Of course, the visual and literary arts require some sort of medium as well. Michelangelo needed marble to enable us to see the image of David that his genius had led him to imagine; Dickens needed print and paper to tell his readers the story of David Copperfield that he had invented. Jackson Pollock needed copious quantities of metallic paint for his 'action' paintings. In this way, sculptors, novelists and painters also rely upon other people to help them bring their artworks to reality: Michelangelo on the stonemason, Dickens on the printer, Pollock on the paint manufacturer. But there is an important difference – no one thinks the stonemason or the printer are themselves artists. Since the stone with which the sculptor has been provided does not play any direct part in making the artwork what it is, and since the story of David Copperfield remains the same irrespective of the typeface used to print it or the paper it is printed on, in neither case does the medium add any artistic element of its own. True, it is the manufacturer who produced paint of precisely the colour that is to be found in Pollock's painting, but Pollock who chose to put it there. The implication is that the people involved in supplying these media, essential though they are, are not themselves artists. Dickens needs the printer, but not in a way that makes the printer a sort of novelist.

Precisely the opposite is true in the performing arts. The cellist Pablo Casals made a recording of Bach's *Cello Suites* that is widely regarded as perhaps their greatest performance. People continue to prefer it to more recent recordings, because it is itself the work of a great artist. Similarly, audiences flocked to see Rudolph Nureyev dance *Swan Lake* and not merely to see Geltser's choreography (or even hear Tchaikovsky's music). Lawrence Olivier's performance as *Richard the Third* was critically acclaimed quite independently of Shakespeare's great drama. In performing art, then, there are *three* aspects to be considered and not just two. From an artistic point of view, the *performer* matters as well as the artist and the audience. It is the crucial role of the player, the dancer and the actor that marks off the performing arts from the plastic and literary arts in which there is no equivalent. Pollock's 'action painting' is misleadingly named if it ever inclines anyone to think that *they* could paint one of *his* paintings.

Painting as the paradigm of art

Despite this rather obvious difference, there has been a strong tendency in aesthetics and the philosophy of the arts to try to conceptualize the performing arts as *something like* the plastic and the literary arts. This tendency has been sustained by the recurring desire amongst philosophers, art theorists and even artists themselves to find a common property or feature that all the arts share, something that will justify their being classified as 'art' despite their evident differences. It is in this spirit that the painter Kandinsky declared 'all the arts are identical. The difference [between them] manifests itself by the means of each particular art. . . . Music expresses itself by sound, painting by colours etc.' (quoted in Chipp 1968: 346–7).

This aspiration to find the thing that all arts have in common will be examined at greater length in Chapter 12. For the moment it is worth observing that one of the motives driving it is a concern with value and status. As we saw in Chapter 1, anything that can claim the title 'art' is generally accorded a higher cultural status than diversions classed as amusement or entertainment. Just as reporters are ranked more highly than crossword setters by editors and readers, though both contribute something of value to a newspaper, so the concert hall is rated above the nightclub and Shakespeare above soap opera, even though all of them provide leisure-time opportunities.

But what is it that elevates something from the realms of entertainment to the realms of art? Previous chapters have considered several suggestions. The point to note here, however, is that, in searching for an answer to this question, it has often been assumed that the great painters and sculptors provide the benchmark. That is why the word 'art' is usually taken to mean painting and sculpture first and foremost, and applied to music or literature only by extension. The *Oxford Dictionary of Art*, for example, is almost exclusively concerned with painting and sculpture while corresponding volumes for the other arts expressly specify music, literature and architecture in their titles. This assumption – that 'art' first and foremost means painting – is most evident whenever a doubt arises about artistic status. If, for instance, someone wonders whether dance is an art, a common approach to settling the issue is to see if it can, in some way or other, be modelled on painting.

An interesting parallel to this way of thinking about value and significance is to be found in science. 'Science' like 'art' is an honorific term, one that bestows considerable status. But what is a science? Just as visual art is taken to be the paradigm case of 'art proper', so there is a tendency to regard physics as the paradigm or benchmark that other subjects must measure up to if they are to be classified as 'sciences'. That is why, in times past, astrology (as opposed to astronomy) was declared 'unscientific', and more recently, why people have sometimes been led to question the scientific status of subjects such as psychology and sociology. When this is questioned, an onus falls on psychologists and sociologists to show that their inquiries are conducted along something like the same lines as physicists.

Yet, to take physics as the paradigm of science can lead to gross distortion. Why should the study of the human mind, or of human societies, be like the study of particles and forces? How could it? Just to take one evident difference: human beings and human societies can learn from each other, physical particles cannot; so in explaining human and social behaviour we have to take account of factors – knowledge and experience – that have no place in explaining the behaviour of particles. We all see how deeply mistaken it would be to try to explain the behaviour of fundamental particles in terms of their knowledge and beliefs, hopes and fears. People have found it less easy to see that it is equally mistaken to try to explain the workings of the human mind in terms that exclude all these. What this tells us is that the *scientific* study of human beings and human societies *has* to be different, since taking physical science as our model would lead us, *unscientifically*, to ignore some crucial facts.

Just as the philosophy of science needs to be aware of the dangers of making one science the model for all, so the philosophy of art needs to be alive to the possibility that taking painting (or plastic art more generally) to be the pattern for all the arts runs a similar risk of distortion. Consequently, we need to consider very carefully whether the idea that painting is the standard to which anything properly called an art must aspire, can really accommodate the performing arts satisfactorily.

A major consequence of treating painting as a paradigm when considering the performing arts is that the principal focus of attention is not *activity* – playing, dancing, acting – but product – the composition, the choreograph, the play. Just as the outcome of the painter's activity is a picture, so (we might think) the result of the ballet dancer's activity is 'a performance', the realization of choreographed movement before an audience. In this way, painting and ballet are conceptualized as the same sort of thing. Both the picture and the performance are 'art objects' that are presented for an audience to appreciate aesthetically.

It is quite easy to conceive of music along these lines. We speak, after all, of music *making*, and might therefore focus our attention exclusively on what is made, rather than the process of making it. If we do, music becomes a sort of 'painting in sound', or 'sonic art' to take another term from Chapter 5. Conceived in this way, music appreciation is rather like viewing a painting, except that it is something we do with our ears rather than our eyes. In a similar fashion, it is possible to think of acting as a way of turning dialogue and stage directions into something perceptible on stage, so that the playwright's visualization becomes visible to the audience. (In times past it was precisely this way of thinking that inclined people to think that the arrival of film would put an end to theatre, though as we saw in Chapter 6, this 'fourth wall' conception does not do justice to film as an art.)

Amongst the performing arts, it might seem least easy to construe dance as a kind of painting. Yet some of the major historical figures in the theory of dance, anxious to secure its status as an art, have enthusiastically advocated a conception of dance that interprets it as 'painting in movement'. The eighteenth century produced two celebrated advocates of this view: the Englishman John Weaver and the Frenchman Jean-Georges Noverre. Both were highly successful choreographers as well as dance theorists, and both thought that the best or highest form of dancing was an art in virtue of being a sort of painting or picturing. Noverre expressly makes the comparison with pictures and painting: '[A] well composed ballet is a living picture of the passions, manners, ceremonies and customs of all nations of the globe . . .; like the art of painting, it exacts perfection' (Noverre 1966: 16).

In taking this approach to dance, both Weaver and Noverre were thinking very much in accordance with an aesthetic common to most writers in the eighteenth century and given its most influential exposition at the end of that century by Immanuel Kant in his *Critique of Judgement* (1790). The Kantian aesthetic, as we saw in Chapter 2, places great emphasis on the contemplation of beauty as the main focus of art, and a consequence of this is that the centre of aesthetic attention must be a beautiful object. What is this object? In painting and sculpture, the answer is easy. The activity of the artist produces beautiful visual objects that we can contemplate and admire, namely painting and sculptures. But what could such aesthetic objects be in the case of performing arts? Music offers an obvious answer – *sonic* objects, pieces of music, identifiable compositions (Beethoven's *Ninth Symphony*, Grieg's *Piano Concerto*, Barber's *Adagio for Strings*, for instance). These are 'things', to be heard rather than seen. Theatre, too, offers objects – nameable plays like Shakespeare's *Othello* or Tom Stoppard's *Jumpers*. We can meaningfully raise questions about such entities, without having to mention any particular performance of them. 'Have you heard Mahler's *Fifth Symphony*?' or 'Have you seen Ibsen's *Hedda Gabler*?' are questions that make just as good sense as 'Have you seen the *Mona Lisa*?'

Dance is more difficult because in general we are rarely in a position to name individual choreographs. The most famous ballets tend to be associated with the composer of the music rather than the choreographer of the dance. Tchaikovsky's *Nutcracker* and Stravinsky's *Rite of Spring* are examples of this. Even so, we still think of these as the names of ballets rather than the names of pieces of music, things that have to be *seen* and not just heard. So it seems possible to identify dances as a further kind of aesthetic object without referring to any individual performance.

Should we, then, think of the performing arts as a kind of painting – in sound, in movement, in theatrical action? It is worth emphasizing that the motive for doing so on the part of Weaver and Noverre was normative, not descriptive. Their intention was not merely to characterize dancing, because the word 'dancing' includes everything from barn dance, through ballroom, to disco. Rather they meant to pick out, and recommend, a kind of stylized dancing that could take its place alongside painting and poetry as one of the 'fine' arts. Their recommendation reflected (and probably contributed to) a widespread movement out of which ballet arose. Ballet, in contrast to barn dance, came to be regarded as having special 'artistic' status. This view of dancing has prevailed. The *art* of dance is distinguished from *social* dancing, and when people claim that dance is an art no less than painting, it is ballet not barn dance that they have in mind.

We can find something similar in the way people think about music. Like dancing, 'music' covers a wide variety of phenomena. Folk singers, church choirs, symphony orchestras, jazz pianists, brass bands, pop and rock groups are only part of this variety. But when people speak of music as an art, they generally have in mind just one of these, the music commonly called classical, but better referred to as the music of the concert hall.

It takes a special effort to remember that the practice of sitting down and giving exclusive attention to a piece of music is relatively new in human history, and it is still relatively rare. Music occupies a large place in every culture, but most of it is not the music of the concert hall, and many cultures have no equivalent of the concert hall. Even in the modern Western world, music is far more frequently heard on other occasions than in classical concerts, very often as an accompaniment to something else – the soundtrack to a film or television programme, the organ during a church service, the military band at a public ceremony – or just as background in a shop or restaurant. Why then do musicologists and philosophers of music tend to take the music of the concert hall as the principal form of music as art?

Once more the answer lies with the aesthetic ideals of the eighteenth century, which was, in fact, the period when concert halls devoted exclusively to music began to be built across Europe. Concert hall music fits the paradigm of the visual arts, or seems to. In the concert hall an aesthetically aware audience attends to an art object – a symphony, a string quartet, a piano concerto – in the way that paintings are attended to in a gallery. It is not difficult, therefore, to think of the music as a kind of 'painting in sound', and indeed it is not unusual to find programme notes referring to the 'colours' of the orchestration or the instruments. But the same conception is difficult to apply to music in its other manifestations. The jazz pianist playing at a restaurant, the brass band leading the parade, the organist accompanying the Church choir, the fiddler entertaining friends at home, are all musicians, and often very skilled ones. None of them fits the conception of 'painting in sound' in the way that the composer writing for a concert audience does. Should this failure to fit prevent us from calling them artists, and if so why? The question invites us to think again about the idea of painting as a paradigm for all the arts.

Nietzsche and *The Birth of Tragedy*

A central feature of the paradigm we have just been examining is this: it seriously diminishes the role of the performer. The conception of music as 'painting in sound', for example, construes players of instruments as merely the means by which a composer reaches an audience. As such, they are not any more artistically significant than the paintbrush or the paint, which are also means. The point can be extended to dancers whom the 'painting in movement' conception also treats as mere means by which choreographers bring their creations to their public. Even actors, if we think of them as simply making visible the playwright's play, become no different to puppets skillfully manipulated by the puppeteer. In all three cases, this implication is obviously mistaken. Musicians, dancers and actors bring interpretative as well as technical skills and abilities to bear upon their performance. Like the composer and the choreographer and the playwright, they too are artists.

Equally important is this fact. There cannot be a painting without a painter, but there *can* be dancing without a choreographer, just as there can be music without a composer. In fact, musicians do not need an audience either, at least in the way that painters need other people to look at their paintings. An improvising jazz group is an instructive example. The musicians are not following any score, and can be playing entirely for their own benefit. Yet, even without either composer or audience, the activity is properly called 'music making'. The music that is 'made', however, is not an art *object*, the sonic equivalent of a painting; it is a *performance*. The music resides in the activity itself, not in its outcome.

The paradigm of music is usually taken to be a nameable work by a famous composer played in a purpose-built concert hall – the Allegri playing Benjamin Britten's first *String Quartet* in London's Wigmore Hall, say. But suppose we reject this model, and take jazz improvisation as the paradigm of music instead. What difference would this make to an account of music *as an art*? In the first place it would require us to identify and explain the aesthetic character of music quite differently from the aesthetic character of a plastic art like painting. If the jazz group is indeed the *paradigmatic* example of music, and if music is an art, it follows that in some of its manifestations, art is not located in objects at all, but in activities. Now the essence of activity is not contemplation, but participation. This shifts the focus of attention entirely away from the presentation of an object to an audience, which no longer seems of any special relevance to understanding music as an art. In short, music is *not* a kind of painting in sound, and it is only if unwarrantedly we give special attention to instances such as the Allegri in the Wigmore Hall that we will be inclined to go on thinking so.

It is this difference, or something like it, that the nineteenth-century philosopher Friedrich Nietzsche (1844–1900) had in mind in his earliest work – *The Birth of Tragedy*. There are, he thought, *two* spirits at work in art:

> Unlike all those who seek to infer the arts from a single principle, the necessary spring of life for every work of art, I shall fix my gaze on those two artistic deities of the Greeks, Apollo and Dionysus. For me they are the vivid and concrete representations of two worlds of art, utterly different in their deepest essence and their highest aims.
>
> (Nietzsche 1886, 1993: 76)

It is a contrast he goes on to describe as '[t]his tremendous opposition, this yawning abyss between the Apolline plastic arts and Dionysiac music'. The Apollonian manufactures dream-like images in paintings, stories and poems, images that intrigue us and invite our passive contemplation. The

Dionysian, by contrast, does not invite contemplation, but seeks to take possession of us. If we yield to its spirit, instead of simply sitting back and watching, we are caught up in activity. Though the language may strike modern ears as somewhat fanciful, it captures something true and important. Some of the arts offer us images that are worth contemplating. These images can be conceptual as well as visual, characters in novels no less than portraits in paintings, but they all invite us to study them carefully by giving them our undivided attention. It is this feature that has led to the concept of a distinctively 'aesthetic attitude' that was discussed in Chapter 2. Other arts, however, offer us something quite different – the opportunity to participate in activities like playing and dancing. It is certainly true that *one* instance of art is that of the spectator in an art gallery carefully contemplating paintings by great masters. But another, equally good instance is the musician who, with voice or instrument, joins in the harmony and rhythm of the choir or band. This is one reason why Nietzsche thinks that:

> Music obeys quite different aesthetic principles from the visual arts, and cannot be measured according to the category of beauty; . . . [A] false aesthetic . . . has grown used to demanding, on the basis of a concept of beauty that prevails in the world of the visual arts, that music should provide an effect similar to that of works in the visual arts – the arousal of pleasure in beautiful forms.
>
> (*ibid.* 76–7)

This 'false aesthetic' is the aesthetic of the eighteenth century, the aesthetic of Weaver and Noverre, the aesthetic of the concert hall. It is 'false' because it is one-sided and takes a single type of art – painting – to be all of art. In this way it distorts our understanding of the performing arts by trying to make them fit an alien model.

The principal theme of *The Birth of Tragedy* is an historical one. Nietzsche argues that if we look back we will find a significant change taking place between early Greek tragedy and its later development. The famous tragedies of Aeschylus (525–456 BC) and Sophocles (c. 492–c. 406 BC) – most famously *Prometheus Bound* and *Oedipus Rex* – reveal the spirit of Dionysus, which is to say a spirit that engages actively with the human condition and even rejoices at the suffering that life requires it to undergo. But at the hands of Euripides (480–406 BC) a change begun by Sophocles is accelerated, and the spirit of Apollo becomes dominant. As a result, instead of taking possession of its audiences in a powerful affirmation of life, the spirit of Apollo fabricates illusory images whose purpose is to distract us from the horrors of existence, and replace activity with dreaming.

We are not concerned here with the historical accuracy of Nietzsche's view of Greek tragedy, or his understanding of Greek mythology. The point relevant to this chapter is simply his distinction between two aesthetic principles, and his contention that the plastic arts and music are quite different.

While one can only involve us in passive contemplation, the other invites us to activity. The significance of this is substantial. It offers a quite different engagement with the art world for those (the majority) who are not possessed of unusual creative talent. We think of painters, poets, sculptors and composers as having special gifts. But nearly all of us can sing, or dance, or play a part.

It would be deeply misleading to describe Nietzsche as a democrat, and his philosophy of art does not especially emphasize participation over creation. Indeed he thinks that on its own the Dionysiac is no less defective than the Apollonian, and that the greatest art requires the two to be united. 'The sculptor', he says, 'has lost himself in the pure contemplation of images', but '[w]ithout a single image, the Dionysiac musician is himself nothing but . . . primal resonance' (*ibid.* 29–30). This is an idea we will return to, but for the moment we can use the distinction he draws between music and the plastic arts to justify an important shift of emphasis. It is one that transforms our conception of 'the audience' from passive recipients to active contributors, and thus extends active contribution to art far beyond the creations of the individual genius.

Performance and participation

'Is this true?' we might wonder. What the previous section showed is that a proper understanding of the performing arts requires us to accord artistic status to performers as well as composers, playwrights and choreographers. But how does this extend to audiences? The answer lies with the concept of participation.

We commonly distinguish between performers and participants, but it can be argued, with respect to music and dance at any rate, that the distinction is not really very important (the case of drama will be returned to). When an audience is invited to participate, those of its members who take up the invitation cease to be the audience and become performers. There is often an unspoken assumption that participation is a kind of half-way house between passive watching on the one hand and full-blooded performing on the other, but 'participation' usually just signals more limited skill than 'performance'; it is not a different kind of relation. Children new to music making who are given an opportunity to join in playing a gamelan, say, will be described as participating, while the more accomplished players will be described as performers. The audience (if there is one) is merely listening. *Both* 'participants' and 'performers' are making music.

The same point can be made with respect to dance. Imagine tourists visiting parts of Spain who try their hand at flamenco. We might describe them as taking part rather than performing, just because their dancing falls rather far short of the most accomplished local people. But 'taking part' and 'performing' are both to be contrasted, and in exactly the same way, with merely watching. The locals are not any more engaged in dancing than the tourists; they are simply better at it. In short, the contrast between performance and participation tends to be confused with that of 'professional' and 'amateur'. If we avoid this confusion we can see that participants are actually performing, albeit not very well on some occasions. Conversely, we can see that the most accomplished performers are not the tools of the composer's sonic creations, but participators in an unfolding activity of music making.

Participation as performance lies at the heart of Nietzsche's account of *The Birth of Tragedy*. Greek tragedy combined music, drama, poetry and choreography, and Nietzsche claims that it is the chorus, not the actors, who are central. Yet, despite this centrality, the chorus is 'the symbol of the crowd' and made up of 'amateurs'.

> Accustomed as we are to the function of a chorus on the modern stage, and the operatic chorus in particular, we are unable to understand that the chorus of the Greeks is . . . more important than the 'action' itself, . . . [and because of this] we cannot discern why it should have been made up exclusively of humble votaries (*ibid.* 44)

The essential point for present purposes is this. As symbol of the crowd and at the same time central to the action, the chorus bridges the gulf between performer and audience. The art in Greek tragedy is not a beautiful image realized by actors which an audience is invited to contemplate (though modern productions may present it in this way); it is a dramatic 'happening' to be caught up in.

Nietzsche believed the essence of Greek tragedy had been lost, but that two millennia later he could detect elements of its rebirth, 'dreams of a future awakening'. Surprisingly, given his profound hatred of Christianity, Nietzsche found these stirrings in the Lutheran chorale – 'as profound, courageous, soulful, as exuberantly good and delicate, as the first luring Dionysiac call' (*ibid.* 110). Once more the somewhat extravagant language may disguise an important truth.

Lutheran chorales are a product of the Protestant Reformation, and as their name suggests, owe their origin to the great German reformer Martin Luther. In pre-Reformation Christianity, polyphony had come to dominate church music; the words of the mass and of motets (anthems) were set to long complex lines of music which it required a great deal of expertise to sing. Moreover the music usually stretched single words out so much that their meaning was lost, with the result that ordinary people attending mass could neither sing nor understand what was being sung. Luther wanted to restore the congregation's role in singing, and so he composed simple devotional poems that could be set to familiar folk tunes or old church melodies, some of which he arranged himself. From this relatively humble origin, chorales developed into sublime works of art, and finally found their greatest exponent in Johann Sebastian Bach. Bach wrote only about thirty chorale tunes, but he harmonized a further 400 or so. More importantly, he wove chorales into his two great *Passions*, the St John and the St Matthew. These are settings of the story of Jesus' capture, trial and execution, as told in the New Testament, and they employ organ, orchestra, solo singers and chorus. But interspersed between the major movements are chorales, short hymns that chorus and congregation both sing.

The *Passions* are amongst the greatest works of art ever created. Yet they were not intended for the concert hall, but for liturgical use – the observance of Good Friday in Lutheran churches, to be precise. There are indeed striking similarities to Greek tragedy, because they combine words and music in the dramatic telling of a powerful story. And within them, the chorales are the counterpart of the Greek chorus. But it is of the first importance to see that, though an integral part of the dramatic work, these chorales are for 'humble votaries' to join in singing; they are not simply for listening to. The result is that when they are sung, the distinctions between participation and performance, audience and artist are completely submerged.

Of course it is possible, and common, for (especially) the *St Matthew Passion* to be given a concert performance, when an audience simply listens to professionals playing and singing. Concert performance of this kind turns religious liturgy into 'art' music. This transformation is most marked when the chorales are heard, and sung even, without any understanding of the words. On such occasions the human voice is converted into just another instrument, one that has its own distinctive timbre certainly, but no more meaning than a flute or a violin. In this transformation, something essential is lost. The hearer merely contemplates the art of the chorale instead of being caught up in it. This is precisely the contrast Nietzsche has in mind when he refers to *two* 'artistic deities'.

The performing arts, then, offer us a distinctive sort of engagement with art. The most straightforward case is dancing. Dancing is neither a sport nor a form of exercise; it is a form of art. There are identifiable dances that the dancers perform – the waltz, the polka from ballroom, 'Stripping the Willow', 'The Dashing White Sergeant', etc., from Scottish country. These performances, however, are to be engaged in, not watched. From the point of view of the spectator, in fact, most ballroom and Scottish country dancing is tedious. Dancing is something to be caught up in.

Moreover, its advantage over other art forms is that it is directly available to almost everyone, and open to both amateur and professional, where these terms refer not to the unpaid and the paid, but to people with quite different levels of skill and ability. This is true of the performing arts per se, and perhaps the most important respect in which they differ from the plastic arts. To appreciate the point fully, consider how differently the distinction between 'amateur' and 'professional' works in painting compared to music and drama. An amateur painter cannot paint a great work. The most that amateurs can do is *copy* the works of great painters. This is just what it means to call them 'amateur'. But an amateur musician *can* play a great work, just as an amateur actor can take a part in a great play. If I have little talent for painting or sculpture, my sole involvement with the plastic arts will lie with contemplating the productions of others. But if I can sing at all, or play an instrument to some degree, I can 'perform' some (not all, of course) of the greatest works ever composed. So too with drama, where people of limited skill are not confined to the role of spectator, but can get caught up in the greatest of dramas by performing in them. This is precisely what Nietzsche is pointing out in his remarks about the 'humble votaries' who comprise the chorus in Greek tragedy.

The art of the actor

We have already noted that to think of painting as a paradigm for all the arts places unwarranted emphasis on 'high' art over 'folk' art in music and dancing. By doing so it inclines us to think in terms of artefacts rather than performances – the choreography of the ballet, the compositions played in the concert hall – thus mistakenly construing the performer as a mere vehicle by which artistic creations are brought to an audience. If we shift the emphasis to jazz improvisation, traditional song or country dancing, we are unlikely to make this mistake, so that attention to folk art acts as a useful corrective.

In the case of drama, however, it is not easy to make a similar change of emphasis, because leaving pantomime and mystery plays aside, there is virtually no 'folk' drama (in Western art at any rate). Drama appears to be quintessentially 'high' art in this sense: the initiative nearly always lies with a playwright. Musicians can make music without a score and most dancing takes place without a choreograph, but actors seem to depend upon a script. What is the dramatic equivalent of a traditional folk tune like 'Greensleeves' or a traditional dance such as 'The Dashing White Sergeant'? There does not seem to be one.

Interestingly, and contrary to what this difference with the other performing arts might be thought to imply, theatre finds artistic scope for actors in other ways. Whereas a score specifies fairly closely what the instrumentalists must play, the script of a play does so much less exactly. The difference might be expressed in this way: the playwright leaves much more space to the actor in the realization of the work. This 'space', however, relates only to certain aspects of the drama. Ignoring certain types of experimental theatre, the plot, the dialogue and the number of the dramatis personae are all laid down by the dramatist. But the *characters* remain incomplete, and it is the task of the actor to complete them as credible appearances on stage or screen.

In early forms of drama – the Greek tragedies already mentioned for instance – actors literally put on the character whose part they played by wearing masks. This gave physical expression to the distinction between the actor and the part, and at the same time prevented the audience from confusing the two. In modern drama, where masks are no longer worn, it is no less essential that the two are not confused. It is the mark of a poor performance when the person of the actress obtrudes into the character she plays. The overshadowing of part by player can also happen not because of poor performance but because of audience recognition. This explains why the central role in a major production is sometimes given to an actor relatively unknown (as was the part of Jesus in Mel Gibson's film *The Passion of the Christ*). Fame on the part of an actor can be an artistic obstacle.

On the other hand, it is equally a failure if a part is simply 'acted out'. This is what often serves to make amateur dramatic productions unsatisfactory. The classic 'ham' is not someone whose own personality shines through, but someone who is obviously acting. Actors and actresses, then, have to fuse their own persons with that of the imagined character whose part they play so that the distinction between performer and performed is imperceptible. One way of expressing this is to say that, for the duration of the performance, the actor must *be* the character. Of course, there is a plain sense in which the character is not a real person, and the actor is. Marlon Brando, a real person, played Stanley Kowalski, an imaginary person, in Tennessee Williams's *A Streetcar Named Desire*. But it is precisely the fact that we can completely identify Brando with Kowalski that makes his performance in the role so outstanding.

One interesting conclusion to draw from this is that it is in the art of the actor that the two spirits of art identified by Nietzsche are most satisfactorily combined. The spirit of Apollo creates images; the spirit of Dionysus takes possession. In Greek tragedy, the image is literally a mask, and the audience is not (or should not be) able to identify the person behind it. In modern drama the audience should not be able to distinguish between the physical person on stage or screen and the imaginary character invented by the playwright. For the audience, in other words, the actor is an image, a product of Apollo. By contrast, the person of the real actor has to be possessed by the image of the character. It is in this way that the Apollonian and the Dionysiac are unified.

There is no reason to think that Nietzsche himself would have endorsed this conclusion. To begin with, *The Birth of Tragedy* was his first work and subsequent works did not much explore its further implications as revise his view of art. But in any case, he identifies the spirit of Dionysus with the spirit of music rather than drama. Is there then some similar unification of activity and image in music? The answer it seems to me is 'yes', but the identification of player and music is less than total. There are several reasons for thinking this.

First, the animating spirit in a theatrical performance is the whole being of the actress – her thought, action, utterance, feeling and physical presence. Now while the musician has to invest thought, action and sensibility in playing a piece of music, it is only by stretching language a little that we can speak of musical performance as requiring his or her whole being. It is only part of their being that it requires. We come closer to total absorption in singing, but it is hugely important that this involves words. When it does not, or when the words are in a language the singer does not understand, the voice is simply another instrument.

Second, what the actor realizes is a whole personality – an imaginary person in fact. 'Anthony Hopkins is Hannibal Lector' is as familiar a grammatical form as 'Anthony Hopkins plays Hannibal Lector'. It is possible to say 'Yehudi Menuhin is the violin in the Bruch' but much more natural to say 'Yehudi Menuhin *plays* the violin in the Bruch' precisely because we think identification somehow overstates the case. How could a person be a non-person?

Third, the term 'image' goes most naturally with the idea of representation, and as we saw in Chapter 5, there are serious limits on the representational powers of music. Pianists who bring the full force of their musicality to a performance of Debussy's *Clair de lune* can only in a limited way be said to be possessed by the image of moonlight since, while the sound of the piece has a certain appropriateness when we think of the moon, strictly there is no image before us or the player at all.

There is a deeper unity to be found between music and its performance, however, once we have abandoned the idea of visual images and representation. Chapter 5 concluded that it is more illuminating to think of musical compositions as created worlds of aural experience. Their creation requires both the imagination of the composer and the music making of the player. The composer imagines this world. The audience apprehends it. But uniquely, performers wander in the world they make, and in this way both contemplate it and are possessed by it.

Summary

This chapter has paid special attention to the performing arts of music, dance and theatre since they differ from the plastic and literary arts in certain ways. Crucially, it seems that a key element in understanding their special nature is to recognize the indispensability of a third artistic element – the instrument player, the actor, the dancer – that bridges the relationship between creator and audience and which has no counterpart in the relationship between author and reader or painter and viewer. The importance of artistic activity has tended to be overlooked in favour of art objects because painting has so often been taken to be the paradigm for all the arts. It is possible to construe music as 'painting in sound' and dance as 'painting in movement', but to do this is as distorting as it would be to insist that all the sciences must be modelled on physics. In *The Birth of Tragedy* Nietzsche tries to lessen the grip of this paradigm by focusing our attention on two spirits at work in art. One has to do with contemplating objects, and the other with being absorbed in activity. This alternative analysis to the dominant Kantian aesthetic enables us to make much more sense of the performing arts and why we value them. However, Nietzsche holds that ideally the best art will unite contemplation and participation. The art of the actor seems to provide a context in which we can make most sense of this idea, but the understanding of music that we arrived at in Chapter 5 also allows us to find a deep unity between music makers and the music they make.

Suggested further reading

Advanced introductory reading

Routledge Companion to Aesthetics (second edition), Chapters 8, 39, 45, 52
Oxford Handbook of Aesthetics, Chapters 33, 34

Classic writings

Nietzsche, *The Birth of Tragedy*

Major contemporary works

Noël Carroll, *The Philosophy of Horror* (1990)
Peter Kivy, *Osmin's Rage: philosophical reflections on opera, drama and text*, second edition (1999)

9

Architecture as an art

The general question on which we have been focused so far is the *value* of art. The arguments of the first four chapters led us to endorse the theory known as 'aesthetic cognitivism'. This holds that art is at its most significant when it deepens and enriches our understanding of what it is to be a human being. The value that lies in the work of the great masters of painting, music and literature is their ability to do this, and in so far as art functions in this way it has a value other than simple beauty and is to be classed, alongside science and philosophy, as more than entertainment. The next three chapters explored the application of this general theory to specific media – sonic, visual and literary arts – and were followed by a fourth chapter investigating the peculiarities of the performing arts.

It is now the turn of architecture. Yet this is an art form where, it seems, we need not even try to apply the general thesis – for three reasons. First, how could a *building* enrich our understanding about human experience or anything else? Second, in the other arts the key concept is 'imagination'. Paintings, sculptures, poems and books depict imaginary scenes, objects and people; actors play imaginary characters. Even if these are based on real people and events, this is incidental to their artistic value. But buildings are necessarily *real*. It is not enough for architects to imagine buildings because a work of architecture must serve a real function. Third, this functional dimension means we do not need any special explanation of the value of architecture. Its value is obvious. Architecture is the construction of buildings with useful functions – houses, shops, hospitals, schools, churches, theatres – and the value of architecture simply derives from the value of those functions.

On the basis of this third point someone might reject *any* normative theory of architecture, not just aesthetic cognitivism, and insist that architecture has purely instrumental value. To do so, however, raises a doubt about whether architecture is an art at all. In general we distinguish art from design, and one obvious way of making the distinction is to say that good design is valuable for some extraneous purpose, whereas art is valuable in itself. Knives, chairs and washing machines can all be beautifully designed, but the test of their value is how good they are for cutting things up, for sitting on and for laundering clothes. Art does not have any use external to it, so what value it possesses cannot be utilitarian. But if artistic value is to be contrasted with instrumental usefulness, and if the value of architecture lies in its usefulness, how can architecture be an art?

The peculiarities of architecture

On the face of it, 'Is architecture an art?' is rather an odd question. How could there be a doubt? Our ordinary ways of thinking and speaking place architecture among the arts, and the great architects are naturally classed with the great painters and poets. The Gothic cathedrals of Northern Europe, the buildings of the Italian Renaissance or Regency London, the American Congress, the Taj Mahal are all widely regarded as examples of artistic magnificence. And among the names of those who have created great and lasting works of art we must surely list Christopher Wren and Fillipo Brunelleschi as well as those of Rembrandt, Mozart and Molière.

Unfortunately, the question of the status of architecture as an art is not so easily settled. This is because architecture undoubtedly has features that set it apart from the other arts. The first of these is indeed its usefulness. Architecture is useful in a way that the other arts simply are not. The outcome of the architect's activity is *essentially* functional. Music and painting can serve practical purposes. It is not hard to imagine examples. The sound of an orchestra, for instance, could be used to drown out a baby crying. A painting could be used to cover an ugly crack in the wall. Such uses are contingent, however. They are not *intrinsically* related to the character of music or painting as art. They are also somewhat fortuitous; as luck would have it the music and the painting turned out to be useful. But even when music and painting serve *aesthetically* functional purposes, the function is still contingent rather than intrinsic. For example, incidental music in the theatre performs an important function by filling the gaps between scenes that changing the set requires, and painted stage sets can contribute a great deal to the overall artistic effect of a drama or an opera. Unlike the earlier examples, these deployments of music and painting serve an artistic function, and so cannot be viewed as simply fortuitous, and consequently cannot be dismissed so easily.

Even so, in neither of these second examples – music and painting in the theatre – can the aesthetic purpose be regarded as essential. This is because, removed from the context of their theatrical use, both have value in their own right. It is possible to listen to incidental music for its intrinsic merits and disregard the contribution it makes to the play for which it was written. Mendelssohn's music for *A Midsummer Night's Dream* is a good example. Indeed nowadays most people probably know it best as a piece of music in its own right rather than as an accompaniment to Shakespeare. Similarly, stage sets and backdrops, though not often exhibited as works of art in their own right, clearly could be. Even more important than the possibility of independent worth is the fact that we can intelligibly *prefer* to listen or look at such things in isolation from their original context, in the belief that they have greater artistic merit on their own. Arguably this is the case with Schubert's music *Entr'actes from Rosamund*, which are rarely heard in the setting for which they were written since the play is now virtually forgotten.

The possibility of independent existence and independent merit is important because it shows that music and painting can fail to satisfy the artistic use for which they were originally intended and yet continue to have aesthetic value. Music that does little or nothing to intensify the drama for which it was written, for instance, may nevertheless succeed as music. The spectacular backdrop of a play that fails may be the only aesthetically interesting thing to emerge from it. A poor film may have an excellent score. Something of the same can be said for sculpture, drama, poetry, and so on. But the same *cannot* be said for architecture. Whatever else architects may be said to do, they build things, and this means that they necessarily operate under certain functional constraints. A building that fails in the purpose for which it is intended is an architectural failure, regardless of whatever other more decorative merits it might have. The simplest mark of such failure is that the building falls down, but there are others of greater interest. The architect who designs a house in which comfortable and convenient living is virtually impossible has failed, however attractive his building may appear in other respects. Something of this sort can be said about some of Frank Lloyd Wright's highly praised houses, despite his express intention to the contrary. The same is true of those who build office blocks, hospitals, universities, factories, and so on. However attractive their appearance may be, if they prove expensive or unpleasant as places of work, they are architectural failures. In every case, the building must satisfy a user, and the purpose of the user is always something other than merely admiring the building. As someone has said, it is important in buying a house to remember that we do not live in the garden.

What this means is that, unlike other art forms, the outcome of the architect's work must have a use, and most importantly, it cannot fail to satisfy this requirement without losing its merit as architecture. Of course, a building erected for one purpose can later serve another. But this does not show that there are buildings without functions; it just shows that no architectural function is fixed. The possibility of *changing* use does nothing to refute the contention that every work of architecture must have some purpose or other.

But why *must* a building have a purpose? Surely there are buildings – the miniature *folies* that decorate eighteenth-century English gardens for instance – with no purpose at all? With this sort of example in mind, it is tempting to think that the purpose of at least some architecture could be mere ornamentation. The ornamental buildings of the eighteenth century, however, are parasitic; they are copies of buildings that did have a function, the temples of Greece and Rome mostly, where sacrifices were offered and oracles consulted for practical purposes. When we admire a building, we cannot merely be admiring how it looks. If we were, a model of the building would suffice. It is not enough, therefore, for a building to be elegant or delightful to the eye. This is confirmed by the fact that although many ruins make impressive sights, it would not have been acceptable for the architect to have built any of them that way. The abbey ruins at Rievaulx in Yorkshire are wonderful to look at and wander around, but they are still architectural *ruins*.

It might be countered that eighteenth-century architects *did* build ruins for the sake of ruins – there is an example in Kew Gardens (though there is something odd about this description of what they did, since 'new ruins' is a contradiction in terms). We might try to accommodate this by saying that the ruins still had a purpose, to be ornamental. This might be described as a purpose of sorts, but it is more plausible to argue that any building whose purpose is *pure* ornamentation is really a kind of walk-through sculpture. Roger Scruton, in *The Aesthetics of Architecture*, provides us with a convincing example. The 'Chapel of the Colonia Guëll' by the Catalan architect Antonio Gaudi (1852–1926) takes the form of a tree-like growth that disguises its character as a piece of engineering. What are in fact supporting pillars look like the trunks of palm trees and the lathes of the ceiling are disguised by being in the form of leaves. But, as Scruton remarks, so extraordinary is it that 'what purports to be architecture can no longer be seen as such, but only as a piece of elaborate expressionist sculpture seen from within' (Scruton 1979: 8).

It seems we must agree that architecture is essentially useful. This is to say, architecture *must* be useful while other arts only have the *possibility* of usefulness. Utility, however, is not the only peculiarity of architecture, not the only thing setting it apart from the other arts. A second feature is the importance of place. A building can be both attractive and functionally effective, but marred by failing to fit its location. It can be so out of keeping with its situation by being too grand or too small, it can overshadow or be overshadowed by the buildings around it, or be in a style that puts it wholly at odds with its surroundings. All these are factors that can contribute to its being regarded as an architectural failure. Irrespective of its other merits, incongruity of place can make a building look ridiculous or ugly. It is this sort of failing that the Prince of Wales had in mind when he famously criticized a proposed extension to the National Gallery in London as 'a carbuncle on the nose of a friend'.

It is difficult to see how the same thing could be said of plays, poems or pieces of music, because these can appreciated in a large number of different settings and contexts. There are some limits. As Scruton points out, it may not be possible to appreciate medieval church music properly in a modern concert hall where the ambience is quite wrong, and it is plausible to think that paintings and sculptures are place sensitive. But in none of these cases does choice or change of location alter the artistic merits of the thing itself. A Palestrina Mass may be poorly suited to the place in which it is sung, but this hardly counts against Palestrina's mastery of music. A huge painting such as *The Night Watch* by Rembrandt (1606–69) may lose a lot by being hung in too small a gallery, but this doesn't make Rembrandt any less of a master. By contrast, a building that does not fit its context does count against the mastery of the architect who built it.

A third differentiating feature is this: architecture makes extensive use of 'ready-mades'. Some of these are part of what is sometimes called the accumulated 'vocabulary' – the Georgian door, the sash window, the pitched roof, for example. Some are items that other trades and professions design and produce – electrical and plumbing systems for example. Technological developments and the invention of new materials also bear directly upon the work of the architect, since the functionality of the building will favour some forms of structure and finish over others. Even the less functional aspects of a building, such as cornices, corbels and turrets, are provided for in a standard vocabulary that architects use, as well as more specialized features like Doric and Ionic columns. This element of assembly has no parallel in the other arts (though the recent innovation of the 'art of the readymade' will be discussed in the next chapter). There are no accumulated features which the poet or composer simply assembles.

To this extent, the architect is more like engineer than artist, and indeed on the strength of the features outlined, we might conclude that the architect *is* a constructional engineer – someone who uses existing techniques and devices to fulfil given functions within a given location, in precisely the way a bridge builder does. But if architecture is a kind of engineering, then using a distinction most closely associated with R. G. Collingwood (1889–1943), but in fact far older than that, we must conclude that it is a craft rather than an art.

Does this classification matter? Against it there is the point with which we began – that our ordinary way of thinking includes some buildings among the artistic masterpieces of the world, and some architects among the greatest artists. St Peter's in Rome began under the direction of Donato Bramante (1444–1514) who is widely acknowledged as an architect, but was later continued by Michelangelo, widely regarded as an artist. Michelangelo was certainly confronted by difficult problems of engineering, especially with regard to the dome, but it seems absurd to suggest that he was a supreme artist when he painted the ceiling of the Sistine Chapel, but not when he worked on the design of St Peter's.

One way round this conundrum is to say that all buildings are works of engineering, but only some are works of architecture. This distinction between 'architecture' and 'mere building' is expressly drawn by the influential modernist architect Charles-Edouard Jeanneret-Gris (1887–1965), better known by the pseudonym Le Corbusier. He wanted, of course, to classify his own buildings as the first, but it is a natural distinction to draw. The classic work *An Outline of European Architecture* by the celebrated architectural historian Sir Nikolaus Pevsner (1902–83) begins with just this distinction: 'A bicycle shed is a building; Lincoln Cathedral is a piece of architecture' (Pevsner 1963: 15). But where does the difference lie? How does the art in a work of architecture relate to the engineering involved in building it?

Form, function and 'the decorated shed'

Pevsner's own answer is this: 'nearly everything that encloses space on a scale sufficient for a human being to move in is a building; the term architecture applies only to buildings designed with a view to aesthetic appeal' (*ibid.*). This is a more complex answer to the question than it might seem at first, because it qualifies 'aesthetic appeal' with the phrase 'designed with a view to'. Does this mean that the move from building to architecture is a matter of the builder's intention? In any case what exactly is meant by 'aesthetic appeal'? Generally this would be taken to the appearance of a building, how it looks. Pevsner means more than this, actually, but if we stick to appearance, we confront a problem. To locate the architectural element in a building's appearance obliges us to conceive of a work of architecture as a 'decorated shed', a useful expression coined by Karstin Harries in *The Ethical Function of Architecture*. Surely when we describe Lincoln cathedral as a work of architecture, we do not mean to say that it is an enormous shed with lots of decorative features?

The problem with the 'decorated shed' conception is that it appears to divorce the building from its appearance, and to make the aesthetically significant element reside in appearance alone. It thus bifurcates the activity of the architect as well, because architects qua architects are not builders at all, but decorators. This seems counterintuitive. When the British Houses of Parliament burnt down in 1834, Sir Charles Barry (1795–1860) was the architect commissioned to construct their replacement. The result was the familiar building that is now the unmistakable image of London. But a great deal of the decoration that adds to the magnificence of the building, both inside and out, was designed by the Gothic-revivalist A. W. N. Pugin (1812–52). If the 'decorated shed' conception were correct, Pugin would be the architect and Barry the builder, which is not how any architectural history would ever record their contributions to this famous landmark.

The problem we are confronted with here can be stated in terms of the familiar distinction between form and function. Buildings must have a function. If, however, that function is satisfied by a variety of forms, from what point of view are we to adjudicate between the different forms a building might take? From a utilitarian or functionalist point of view it seems to make no difference. If two different forms serve the same function equally well and function is what counts, must we not regard them as equally good pieces of architecture?

What counts against this strictly utilitarian point of view is that the form of buildings does seem to matter. Indeed there is a measure of absurdity in even attempting to deny this. While there is no escaping the fact that how well a building serves its function is important, the finest buildings are commended and admired at least as much for their appearance. In other words, people care not just about how efficiently functions are satisfied, but how buildings look.

Can we not just say that both form and function matter independently, and that the architectural point of view is best thought of as a combination of different interests and considerations? There is obviously something right about this. Structural soundness, functionality and an attractive appearance are all important in architecture. The question, however, is just how the first two (structure and purpose) and the third (appearance) might be related. Is there some way in which these different interests could be *fused*, and thus give architecture the integrity of an art?

If we simplify matters by combining structure and purpose under the conception of 'function', we are faced with two possibilities. One is that form and function in architecture are quite independent, and held together contingently by the fact that some of those who build functional buildings also care about their form. The alternative is that precisely what makes a building a work of architecture is that its form and function are intimately related in some way.

Consider the first possibility. Is it possible to build in such a way that form and function are divorced, but given equally close consideration? Sometimes it seems that we can. For example, Orchestra Hall in the city of Minneapolis aspires to this sort of separation. The inside was designed independently of the outside because the dominant consideration (as befits a concert hall) was acoustic. Consequently behind the stage there are large blocks projecting at odd angles from the wall. Probably many concert-goers regard these as an unusual or extravagant decorative feature, but their purpose is not decorative at all. It is the absorption and reflection of sound. Around this acoustically designed hall an outer shell has been erected. In its construction the prime consideration has been how the building in its location looks to the passing observer, who may have no interest in its function as a concert hall at all.

Such a building is a 'decorated shed' in the sense that its properties as a shed – acoustic adequacy – have been addressed independently of how it can add decorative interest to the city in which it stands. But analyzed in this way, what is so wrong with the decorated shed? Theorists can *assert* that works of architecture ought to have a unity, but by what aesthetic or artistic principle is such an assertion to be validated? If those who want to go to concerts and those who want their city embellished by impressive buildings are both satisfied, the builder/architect can claim to have done everything required.

Façade, deception and the 'Zeitgeist'

A more modest assertion would be that while form and function *can* be divorced, it is better when they are unified, because the decorated shed has an aspect of fraud or deception about it. This is often the thought behind objections to façade. When joint stock banks were first establishing themselves in Britain they were risky ventures, and the banks that succeeded were those that managed to create and sustain confidence on the part of savers and investors. One way of doing this was to commission large buildings with imposing façades, often with classical features – Corinthian columns and the like – that had no real function in the building. Their purpose was to lend to the chancy business of banking a false appearance of venerability. In a similar fashion, post-revolutionary architecture in the USA, especially the US Congress, used a classical style of architecture to lend the new republic the appearance of a historical solidity it did not really possess. The grandeur of the architecture belied the fragility of the political institutions within. One way of describing this slightly shameless pillaging of the outward appearance of the temples and public buildings of the ancient world is to say that a distinctive architectural style was simply being exploited to create an illusion. The form of the building was chosen to cast a misleading light over its true function, whereas architectural integrity requires a kind of openness and honesty.

Augustus Pugin, whose work on the British Houses of Parliament was referred to earlier, expressed something like this view when he said that 'every building that is treated naturally, without disguise or concealment, cannot fail to look well' (quoted in Watkin 1984: 103). There is of course a difference between the rejection of ornamentation and façade and the rather bolder idea that naturalness and 'honesty' in building guarantee its aesthetic success. But both suggestions arise from one line of thought: that good architecture must meet higher standards than merely that of a pleasing appearance.

David Watkin, who quotes Pugin on this point, vigorously repudiates his way of thinking. Watkin rejects what he sees as alien moralistic ideas introduced into architecture by Pugin in order to defend the revival of Gothic for which he was famous. But Watkin finds the same kind of thinking in the writings of Nikolaus Pevsner (quoted earlier in this chapter) who took just the opposite view from Pugin on the matter of revival. Pevsner was famous for his endorsement of modern architecture, but this endorsement arose from a belief in architectural 'honesty', which requires the architect to be 'true' to the times. In another famous book – *The Buildings of England* – Pevsner says about the architecture of 1950s London:

> [I]t ought to be recorded first that the neo-classical, neo-Georgian spectre is even now not yet laid. In no other capital known to me would it be possible to see major buildings still going up which are so hopelessly out of touch with the C20.
>
> (Pevsner 1972: 111)

Pevsner thinks that architecture can be either 'true' and 'honest' in the appearance it presents to the world, or that it can be false and deceptive. Façade and ornamental copying are defects in architecture because they get in the way of honesty. They present an appearance at odds with the reality. Watkin, by contrast, is contemptuous of any such attempt to make architectural worth subject to independent non-aesthetic standards. Who is right about this?

To answer this question we need to determine where a standard of 'truth' in architecture could come from. The quotation from Pevsner suggests an answer: architecture is false or deceptive if it does not reflect the Zeitgeist, or spirit of the times in which it is constructed. Pevsner is not alone in this view. In fact it is a thought shared by a school known as *Kunstgeschichte* or the historical school of art. The idea takes more and less ambitious forms. One of its most ambitious statements is to be found in the writings of the German theorist Wölfflin.

> Architecture is an expression of its time in so far as it reflects the corporeal essence of man and his particular habits of deportment and movement, it does not matter whether they are light and playful, or solemn and grave, or whether his attitude to life is agitated or calm; in a word, architecture expresses the '*Lebensgefühl*' [feeling for life] of an epoch.
>
> (quoted in Scruton 1979: 53, brackets added)

Others have said the same with respect to other art forms. The painter Kandinsky held that:

> Every work of art is the child of its time. . . . It follows that each period of culture produces an art of its own, which cannot be repeated. Efforts to revive the art principles of the past at best produce works of art that resemble a stillborn child. For example, it is impossible for us to live and feel as did the ancient Greeks. For this reason those who follow Greek principles in sculpture reach only a similarity of form, while the work remains for all time without a soul. Such imitation resembles the antics of apes: externally a monkey resembles a human being; he will sit holding a book in front of his nose, turning over the pages with a thoughtful air, but his actions have no real significance.
>
> (Kandinsky 1947: 129)

It is not hard to see how this stinging condemnation is to be applied to architecture. Those who seek to copy the building styles and ornaments of the past can only succeed in producing slavish and hence lifeless imitations. Each era must speak for itself, find its own voice, and in so far as architects and other artists fail to meet this challenge, their work is 'false'.

The view espoused by Wölfflin and Kandinsky, and in a milder form by Pevsner, is generally known as 'historicism', the theory that history determines both possibilities and necessities for the art and culture (including the religion and morality) of each 'epoch'. It is a view that derives in large part from the philosophy of G. W. F. Hegel (1770–1831) whose philosophy of art was outlined at the beginning of Chapter 4. However, there is a simpler account of the falseness of façade in architecture that can be separated from this Hegelian context. We do not need to invoke ambitious theories of the Zeitgeist or spirit of the age in order to think that the copying of styles and the extensive use of façades can rightly be called 'deceptive'. The chief point of building in this way, after all, has often been to make things seem other than they are. What the architect aims to do, and is paid to do, is to disguise the relatively mundane function of a building by a grand exterior (as in the case of some nineteenth-century department stores), or to create a misleading impression of the history and solidity of a company (in the case of the early banks).

With these examples in mind, it seems plausible to say that, other things being equal, it is better to avoid such deception if we can. We need not defend such a view with historicist theory or high-minded moralizing, because it amounts to no more than saying that a building which declares its function openly, and at the same time succeeds in 'saying' everything the façade was intended to, is preferable just because it has the added element of integrity. The qualification 'if we can' is important here. Such integrity may not be possible, and the use of decoration copied from classical or other styles may be the best the architect could do. But we can still agree that in an ideal world the architect would have no need to disguise, and that it would be the mark of a particularly gifted architect to find a way of securing this integrity when others could not. It may be faintly ridiculous (as Watkin alleges) to castigate 'non-modern' styles of architecture for 'dishonesty' in the way Pevsner does. But it is not ridiculous to hold out as the ideal in architectural achievement, the construction of an integrated building in which none of its features can be dismissed as copying, or relegated to the category of façade and mere decoration.

To accept integrity of structure, purpose and appearance as an ideal does not tell us how it is to be attained. We still need to know in the abstract how form and function are to be integrated. But we may conclude on the strength of the argument so far that an architecture in which form and function are treated separately falls short of an ideal. What makes it an ideal is that organic unity is widely accepted as a mark of achievement in a work of art. In poetry and painting, this unity is between form and content. In architecture it is one of form and function. But in so far as such a unity is possible, this will enable us to explain what it is that makes architecture an art. But how is organic unity between form and function to be achieved? Initially, there appear to be two possibilities. Either form follows function, or form determines function.

Functionalism

The first of these possibilities – that form should follow function – is recognizable as an architectural slogan coined by the American architect Louis Sullivan, although it expresses a view that influenced architecture on both sides of the Atlantic for the larger part of the twentieth century. 'Functionalism' is a normative conception of architecture, a doctrine about how architects *ought* to build. It was promoted with campaigning zeal among architects themselves who took it to imply the rejection of everything decorative. Its most extreme statement is to be found in a remark by the architect Adolf Loos – 'ornamentation is crime'.

The belief that function should determine the form is usually associated with modernism rather than neo-classicism in architecture. Yet this is the view (though not the slogan) of Augustus Pugin, to whom reference has been made twice already. Pugin believed passionately in the superiority of the 'Pointed' style of architecture associated with medieval Christianity. Its revival was known as the neo-Gothic, and promoted by Pugin in several architectural treatises as well as a large number of buildings exemplifying the style. This extraordinary productivity in the space of a short life (he only lived to the age of 40) did much to make the neo-Gothic dominant in nineteenth-century British architecture. A vast number of churches in this style were commissioned, but so too were public buildings, of which Manchester City Hall is perhaps the grandest.

It was Pugin's view that every feature of a building should be necessary for convenience or construction, and consequently that ornament should be limited to the essential structure of the building. It should be the concern of architecture to serve the business of living, and the best architecture did this superlatively well. This is what made him a functionalist. But Pugin was also an enthusiastic Christian, and believed that since the best form of life was Christian, the best form of architecture was to be found in that period when life was most extensively Christianized, namely medieval Europe. This is how he arrived at the conclusion that functional building is best realized in the pointed architecture of the Gothic period, and that is why he advocated a return to it.

To say that form must follow function is another way of saying that a building should be constructed in accordance with its use. There is some obvious truth in this. A school which was so organized that it made teaching virtually impossible – the teacher's voice did not carry, the blackboard or screen was hard to see, there was no storage space, and so on – would be an architectural failure. Similar constraints apply to more general functions: the building should keep out the wind and rain, and protect against extremes of heat and cold, etc. But though close attention to general and special functions will determine many features of the building, it cannot determine them all. For example, a school will serve its function just as well whether yellow or red brick is used for its walls, and even the more obviously architectural features of a building may remain indeterminate when the demands of function have been apparently satisfied. Functional considerations can make a pitched roof preferable to a flat one, but this will not determine whether the gables are crow-stepped or not.

Formalism and 'space'

Form then *cannot* simply follow function, for even in buildings of considerable functional complexity, an exclusive focus on function would leave too many issues concerning its construction undecided. Sometimes 'architectural functionalism' is understood as the normative view that since it is only the functional aspect of a building that matters, architects should eschew the kind of extravagance one finds in the *Jugendstil* buildings of the early twentieth century, and construct buildings of the stark and unadorned kind associated with modernism. However, there are two errors here. First, the failure of function to determine form is a logical failure, not the practical one of ignoring simplicity. *Jugendstil* buildings, like the buildings of Gaudi, are exuberantly decorative it is true, but the point is that even a wholly determinate description of function cannot be made to imply a determinate description of form. Second, the sort of austerity characteristic of modernist buildings is not the logical consequence of a belief in functionalism, but precisely its opposite, the belief that function should *follow* form.

The principal influence on modernist architecture was Le Corbusier, whose insistence on the difference between architecture and 'mere building' was noted earlier. Le Corbusier's conception of architecture is of a pure art which explores space and shape through the medium of construction. This conception developed out of 'stripped Classicism', an architectural school which aimed to purify imitative neo-Classicism by stripping it of all mouldings, ornament and detail, leaving visible only the structural and proportional elements. One of Le Corbusier's early buildings (the Villa Schwob 1916–17) was of this kind, but it was the wholesale destruction brought about by the First World War that stimulated him and others to establish CIAM – the *Congrés Internationaux des Architects Moderne* – in 1928. The aim of this organization was to promote a revisionary conception that would make architecture a contributor to the rebuilding of European society. Viewed in this light, the role of the architect changes. No longer the servant of historically conventional or politically sanctioned functions, architects assume a far greater significance than that of simple builders, designers or engineers. Their place is alongside visionaries and opinion formers and their role is to show people how to live.

The influence of this line of thought was most marked in the design of housing. Here architects set out not to satisfy preconceived ideas of domestic accommodation but to show what domestic accommodation could be. The examples are legion, but in his famous *Unité d'Habitation* in Marseilles, Le Corbusier himself supplies the classic example – 337 apartments on top of massive *pilotis* or pillars of concrete marked with the lines of the timber shuttering into which it was poured. It was a model of public housing that was to be followed thousands of times in many countries.

The aim at the heart of this school of thought was the opposite of Pugin's. Whereas he accepted medieval Christianity as the right way to live, and saw the Gothic style of building as its architectural expression, modernists like Le Corbusier thought that architecture ought not to passively accept but to actively fashion ways of living. The relative simplicity of the style and lack of ornamentation arose not from a desire to let function determine form but from a realization, and confinement, of function within geometrically simple forms, namely, the artistic exploration of space itself.

CIAM's definitive statement was *The Athens Charter* of 1933. Together with the German modernist school known as Bauhaus (after *Das Staatliche Bauhaus Weimar* whose first director was Walter Gropius (1883–1969)), the influence of this conception of architecture across Europe and the United States was immense. It even reversed the roles of architect and client in accordance with its theories, for whereas formerly clients had decided what sort of building they wanted and had found someone to build it, increasingly they turned to architects to tell them what sort of building they *ought* to want, the theme of Tom Wolfe's polemical book, *From Bauhaus to Our House*.

But the result, as almost everyone concedes, was widespread failure to satisfy need. Houses and apartment blocks were built in which no one wanted to, or could, live and gigantic offices were created in which working conditions were often intolerable. This functional failure was illustrated most dramatically in 1972 when the Pruitt-Igoe flats in St Louis, Missouri, which had won an award from the American Institute of Architects only seventeen years before, were blown up at the unanimous request of the residents, because they had proved impossible for daily living. Similar steps have been taken elsewhere. In October 1990 the largest ever controlled destruction of buildings took place when eight huge blocks of British council flats in the same modernist style were destroyed in under three minutes. Not only was life in these buildings intolerable, but their construction was so poor that it would have been prohibitively expensive to repair them.

'Modern' architecture is now almost universally deplored and generally regarded as having failed. It is easier to record this failure than explain it adequately. One of its causes was undoubtedly the disregard for historical accumulation that the modernist school displayed. An early declaration of CIAM expressed the intention that 'It is only from the present that our architectural work should be derived' and this meant ignoring the experience of the ages in satisfying the real needs of the people who were to make use of that work. Generally the modernists were undeterred by popular opposition to their plans because they believed that people would have to be educated in the new architecture, and shed their preconceptions of what the experience of living in a building should be. Le Corbusier himself took this view of objections to his designs, believing that his work constituted a crusade against unthinking convention. However, the aim of 'teaching people how to live' falls easily into the assumption that they have no worthwhile opinions of their own on the matter, and not surprisingly, the buildings the modernists constructed were almost invariably regarded as unsatisfactory by those for whom they were intended.

It is a fact about human beings that they tend to cling to the tried and the familiar and resist anything new. This creates difficulties for the truly innovatory. Nevertheless, the opposition to modernism in architecture can be seen to be based on something deeper than mere conventionality, and evidence for its depth lies in the fact that it eventually led to the defeat of the modernist school. It is *real* needs and purposes that many modern housing schemes, schools and office blocks have failed to meet.

But this failure arises at least in part from a philosophical flaw in the modernists' central idea. Just as function cannot wholly determine form, so form cannot wholly re-conceive function. The form of a building must in part be determined by its function, whether consciously or not, because the function is to a large extent independently determined. A multi-storey parking lot, for example, could have a design which explores volume and space in a manner so striking that it thoroughly alters our idea of what a parking lot could be. Even so, in the end it must satisfy the purpose of housing cars safely and conveniently. Moreover no artistic conception, however brilliant, can make a multi-storey car park into a dwelling place because people are not cars, and they both want and need a different sort of shelter. Differing needs and practical requirements mean that car parks and houses have to differ in form and construction, and the most imaginative architecture cannot change this. In short, aesthetic form can no more determine function exhaustively than function can determine form.

Résumé

We have now considered three possibilities: first, that form and function in architecture may be treated quite separately; second, that form must follow function; and third, that architectural form can re-conceive the functional. Interpreted as normative principles of architecture, while none of these has proved satisfactory, each has something to be said for it. Clearly it is possible to deck a strictly functional building with ornamentation, and this has often been done. The most we can say in criticism is that a greater degree of organic unity is an intelligible ideal. It is one to which almost all generations of architects have aspired, and this is an aspiration relevant to architecture as an art since the ideal of organic unity is characteristic of other arts.

The attempt to seek this unity by making form follow function is not flawed because it results in plain or ugly buildings. On the contrary, as a matter of architectural history the 'high priest' of functional architecture, A. W. N. Pugin, was responsible for many beautiful buildings. The flaw lies in the fact that it is logically impossible to determine every formal feature of a building by appeal to function alone.

If modernist architecture is any guide, to seek organic unity the other way round – starting with form and exploring function by means of it – does lead to unattractive and undesirable buildings, but this is not the major flaw in such a search. Once more there is a logical gap that cannot be bridged. The functions a building must serve if it is to be satisfactory are in large part 'given' by independent needs and requirements, and no amount of architectural imagination can transform these functions further than the objective needs upon which they are based will allow.

On the strength of the argument up to this point we can say the following. Form must in part be pre-determined by function but never wholly so. Architectural innovations in enclosure and usage can enhance and enlarge our ideas of how given functions could be satisfied, but they cannot completely re-fashion them. What is required, then, is a conception of architecture in which both form and function have a measure of independent specification, but *complement* rather than compete with each other. One possible way in which this complementarity might be achieved is through a style of building that both *serves* and *expresses* the function, thereby establishing a mutual re-inforcing of the relationship between construction, purpose and appearance.

Architectural expression

How might the form of a building – its structure and appearance – express the function it is intended to serve? It is not difficult to say *in the abstract* how this could be done. A building is an organic unity when its most striking architectural features not only serve its function satisfactorily, but also convey the idea of that function to an observer. The problem is to see just how it is possible. How could architectural features convey ideas? We can easily imagine a restaurant, say, that serves its purpose well from the point of view of the chef, waiter and customer, and which is attractively designed. But it seems absurd to suppose that its lines or colour might in any sense convey the idea of 'good food'. The same sort of absurdity attaches to similar interpretations of much grander buildings. How could St Pancras railway station in London, though undoubtedly impressive, be thought to express the idea of travelling by train? Besides, there is a further question about what exactly the idea to be conveyed is. Should it be cooking or serving or eating good food? Should St Pancras say 'travelling by train' to the spectator or just 'travelling', or even more abstractly 'movement'? It is not so much that we find it difficult to answer these questions but that they seem inappropriate questions to raise.

It is easy to raise such difficulties and make them out to be absurdities, yet we can overlook real possibilities. It is not absurd to think that a building might express *some* ideas – grandeur or elegance, for instance – and it is not too difficult to connect these with the function a building might have. For instance the Marble Hall in Holkham Hall, Norfolk, England, is rightly described as both elegant and grand, a fine blend of classical and Baroque styles in fact, and its purpose was to allow both guests and hosts to display their elegance and grandeur. The Marble Hall may thus be said both to show and to serve elegance. In this way its form expresses its function.

But yet more plausible as examples of buildings which express ideas closely associated with the function they are intended to serve are the medieval churches of Western Europe. It has been pointed out many times that everything about a Gothic cathedral, but especially the spire, draws our attention upward, just as the minds and souls of those who worship in it should also be drawn upward. The gigantic nave of the cathedral at Rheims must fill those who stand in it with a sense of how small and fragile they themselves are. The important point is that this is an attitude singularly appropriate for those entering the presence of God. Similar remarks can be made about church architecture of other periods. It has been observed, for instance, that the colonnades which Bernini built around the piazza at St Peter's in Rome 'providing welcome shade in the midday sun . . . suggest the embracing, protective arms of Mother Church, wrapped around the faithful in the piazza . . . [and] . . . draw the eye to the steps or to the window and balcony in the Vatican palace from which the Pope gives his blessing' (Nuttgens 1983: 200). Whether this is the correct interpretation of this building is not the crucial point here. What matters is that remarks of this sort are both plausible and intelligible. This is enough to show that architecture *can* unify form and function in just this way: the form can express as well as serve the function.

Architecture and understanding

There is then at least one way in which architecture can be conceived as unifying form and function and, in so far as this is the case, we can regard architecture as a form of art and not simply design or engineering. But given the general conclusions of Chapter 4, this question remains: if art at its best is a source of human *understanding*, can architecture be art at its best? In other words, is there any sense in which architecture can contribute to understanding? What the argument of this chapter has shown (against both functionalists and formalists) is, first, that there is an architectural version of organic unity as an artistic ideal, and second, that some of the greatest works of Western architecture can be interpreted as realizing this ideal.

The ideal is architecture in which the form of the building conveys the idea of its function. This is not always the case, even for some very fine buildings, but when it is there is this further question: can the architectural expression of an idea enhance or enrich our understanding of that idea? Chapter 4 began with a quote from Nelson Goodman, one of the best-known exponents of aesthetic cognitivism. Goodman's short essay 'How Buildings Mean' summarizes the central idea of aesthetic cognitivism as the view that 'the excellence of a work is a matter of enlightenment rather than pleasure' (Goodman 1992: 375). Goodman then applies this view directly to architecture.

> A building, more than most works, alters our environment physically; but moreover as a work of art it may through various avenues of meaning, inform and reorganize our entire experience. Like other works of art – and like scientific theories – it can give new insight, advance understanding.
>
> (*ibid.*)

Buildings can both represent and exemplify. 'If a church represents sailboats, and sailboats exemplify freedom from the earth, and freedom from the earth in turn exemplifies spirituality, then the Church refers to spirituality by a three link chain' (Goodman 1992: 373). This might still leave it unclear how a work of architecture can enhance our understanding. One suggestion would be that the character of the building prompts us to think in new or different ways. Roger Scruton discusses the cathedral at Amiens in something like these terms. Looking at its West Front, he says,

> we are compelled to believe that what we see is a mass of masonry, and therefore to see that it is so. But we are not compelled to attend to the building in such a way that the thought of the celestial city seems an apt or appropriate expression of our experience. It is an activity of ours to attend to the cathedral in this way.
>
> (Scruton 1979: 85)

The contrast here between being compelled to see the cathedral as a mass of masonry, but being able to see it as a representation of the heavenly city, draws attention to the fact that looking at a building as architecture is not a matter of passive sense perception but of active imagination. Like any exercise of the imagination it has to be free, but for this very reason it results in new experiences, and thereby an enhanced understanding. The cathedral at Amiens has immense solidity; the very form this solid mass of stone has been given invites us to think of a spiritual substance and hence of a heavenly rather than an earthly dwelling place. As with Nuttgens's explication of Bernini's colonnades, the crucial point is not the accuracy of Scruton's interpretation but its intelligibility. It is not fanciful to speak of great architecture in this way, which shows that architecture can have the sort of meaning and significance we have found in the other arts.

How widely, and to what extent, architecture illuminates ideas for us in this way is another question. Great cathedrals are probably among the most immediately plausible examples to cite, but works of civic architecture are as well; Goodman discusses the Sydney Opera House in this way. Still, architecture, like the other arts, has a great deal of variety and this includes varying degrees of profundity and importance. In the case of many buildings, perhaps the vast majority, it would be absurd to attribute to them an ability to enhance our understanding of human purposes and the human condition. The conception of architecture we have been concerned with here is an ideal. The fact that it is only occasionally and mostly imperfectly realized should not lead us to decry the more obvious values of beauty and utility which many buildings possess. Just as in the other arts, there is a scale of values, and those at the lower end are not any the less values.

Summary

Unlike the other art forms, architecture seems to have a special feature relevant to its value: it is useful. Its usefulness explains its value, however, only if we focus on the function of buildings to the exclusion of their form. Yet it is the form of the building in which the art of architecture is usually supposed to lie. Architecture plainly must have both form and function. The central problem in the philosophy of architecture is to explain the relation between them that allows us to classify architecture as an art.

For the last 100 years or so, architectural theory has seen a sustained rivalry between functionalism and formalism. The first believes that the form of a building should be determined by the function it is meant to serve, while the second thinks that functions should be re-conceived through the architect's exploration of form and space. To a large extent this rivalry is based upon a false dichotomy. All buildings need both form and function and neither can wholly determine the other. An alternative idea is that unity of form and function in architecture can be achieved by the relation of expression: the form of a building can give public expression to its function. This account of the way in which architectural form and function can ideally be unified has the advantage of enabling us to explain the value and importance of many great architectural achievements.

Does this explanation of the value of architecture connect in any way with a cognitivist aesthetic? It is plausible to interpret some of the very finest buildings as being vehicles for the exploration and elaboration of certain human ideals. The spiritual aspiration characteristic of religion is an obvious example of an ideal embodied in some of the finest buildings of Western Europe – the great cathedrals – but other fine buildings suggest that the ideas of social elegance and royal grandeur, civic pride and political stability can also be given architectural embodiment. The power of a building to convey an idea may be relatively rare, but its possibility shows that while the value of architecture extends over a range – usefulness, durability, attractiveness, and so on – cognitive value enables us to explain some of its finest accomplishments.

Suggested further reading

Advanced introductory reading

Routledge Companion to Aesthetics (second edition), Chapter 50
Oxford Handbook of Aesthetics, Chapter 24

Classic writings

Nikolaus Pevsner, *An Outline of European Architecture*

Major contemporary works

Roger Scruton, *The Aesthetics of Architecture* (1979)
Karstin Harries, *The Ethical Function of Architecture* (1997)

10

Modern art

The break with tradition

The tradition of European art can be traced back to the world of classical Greece and Rome. For a considerable stretch of European history – roughly AD 400–1400 – this ancient inheritance was largely in abeyance. Even the casual visitor to any major art gallery can see that the paintings and carvings of the medieval period bear relatively little resemblance to the faces and figures on Greek and Roman remains. This is partly because some of the skill of painting and carving lifelike resemblances seems to have been lost. Medieval saints, often surrounded by birds and fishes, or armies of knights on horseback, look much less like real people and animals than do the marble busts and bas-reliefs that can still be seen in the ruins of ancient Athens. This is not to say that the art of the medieval period was necessarily inferior. Paintings of the period are noted for the vibrancy of their colour and narrative content, and Gothic architecture, which owes almost nothing to the architecture of the classical world, is amongst the finest we possess. But the Renaissance which began in Italy in the fourteenth century, and whose influence spread across much of Europe, sprang from the rediscovery of classical styles and methods in painting, sculpture and architecture, as well as Latin poetry and Greek drama. Combined with the Christian influences of the medieval period, the result was an astonishing explosion of artistic creativity whose magnificent results are still to be seen and treasured.

The classicism of the Renaissance influenced European art and architecture for a very long time, but eventually alternative styles and schools developed in all the arts. Some of them, such as the Baroque of the seventeenth century, are evidently continuous with the classical, others such as the Flemish School of painting in the sixteenth century much less so. But all of them melded in one way or another into what we might call a continuing tradition. Throughout most of this period, the arts owed their existence and vitality to patrons. The greatest of these was the Christian Church, in both Protestant and Catholic forms. The Church's inspiration, encouragement, use and commissioning of paintings, sculpture, architecture, music, literature and drama was immense. Cities and states, guilds and corporations, as well as aristocratic households and wealthy individuals were also important patrons of what came to be known as the 'fine' arts. This meant that, apart from the access given to ordinary worshippers in cathedrals and larger churches, to a great extent the arts were the private preserve of the wealthy and powerful. There were no art galleries, town libraries or concert halls in use by ordinary people who would in any case have had neither the time nor the money to make use of them.

This position changed in the course of the late eighteenth and nineteenth centuries, precisely the period in which the art gallery, the pubic library, the concert hall, the theatre and the opera house became familiar buildings in most towns and cities. Cheaper printing, better transport, increasing prosperity, and, later, the development of photography, all combined to make the arts popular and interest in them became widespread to an extent that was previously unknown. Popularity, however, did not mean *populism*. Print runs, attendance figures and commissions show that the concert hall, the opera house, and so on could command similar levels of popular enthusiasm to music halls, public parks and pleasure gardens, which also made their appearance at this time, but the works that commanded this enthusiasm came from some of the greatest creative artists of all time – Beethoven and Mozart, Dickens and Tolstoy, Ibsen and Chekov, Constable and Renoir, Gaudi and John Nash (who built much of Regency London). These are just a few names from a very long list of people working in all the arts with exceptional genius.

Their artworks continue to attract and inspire, but most histories of the arts agree that early in the twentieth century a great change took place and the long tradition of Western art was broken. In fact, the phrase 'the break with tradition' appears as a chapter heading in several major histories that are otherwise unrelated, including both Gombrich's *The Story of Art* and Gerald Abraham's *Oxford History of Music*. It is this break with tradition that gave rise to 'the modern' – in music, literature, theatre, architecture and the visual arts. In all these genres we can identify works that at the time of their creation seemed so radically different from what went before as to be unintelligible to their public – Stravinsky's *The Rite of Spring*, Picasso's *Demoiselles d'Avignon*, Joyce's *Ulysses*, Eliot's *The Wasteland*, Beckett's *Waiting for Godot*, Corbusier's *Unité d'Habitation* are among the most famous examples. With the possible exception of the last, all these works have subsequently come to be regarded as 'masterpieces'. How can they then at the same time be regarded as works that broke with tradition? In what respect is *modern* art so radically different?

Experimental art and the avant-garde

There are two obvious features of works such as Stravinsky's *The Rite of Spring*, Picasso's *Demoiselles d'Avignon* and James Joyce's *Ulysses*. First, they were intentionally novel. Their creators were trying out new ways of composing and writing that consciously moved away from established methods and styles. Stravinsky abandoned familiar styles of melody and harmony, which made music dissonant and totally unpredictable to the listener, the opening theme being a loud, pulsating, dissonant chord with jarring, irregular accents. The figures in Picasso's painting are grossly distorted and have no trace of what is usually taken to be visual beauty. Joyce used 'stream of consciousness' writing instead of the narrative form so characteristic of Dickens or Trollope, ending *Ulysses*, famously, with Molly Bloom's 64-page monologue. Second, all these works met with a very negative reaction on the part of the public, the critics and fellow artists. Picasso's painting, declared incomprehensible by his contemporary Henri Matisse (1869–1954), was not publicly exhibited until thirty years after it was painted. Copies of Joyce's novel were burned in New York, and it took fourteen years to be published in England. At its first performance the music of Stravinsky's *The Rite of Spring* was drowned out by the hissing and jeering of the Parisian audience, and ended in a riot!

Still, even taken together, these facts are not sufficient to characterize the radical break with tradition that is thought to be the distinguishing feature of 'modern art'. That is because all of them are marks of *any* experimental art, and experimental art can be found in all periods. Some of Beethoven's compositions, for example, were regarded by contemporaries as wild and unintelligible. Rodolphe Kreutzer, the violinist for whom he wrote his *Kreutzer Sonata* (1803), is said never to have played it because he could not understand it. The poetry of Gerard Manley Hopkins (1844–89), with its highly innovative use of stress, was rejected by the first anthology to which he submitted it, and was judged by his friend and fellow poet Robert Bridges (1844–1930) as being too experimental to prove acceptable to the public.

Both Beethoven's music and Hopkins's poetry, of course, came to be widely admired and regarded as major advances in their respective genres. However strange they seemed initially, this strangeness faded and they were eventually absorbed into the artistic tradition. This general pattern is one we should expect. While experiment and innovation are intrinsic to creativity, conservatism is a tendency in every public, including the public of the art world. These two facts ensure that experimentalism and initial resistance to it will be found in the creative arts during all periods of their history. Consequently, even in combination they cannot adequately characterize the degree of radicalism that is the mark of 'modern' art.

What then can? Sometimes this question has been answered by an appeal to the concept of the 'avant-garde'. This expression is simply French for 'advance guard', of course, and if taken to mean no more than this, can hardly do much to explicate the radical nature of modern art. An advance guard is a group that sets out before the general body of travellers, soldiers, settlers or whatever, in order to explore unknown territory. But in due course the rest follow. Interpreted this way, Beethoven would fit the metaphor of the 'avant-garde' perfectly. His explorations of symphonic music sketched out the ground for the great symphonists of the nineteenth century, composers such as Brahms, Mahler and Tchaikovsky. However, as it is normally used in this context, the term 'avant-garde' means more than just exploring new ground. It carries implications of rebellion. The avant-garde does not merely set out on something new in painting, music or literature; it rebels against and usually rejects the tradition out of which it has been born, and in some of its forms it goes further by seeking to subvert and undermine it.

For example, serialism in music, the creation of Arnold Schoenberg (1874–1951), deliberately and expressly abandoned its inheritance of harmony in favour of an entirely invented system of composition that would produce sounds different to anything that had hitherto been heard. The aim was twofold: to find a way forward from a tradition of music that Schoenberg and his followers believed to be exhausted, and at the same time to reveal its exhaustion. So too, Cubism in painting abandoned the great techniques of perspective, foreshortening and modelling in an effort not only to depart completely from representational art (in a way that Impressionism had only partially done), but to reveal the essential illusion that underlies it – the illusion that three dimensions can be reduced to two. In a similar spirit, the Theatre of the Absurd abandoned plot and dialogue in favour of meaningless repetition and pointless action with the intention of making the shapeless, non-narrative nature of actual lives apparent on stage. It would thereby expose (its proponents imagined) the extent to which traditional theatre misleads by imposing narrative form on the necessarily formless, and turning lives into 'life stories'.

This notion of the avant-garde as subversion can be extended to the very idea of art itself. Unlike the innovations of a Beethoven or a Hopkins, the radical art of the avant-garde has never succeeded in winning wide popular support. Concert audiences fall when the programme is Stockhausen or Boulez rather than Mozart or Beethoven. Amateur theatre groups rarely choose to stage Beckett. Picasso is something of an exception, but generally reproductions of landscape and portraiture are far more common than reproductions of Cubist works. Experimental novels sell in tiny numbers, while the sales of Dickens and the Brontës approached the level of the modern 'blockbuster'. And as we noted in the previous chapter, some works of modern architecture have actually been destroyed by popular demand. Yet more recent innovations – Damien Hirst's cow in formaldehyde, Tracey Emin's unmade bed and the solitary walks of the 'land' artist Richard

Long – fail to secure anything like popular admiration. This is chiefly because in the minds of the general public, modernism and its successors now prompt a familiar question – 'But is it art?'

Artists of the avant-garde have their explanation for this unpopularity. Anything truly innovative will be challenging, and if its purpose is in part to subvert established ways of thinking and doing, it will inevitably seem threatening also. As a response to criticism, however, this runs the risk of committing the logical fallacy known as 'affirming the consequent'. From the fact (if it is one) that great art is always challenging or even threatening, we cannot draw the inference that art that is challenging or threatening is thereby great. This is identical to a standard error that logic textbooks warn against: 'If it has been raining, the streets will be wet' does not imply that because the streets are wet it has been raining. Something else could have caused the same effect.

So too with the argument about art. It assumes that resistance to new works arises from their novelty. This does not follow. There are other reasons to reject them – that they are pretentious, for example, or wholly without artistic merit. In any case, the claim that all great works will be thought 'challenging' is false; Brueghel's pictures, Mozart's music, Jane Austen's novels, Barry's buildings were never seen as challenging or threatening. Furthermore, though the distinction may be hard to apply in any particular case and for that reason likely to be contested, if there is *any* boundary between art and non-art, it must be possible to be mistaken about what falls either side of the boundary. So it is reasonable in principle to think that *some* of the new things that people called 'artists' come up with will fail to be art at all. Why should art be art simply because this is what its creator calls it, any more than medicine is medicine if its manufacturer declares it to be so?

It is true, however, that some of the art described as avant-garde has set out to be revolutionary by throwing doubt on this very boundary, the art/non-art distinction itself. It has set out to question the very idea of 'art' as something set apart from ordinary life and experience. Its intention in doing so is to break the dominance of a 'canon' of masterpieces, whether in literature, music or the visual arts. The rejection, destruction even, of the canonical in art challenges the authority of the art establishment, part of whose self-understanding is the ability and the right to determine what is and is not artistically valuable. In so far as this establishment is largely the preserve of a social or cultural elite (as many artists have contended), then the challenge presented by the avant-garde does indeed amount to a threat to the power and prestige of that elite.

This is of course a description of the avant-garde's self-perception – how it sees *itself* rather than how others have assessed it. Since part of the purpose of this chapter is to ask how it *ought* to be regarded, the validity of its self-perception is a subject to be investigated. It is useful to begin this investigation with a central example – the episode that inaugurated the art of the readymade.

The art of the readymade

In 1917 Marcel Duchamp (1887–1968), a French–American artist, sent a manufactured enamel urinal, which he entitled *Fountain* and signed R. Mutt, to an exhibition in New York. He was responding to an announcement by the organizers in which they said that they were willing to consider *anything* for inclusion. They meant, we may suppose, that they would not confine their exhibition to either traditional or currently fashionable styles of painting and sculpture, and it is uncertain whether Duchamp was making a serious statement, or whimsically taking their announcement literally. At any rate, his 'exhibit' was rejected, understandably. By the time a later exhibition was staged, however, opinion had changed and it was thought that true open-mindedness required that *Fountain* be accepted. With its inclusion in the exhibition the art of the readymade was born.

Duchamp's was the first, but arguably not the most famous, example of a 'readymade'. More famous was *Brillo Box* by Andy Warhol (1928–87). This soap pad box is not a readymade in the literal sense, since it did not come straight from the store, though the thing exhibited looked more or less like a commercially produced Brillo box. In any case, the differences between Duchamp and Warhol are of no great consequence for present purposes. Duchamp is generally allied with Dadaism, while Warhol is usually described as a proponent of Pop art. But then Pop art is sometimes described as neo-Dadaism. Whatever name we use, the move is the same – to challenge conventional conceptions of art by putting readymade objects in an artistic context.

This move is not confined to visual art. A corresponding move is to be found in music, where it is associated chiefly with the American composer John Cage (1912–92). Cage invites just this comparison, in fact, by entitling one of his pieces *Music for Marcel Duchamp* (1947). His most famous (or infamous) 'composition', however, is *4′33″* in which a singer or instrumentalist appears on stage for four minutes and thirty-three seconds but without making any sound. Half-way through, the 'performer' turns over the pages of the 'score', and at the end of the specified time, takes a bow. The idea is that the audience, faced with a performer in a concert hall setting, will give to the accidentally occurring sounds around them, the same sort of attention that they would give to music. In this way, ordinary sound is turned into an art object for aesthetic attention. A similar phenomenon is to be found in film and dance. Warhol famously shot a film – *Sleep* (1963) – that consisted of nothing other than a real-time film of a man asleep for six hours. The choreographer Yvonne Rainer's *Room Service* consists of a group of dancers moving a mattress in the most ordinary fashion.

The purpose in all of these examples is the same. The 'art' we have been brought up on, whether it be music, sculpture, film or dance, consists of deliberately created objects with aesthetic properties sanctioned by tradition. This means that our aesthetic awareness is confined by preconceptions about what art ought and ought not to be like. But real aesthetic awareness needs to break free of these preconceptions, and the art of the readymade enables us to do this. It thus makes possible 'the transfiguration of the commonplace' – the title of a book by the influential philosopher of art, Arthur C. Danto.

In the hardware store, the urinal and the Brillo box are part of the world of the 'commonplace'. What is it that transfigures them into artworks? One obvious difference is change of location. They have been removed from the shop and placed in the art gallery. There are two ways in which this might be thought to transfigure them. One is simply the change of place itself, and the other is the way that seeing them in this context changes our attitude to them.

Michael Craig-Martin's 'work' *An Oak Tree* (1973) is another example of a readymade. It can be found exhibited in London's Tate Modern. *An Oak Tree* consists of a glass shelf such as one might find in a bathroom. On it sits a glass of water, and below to the left is a short text that explains what Craig-Martin says the exhibit means. The shelf is so commonplace that probably a large number of people who come to see the exhibit have just such a glass shelf in the bathroom at home, possible even an identical one, since it is a readymade. At home, it is not a work of art; in Tate Modern it is. How could mere change of place bring about this difference? If the very same shelf was to be found in the *washrooms* of the gallery (which it may, for all I know) it would not be a work of art there. So it must be its location in the exhibition hall that is important. Now if this were all there is to the transfiguration of the commonplace into work of art – a move from an ordinary place to a special place – it would run deeply counter to the idea at the heart of the avant-garde as we have been exploring it, because it would mean that a commonplace object becomes a work of art when the directors and curators who run such places bestow this status upon it by putting it on show in the exhibition hall. In this way, ironically, the rebellion of the avant-garde not only secures, but relies upon the approval of the very establishment it seeks to subvert. Having set out to show that there is nothing special about the art of the gallery, they have shown that it is only the gallery that matters, artistically speaking. Its success, we might say, is its failure.

Duchamp, who began the whole movement of readymades, made precisely this point: 'When I discovered readymades I thought to discourage aesthetics . . . I threw the bottle rack and the urinal in their faces and now they admire them for their aesthetic beauty' (quoted in Chilvers and Osborne 1997: 172).

But if Duchamp meant what he said (for many of his utterances on these matters are contradictory), then the purpose of the readymade is not in fact to challenge and extend preconceived ideas of art. Rather, its purpose is to explode the idea of art and the aesthetic altogether. In this case the label 'art' means nothing, and art galleries, concert halls and the like should be closed down.

The alternative to simple change of place is the way this re-location alters our attitude. This is plainly the purpose of Cage's 'composition' and of Yvonne Rainer's 'choreography'. By staging their 'works' in the concert hall and the ballet theatre respectively, both of them want us to treat everyday sound and everyday movement as we treat art music and art movement. The commonplace is thus transfigured by the attitude we bring to bear upon it. What is this attitude? The answer seems obvious – the aesthetic attitude. The problem with this answer is that it invokes a concept that the arguments and analysis of Chapter 2 showed to be highly questionable. If, as George Dickie plausibly argued, 'the aesthetic attitude' is a myth, it can hardly be used to rescue the art of the readymade. The heart of the difficulty, it will be recalled, is this. To explain what makes something aesthetic in terms of an attitude that we bring to it, is either vacuous or circular. Among all the points of view from which we consider items in our experience, there does not appear to be a psychologically distinct 'attitude' that we have reason to label 'aesthetic'. If, on the other hand, 'aesthetic attitude' is simply the attitude we *ought* to bring to art objects (practical disinterestedness, or whatever), then to define an art object in terms of such an attitude is circular – 'an art object is any object to which we ought to bring the attitude we ought to bring to art objects'.

To the question 'But is it art?' then, the advocate of the readymade has two answers, neither of which is satisfactory. The first – 'it is if the artworld says it is' – undermines its claim to be the art of the avant-garde. The second – 'it is if we regard it in the way we ought to regard art' – is question begging. Precisely what we want to know, and what is at issue, is whether we ought to regard readymades as art.

We might try to avoid this dilemma by denying that the alternatives change of place/change of attitude are exhaustive. Another possibility is that, by changing place, the object in itself takes on new properties. This is what Danto argues in *The Transfiguration of the Commonplace*, where he discusses both Duchamp's *Fountain* and Warhol's *Brillo Box*. The urinal which became *Fountain* was mass produced, and thus shared identical properties with a great many others – whiteness, smoothness and so on. Placing it in an exhibition does not change these properties. Its whiteness does not suddenly gleam 'like Kilimanjaro' or have 'the white radiance of Eternity' (to quote Danto's faintly mocking expressions). But what it does do is make the urinal take on a new set of properties, 'properties that urinals themselves lack: it is daring, impudent, irreverent and clever'

(Danto 1981: 93–4). The urinal in the art gallery has a wittiness that the urinal in the store lacks. That is why we are likely to smile at one and not the other.

At one level, this defence of the readymade as art is plausible, but not at the right level. The properties Danto lists – impudence, irreverence and so on – are only perceptible if and because we know that there is something odd about placing a urinal in an art gallery. What makes us smile is not the urinal, but the idea of a urinal in an art gallery. Strictly, it is Duchamp's act of putting it there not the urinal itself that is impudent, irreverent, etc., just as it is his painting a moustache on the *Mona Lisa* (another of his famous 'works') that is daring, impudent, irreverent as the 'Mona Lisa with moustache'.

One way of expressing this difference is to say that the *idea* of a manufactured urinal in an art gallery is novel, something original, that no one had thought of doing, and rather intriguing once it is done. Perhaps this is correct, but if it is, the aesthetic value of originality attaches not to the work but to the *idea* or the concept. This analysis has the advantage of signalling a further move – to readymade art's successor, conceptual art.

Conceptual art

Craig-Martin's *An Oak Tree* has a text attached which asserts that 'the actual oak tree is physically present but in the form of the glass of water'. Tate Modern's website goes on to say this:

> *An Oak Tree* is based on the concept of transubstantiation, the notion central to the Catholic faith in which it is believed that bread and wine are converted into the body and blood of Christ while retaining their appearances of bread and wine. The ability to believe that an object is something other than its physical appearance indicates requires a transformative vision. This type of seeing (and knowing) is at the heart of conceptual thinking processes, by which intellectual and emotional values are conferred on images and objects. *An Oak Tree* uses religious faith as a metaphor for this belief system which, for Craig-Martin, is central to art.
>
> (www.tate.org.uk/servlet/ViewWork)

It is unclear how this explanation is supposed to relate to Craig-Martin's work. Is *An Oak Tree* itself the transformative vision, or is it supposed to cause transformative vision in those who look at it? And if so, what is transformed, and into what? Actually the claim that 'the ability to believe that an object is something other than its physical appearance indicates requires a transformative vision' sounds like an empirical generalization, so that if it is false, however *An Oak Tree* is supposed to work, it fails. All these are natural questions in search of an answer, and they make Craig-Martin's 'artwork' problematic.

Still more problematic is Tracey Emin's *My Bed* (1999), a 'work' short-listed for the Turner Prize. *My Bed* is literally the artist's unmade bed, complete with used condoms and stained sheets. For a number of reasons, not least Emin's own attitude and behaviour, this caused great controversy, and in the world of 'modern' art, controversy is often taken to be a mark of artistic success in itself. But as we saw earlier, whether a work is artistically significant or not depends on what has caused the controversy, and what settled opinion is after the controversy has subsided. Stravinsky's *The Rite of Spring* caused controversy, largely because of its dramatically different style – no melody to speak of and rhythm the dominant element. But subsequent musical analysis, together with the recognition that the whole work is a ballet, revealed important aspects of the work which audiences and critics came to focus on as its artistic merits, indeed its genius. What of *My Bed*?

As with *An Oak Tree*, explanations of *My Bed* have been conceptual in the sense that they have focused on the ideas behind it – what it 'says'. Thus one commentator writes: 'marooned in the raging sea of a woman's tortured emotions, *My Bed* . . . might be located within the disjunctive yet overlapping contexts of sexual politics, homelessness and displacement at the end of the twentieth century' (Deborah Cherry, SHARP *www.sussex.ac.uk/units/arthist/sharp*). Such an explanation forges connection between this 'work' and contemporary social issues, but it does so through Emin's autobiography, not through the visual properties of the work itself. The meaning of the work lies in the ideas about 'sexual politics, homelessness and displacement' in the midst of which it is located.

Suppose we were to agree that Emin is making a statement of some political or social significance, and doing so in virtue of her extraordinarily chequered life. This question would still arise about the form of her 'statement' – 'Is it art?' This question is not quite as open as it may sound, because it is really the question 'How *could* it be art?' This deeper doubt arises because there is no identifiably *artistic* input from the artist into the object itself. Duchamp's 'impudence' is to be found in the gesture of submitting a urinal to an art exhibition. It is not to be found in the urinal itself, for the simple reason that the urinal owes nothing of its appearance to Duchamp. So too, properties of Craig-Martin's bathroom shelf owe nothing to any craft or skill of his. The arrangement of Emin's *My Bed* may have been her own work, but since it changed as it moved to other locations – in Tokyo for example – we may conclude that the precise arrangement was not crucial to the 'statement' that it was making.

The problem is one that applies to all readymades. Some of these may be very beautiful, or in some other way well worth looking at, but where is the *artist's* art? By the nature of the case it cannot lie in the making of the objects since these are *ready*mades. It must therefore lie in the ideas connected with them or prompted by them. But this, it seems, makes the artist a philosopher (for want of a better word) because, to quote the Tate commentary again, it is 'conceptual thinking processes, by which intellectual and emotional values are conferred on images and objects' that are 'central for art' of this kind. We do not need to be dismissive of these artists, or contemptuous of their ideas, to ask why we should need, or benefit from, *visual* art, if it really is the case that the processes are *conceptual*. Why does this not mean that art is to be replaced by philosophy?

Here the parallel with the Catholic doctrine of transubstantiation which the Tate commentary invites us to draw is instructive. This doctrine is not a transformative *vision*, but a metaphysical *explanation* of how the real nature of a thing can differ radically from its appearance. It is crucial as to whether the explanation succeeds (as many have thought it does not). How can bread and wine turn into flesh and blood without changing their external appearances? This is a complex conceptual question, so that to interpret the doctrine as a 'transformative vision' would amount to answering it with an assertive (and question begging) gesture – waving consecrated bread and wine and simply saying 'See!' If, then, we press this analogy, the conclusion we must draw is that conceptual art is bad metaphysics, since it cannot do more than assert its (strange) ideas. Actually, out of the art gallery, it cannot even do this. *An Oak Tree* was on its way to an exhibition in Australia, carefully packaged, when it was stopped by the Australian Agriculture Department whose rules forbid the importation of botanical specimens. But the exhibiters quickly explained that it was not *really* a tree! No Catholic would ever say this of the Host.

The market in art

The path we have followed is this. The art of the avant-garde has revolutionary aspirations because its aim is to call into question the art/non-art distinction. One prominent way of doing this has been to put the ordinary in places of exhibition or performance – ordinary sounds, ordinary movements and, most notably, readymade items. The difficulty with this attempt at a 'transfiguration of the commonplace' is that it raises important questions about just what is doing the transfiguring. By the very nature of the case there is nothing especially artistic about the object, but to rely solely upon the prestige of the gallery or the acquired authority of the exhibiters to effect the change would undermine the subversive purpose of the avant-garde, while focusing on an altered mentality in the listener or spectator would invoke the explanatory circularity of 'the aesthetic attitude'. This is what leads to a focus on the ideas or concepts related to the 'works' either as cause or consequence. But in effect this turns art into philosophy since it makes 'conceptual thinking processes' rather than visual or aural perception central to art, and thereby discards the perceptible as an artistic medium. In so far as 'modern' art is the art of the avant-garde, then, it seems to have set itself upon a course that ends in its demise. 'Modern' art is the end of art (as indeed Duchamp in some of his moods wanted it to be).

Yet if we deny modern art the status of art properly so called, and decry its pre-eminence, there is this difficulty confronting us: how can the art establishment have gone so badly wrong in taking it seriously? The claim that most modern art is not art at all may confirm the opinion of the ordinary person in the street, but it is a fact that major galleries display work of this kind, eminent critics review it, often favourably, and large sums of money are paid for it. Prestigious awards such as the Turner Prize regularly consider it, and from time to time readymade and conceptual art has been preferred to all other types of entry. Could it be the case that all these people are mistaken? If they are, there is a comparable error to be found in other arts. Eminent musicians and concert halls have programmed 'performances' of Cage's *4′33″* and Yvonne Rainer's *Room Service* was premiered in New York. What are we to make of these facts?

Earlier it was observed that, until the nineteenth century, the vitality of the arts relied upon patronage. During the nineteenth century, creative artists of every kind were successful because they were popular. In this respect, the nineteenth century was probably highly exceptional, because by the second half of the twentieth century, patronage had resumed its traditional role. For the most part, this has been the patronage of the State, though the personal fortunes of industrialists and businessmen have generated significant private patronage as well, especially in the USA. But a further, and arguably quite new, element is the phenomenon of art as investment, most marked in the visual arts, though there are some instances in other media also.

This investment takes two forms, which affect each other through their impact on the price that art can command. First, there is the investment of art galleries in their collections. The sums involved are often immense, partly because among the major players are foundations with enormous resources at their disposal, chief among them Guggenheim and Getty. But alongside these private benefactions are galleries that can call upon national purchasing funds, and strike government-approved tax deals with potential donors. Compared with State expenditures on armaments, public health or social provision, spending on the arts is low, but it is still large enough to inflate art prices enormously.

Speculative investment on the part of both individuals and institutions adds to this price inflation. It is common for company pension funds to buy Old Masters, for example, and to hold significant numbers of artworks as part of their portfolio of investments. Similarly, some individuals have made substantial sums 'investing' in art. The purchase of artworks is not properly speaking a form of investment because, unlike oil wells or software companies, they are a wholly unproductive asset. Any return on the money invested, accordingly, must come from an increase in the resale value. Interestingly, this increase has nothing to do with the aesthetic merits of the work in question. Nor need it have anything to do with demand. An increase in the resale value is assured only if sufficient people *believe* that there will be such an increase. If they do, then they will be willing to purchase at a higher price, in the expectation of a return on the capital value of *their* investment.

What is sometimes called the market in art is not a proper market at all, because there are no proper supply and demand relations. The demand for Old Masters does not decline as the price rises, and even the most dramatic price rise cannot increase their supply. Galleries may for a time purchase fewer works, but this does not lead to a fall in price. It simply results in their seeking larger purchasing funds. And of course, further down the chain, demand properly so called disappears altogether. If art galleries had to increase their admission charges in line with the rising price of artworks, then fewer people would attend them and revenues would fall, thereby creating a downward pressure on prices throughout the system. This is precisely what has happened with some recording artists and record companies. But since most galleries are free at the point of entry, the public attending them is completely indifferent to the cost of what they see there.

Given a circumstance in which there are a large number of purchasers chasing relatively few items, it is not surprising that there is a spill-over effect. If the supply of Old Masters cannot be increased, the work of new artists can. Public purchase and speculative investment mean that these works can also fetch very high prices (*My Bed* sold for £150,000), and galleries that could not hope to compete with the Getty Museum can 'specialize' in new works whose price is likely to fall within their purchasing power. The effect is that these new artworks have a value and are sought after. It is easy to see how this *contextual* value comes to be confused with *intrinsic* value, and easier still to see how contemporary artists who are able as a result to earn large amounts of money win respect for the value of their work. But of course all this is compatible with their artworks having little or no *artistic* value. A large number of galleries and collectors would pay a very large sum of money to have Duchamp's original *Fountain* in their collection when they could obtain an indistinguishable antique urinal for far less. The additional value derives not from the intrinsic character of that particular urinal, but from its history and the fact that there are so many other eager potential purchasers.

Art and leisure

The commercial value of modern visual and plastic art is unquestionable, but the idea we are considering here is that this simply creates an illusion of artistic value. Faced with this contention, advocates of modern art can point to other evidence that might justify both the high price of its purchase and the cost of its curatorship, namely the success and popularity of many modern art exhibitions. It can be claimed with truth that both established and new galleries dedicated to modernism attract high numbers of visitors on a regular basis, and exceptional numbers for special exhibitions. London's Tate Modern is a notable example; people have flocked to it since its opening. The Guggenheim in Bilbao is another. Just by itself it has increased tourism very significantly. Regardless of the art establishment, people go to modern art exhibitions in large numbers. Do these numbers not demonstrate that modern art has a value other than its purchase price?

The answer is: not necessarily so. Consider this parallel. In the nineteenth century, most Europeans laid great store by the Christian religion. Churchgoing was not as high as is sometimes imagined, but it was extensive, and so was church building. Churches were at the centre of important social networks that connected them with schools, colleges and hospitals. In the course of the twentieth century, Western Europe became widely secularized. Interest in religion and belief in its value declined dramatically, in some countries to the point where practising Christians are now a very small minority. Yet in some of these same places, the numbers of people passing through the doors of the great cathedrals are almost certainly at an all-time high. The explanation is to be found in tourism, which modern modes of transport and comparative wealth have made possible for millions of ordinary Europeans. Cathedrals are popular tourist venues, and the result is that the absolute number of people entering them each year is larger than at any point in their history. Clearly, though, it would be a great error to infer from this fact that belief in the value and importance of religion is correspondingly high. The majority of people who visit these places see them as having purely historic and aesthetic interest, and thus recreational value. They are no longer alive to the religious value that these buildings had for those who built them (and still have for a small minority of course).

Now a similar phenomenon may be at work with respect to art galleries and museums. If so, the fact that people visit them in large numbers does not permit us to conclude anything about the artistic value of what they find there, or of their attitude to it. As the parallel with religion implies, the explanation may lie in the recreational value of the art gallery and museum. People with a lot of leisure time need places to spend it, and galleries provide them. If this *is* the principal driver, it is likely to be reflected by their spending a higher proportion of the visit in the museum café, tea room and souvenir shop compared to the amount of time spent with the exhibits. There is some reason, largely anecdotal, to think that careful consideration of the evidence would confirm this.

Visitor numbers would be more compelling evidence of popular attitudes to art if normal market forces operated, but they do not. Tate Modern is a former electricity power station that cost £57 million to convert. This large sum was met from Britain's National Lottery, and there is no attempt (as there would be in a cinema for example) to recoup this from charges. People are not compelled to choose between expenditure on their visit to Tate Modern and other alternatives because they are able to visit an unusual building and a superb facility at *no* cost. In other places there are charges, but these are generally very low in comparison to other recreational activities. No museum or art gallery would attempt to charge the sort of sum that people readily spend on dinner at a good restaurant.

The purpose of these considerations is not to urge the desirability of charges to museum and galleries. There are quite independent reasons for thinking that admission to art galleries ought to be free, but in any case this is not the issue under examination. The point is that without a price mechanism compelling choice, the number of visitors attracted to an art exhibition is inconclusive evidence for any claim about the value that the exhibition has, or is believed to have by those who attend it. This is not something peculiar to fine art. People watch TV soap opera in very large numbers. Since they are not compelled to, we can infer from this that they like to do so. But we cannot infer much more. If the soap operas became pay-to-view, numbers might drop drastically, or not at all, depending upon alternatives. At that point viewing figures would be much better evidence for popular attitudes.

So too with the fine arts, though there is *some* evidence to go on. As was noted earlier, modern music finds it hard to attract an audience. Concert halls and impresarios who cannot call on any form of subsidy would be out of business very swiftly if they did not take serious account of this fact. Organizers of arts festivals know that while some income can be generated by ticket receipts from performances of music, dance and drama, it is virtually impossible to generate income from video installations. People will go to see them, but not if they have to pay to do so. Both examples underline an important possibility – that massive public (and private) expenditure on modern art, together with free access, gives rise to a misleading impression of the real value that the general public places upon it.

The general theme to be emphasized is this. There is a cultural complexity about the contemporary world of the arts that makes inferences from their social and economic impact a hazardous business, and weak ground upon which to assert (or deny) their value and importance. This is not a conclusion confined to modern art, of course. Visitor numbers at the Rijksmuseum in Amsterdam, the Prado in Madrid or the Louvre in Paris are all hugely inflated by the fact that these are tourist attractions as well as art galleries. But no one thinks to defend Rembrandt's artistic genius in terms of annual ticket receipts at the Rijksmuseum. A proper estimate of artistic worth focuses directly on his paintings and assesses them in terms of long-established values – the beauty, skill and creative imagination they display.

But the appeal to visitor numbers *is* called into play by the defenders of modern art exhibitions. Yet for the reasons we have been exploring, it cannot be regarded as a satisfactory way of answering this question: is the music, drama, painting any good? When we ask this question directly, the arguments of this chapter show that a question mark arises over the art of the avant-garde. Its desire to rebel against the tradition out of which it sprang implies an abandonment of that tradition and the values embedded in it. Yet it continues to trade on the special status of the gallery and the concert hall. As a result, its appearing to retain something of the aesthetic value that the masterpieces of the tradition possess may be an illusion generated by a new culture. Increased arts spending on the part of self-consciously democratic states, high levels of disposable income and a huge rise in the amount of leisure time have altered the world of the arts dramatically. Art is now both commercially significant and a matter of public policy. This new context is inclined to distract us from the fact that real and enduring artistic value can only be determined by critical scrutiny rooted in a cogent philosophical aesthetic.

Summary

The twentieth century witnessed an important rupture in the tradition of European art. In pursuit of new and different styles of creativity, artists in all the major forms – painting, sculpture, music, literature and architecture – produced works that shocked and startled. Though this reaction was highly negative, it was frequently welcomed by the artists themselves, as evidence of their being in the avant-garde, so that rejection became an accolade. However, this self-understanding should be subjected to critical evaluation. Welcoming something without reason is not more defensible than rejecting it.

The crucial question is this: if avant-garde art rejects its forbears, and discounts audience response, how can it claim *any* artistic respect or validity? The art of the readymade shifts attention from artwork to artist. The next step is from art to idea. But this emphasis on ideas, and the move to make the conceptual central, implies that art is ultimately to be replaced by philosophy. Is this then the end of art, or at least visual art? A countervailing fact is the commercial value of modern art and its popular success at a certain level. However, neither of these can be taken at face value. The prices commanded by modern artworks reflect distorting commercial conditions rather than an independent appraisal of their value, and visitor numbers at exhibitions and the like are more likely to be indicative of increased leisure time than of a rising level of artistic or aesthetic interest.

To arrive at this conclusion assumes the possibility of objective critical judgement. Is such a thing possible? This is a question that was considered briefly in Chapter 1. But it needs both more general and more detailed investigation, and this is the starting point of the next chapter.

Suggested further reading

Advanced introductory reading

Routledge Companion to Aesthetics (second edition), Chapter 38
Oxford Handbook of Aesthetics, Chapter 45
See also Cynthia Freeland, *But is it Art?* (2001)

Classic writings

P. Bürger, *Theory of the Avant-garde*

Major contemporary works

Arthur Danto, *The Transfiguration of the Commonplace* (1981) and *After the End of Art* (1997)

11

The aesthetics of nature

The previous chapters have been based upon the assumption that the best way to think about art is a normative one, that is to say, one concerned with its value. In the end, though, to be able to say that art *has* a special sort of value depends upon our being able to make substantial value judgements about particular works of art. Music is important if and only if we can show that, critically considered, those compositions and performances generally heralded as great, truly *are* great; a novel enriches us only if it truly is enriching; and so on. More especially, anyone who holds a cognitivist account of the value of art such as the previous chapters have advanced and defended, will have to be able to show, of any given work, that objectively speaking it does indeed have the cognitive value attributed to it. In short, a normative approach to art and a cognitivist explanation of its value depend crucially on being able to distinguish between sound and unsound judgements about what is and is not aesthetically valuable.

Objectivism vs subjectivism

Here, though, we encounter a familiar philosophical problem, one of the most widely discussed in aesthetics. Is the objective assessment of aesthetic value actually possible? A great many people suppose, to the contrary, that aesthetic judgement is essentially *subjective* – a matter of likes and dislikes, rather than truth and falsehood (a view they often apply to value judgements in general). Their philosophical champion is David Hume whose essay 'Of the Standard of Taste' was considered briefly in the first chapter of the book. If we take the idea of aesthetic *taste* seriously, Hume thinks, we have to allow that it 'has a reference to nothing beyond itself' and thus that 'to seek the real beauty or the real deformity is as fruitless an inquiry as to seek the real sweet or real bitter' (Hume 1963: 238–9).

The same point is stated even more emphatically in another of Hume's *Essays* – 'The Sceptic'.

> If we can depend upon any principle which we learn from philosophy, this, I think, may be considered as certain and undoubted, that there is nothing, in itself, valuable or despicable, desirable or hateful, beautiful or deformed; but that these attributes arise from the particular constitution and fabric of human sentiment and affection. What seems the most delicious food to one animal, appears loathsome to another; what affects the feelings of one with delight, produces uneasiness in another. . . . This conclusion every one is apt to draw of himself, without much philosophy, where the sentiment is evidently distinguishable from the object. Who is not sensible that power, and glory and vengeance, are not desirable of themselves, but derive all their value from the structure of human passions, which begets a desire towards such particular pursuits? But with regard to beauty, either natural or moral, the case is commonly supposed to be different. The agreeable quality is thought to lie in the object, not in the sentiment.
>
> (Hume 1963: 164–7)

The state of general opinion changes, and what Hume here describes as 'commonly' supposed is commonly supposed no longer. On the contrary, most people now share Hume's view on this question – or at least something like it. His conception of the subjectivity of taste is a sophisticated one. It allows for the idea of an *educated* taste, for instance, and to this degree it is perhaps rather less in accord with contemporary versions of subjectivism. Nevertheless, one interesting feature of the first passage I quoted is what it presupposes about *objective* judgements – that they must correspond with (or more generally reflect) an external reality. This may be called a 'metaphysical' assumption, and the idea at work in it – an idea frequently lying behind contemporary defences of subjectivism – is simply stated. Facts are out there in the world; beliefs are inside our own minds. Arriving at the objective truth is a matter of getting these internal beliefs to correspond with the external 'facts'. When they do, we are possessed of the truth; when they do not we are in error. But where there *is* no external fact of the matter, evidently, there can only be assertion of a purely subjective nature – expressions of personal taste, statements of individual preference and so on. If we add to this general metaphysical picture of truth and knowledge the further contention that aesthetic judgements are *at least in part* about what appeals to us or what we find attractive, it seems to follow that they have to be subjective. We like what we like and though what we like must fix upon an object (this book, that piece of music), there is no external 'likeableness' with which our liking could, or should, *correspond*.

This is a very common view, so common, in fact, that generally the onus of proof is thought to lie on the person who wants to disagree with it. How *could* aesthetic judgements be objective? This is frequently used as a rhetorical question (one that assumes what the answer to it is). Here, however,

I shall interpret it as an *open* question whose answer we have yet to arrive at. We can start to answer it by pointing out some fairly obvious difficulties that the subjectivist must overcome. The first is this: an ancient and familiar slogan claims *de gustibus non disputandum* – about matters of taste there is no disputing. Suppose this is true. About aesthetic matters, however, there is *as a matter of fact* a great deal of dispute. There are critics who make a livelihood disputing the relative merits of films, musical compositions, concert performances, plays and novels. There are also, in all the arts, established competitions that rely on the possibility of deliberation in aesthetic judgement – the Booker Prize, Young Musician of the Year, the Turner Prize, the Nobel Prize for Literature, the Cannes Film Festival, and so on. If, as subjectivism contends, aesthetic judgement is a matter of personal taste, does it not follow, somewhat implausibly, that all these familiar institutions are based on a mistake? Its implication seems to be that while the judges *appear* to judge on merit, in *reality* they merely vote in accordance with their personal preferences, because this is all they *can* do – if, that is to say, subjectivism is true.

A second interesting fact is that aesthetic judgement can be very extended. Whereas there is not much to say about ice cream, or different beers, or alternative recipes, except 'It's creamy, and I like creamy things' or 'It brings out the taste of the chicken, and I like the taste of chicken', it seems that entire books can be written in explication of the preference for the metaphysical poets, Beethoven, *Bleak House*, Impressionism or *film noir*. How many ways is it possible to go on saying 'I like it', 'I don't like it' and at what length? Could it really be true that a personal preference can take several hundred pages to express?

Third, there does seem to be some scope for rational justification in aesthetic judgement that has no counterpart in some other expressions of taste. If I say I don't like Mozart, or Abstract Expressionism, or modernist architecture, I can be asked to give my reasons. *Why* don't you like Mozart? Even if it is true that the business of reason giving runs out fairly soon (though this is a matter that warrants further examination), it is nevertheless hard to deny that there is a significant difference between these cases and, say, disliking chocolate cake. 'Why don't you like chocolate cake?'; 'I just don't' seems to be the only thing we can say. Such a dislike is, in Hume's language, 'an original existence', something that can be recorded but about which there is nothing much else to be said. This is not how it is with Shakespeare's plays, apparently, about which a vast amount can be (and has been) said.

Fourth, in adducing reasons for my preference for a work of art (as for any object over which rational judgement ranges), there is at least one constraint that I am rationally obliged to acknowledge, the need to refer to features that the work actually possesses. I cannot plausibly say that I do not like *The Waste Land* because I do not like limericks, for the obvious reason that *The Waste Land* is not a limerick; I cannot give it as my reason for liking pre-Raphaelite painting that I prefer abstract to representational art, since pre-Raphaelite painting is as far from abstract art as one can get; I cannot justify my distaste for modernist architecture in terms of a more general dislike of excessive ornamentation, because famously modernist architecture eschews ornamentation; and so on. In short, aesthetic judgement must accord with the actual features of the work about which it is a judgement, and cannot therefore be wholly a matter of brute preference. If preference is what it comes down to in the end, it must be a preference tempered by reasons.

These are important facts confronting subjectivists who have to find an explanation for them. One way of doing so is to locate the fundamentally subjective nature of aesthetic judgement at another, perhaps more sophisticated, level. It is true, they might say, that unlike the case of culinary preferences, there are lots of things we can say about, and in explanation of, our preferences for particular works or schools of art. It is also true that these preferences have to be grounded in actual features of the works in question if they are to have any relevance and interest. Nevertheless, the possibility of extended 'criticism' only shows (or so the subjectivist can claim) that aesthetic judgement can be more *complex* than the simple expression of taste that we might have for food or drink; it does not show that at bottom it is radically different. Both are essentially subjective, but the aim of aesthetic judgement is to go beyond the expression of *simple* preference, and formulate something more sophisticated, namely a personal interpretation of the artwork.

Art and interpretation

It is only fair to acknowledge that it is possible to take a subjective view of art without thinking that aesthetic judgements are a matter of simple 'gut reaction'. Indeed, Hume himself held that there is an important difference between simple preference and educated taste, the latter being the outcome of education and a mark of refined discrimination. Still, even allowing for this, subjectivists about the arts hold that there is an essential difference between describing a work of art and interpreting it. The subjectivity of aesthetic judgement lies in the interpretation, because while the *description* of a work can be right or wrong, there is no one right *interpretation* of a work of art. Shakespeare's Hamlet is unquestionably the Prince of Denmark, but whether the play shows him to be weak-willed or morally scrupulous is open to interpretation. Indeed, it is often claimed that art's special interest, in contrast to science, lies precisely in the fact that great works of art admit of many 'meanings'. They not only sustain, but actually *invite* a large measure of freedom in individual or personal interpretation. Unlike the student of physics or geology, who must 'track' the way the world is, the student of literature (to use a phrase of Jacques Derrida's) can 'play upon the text'.

Now this way of thinking can be made to accommodate several of the difficulties for subjectivism canvassed in the previous section. For example, the fact that in the arts people are not stopped short by the doctrine of *de gustibus non disputandum*, but do engage in sustained discussion, can be explained as a function of complexity and the competition between rival interpretations. Complexity allows for extended articulation and rival interpretations compete for the allegiance of readers and audience just as rival political ideals do. But we have no reason to conclude from this that either can be 'proved'.

A believer in the subjective character of 'interpretation' can allow, even, that between rival interpretations there can be a measure of adjudication – one interpretation might be more comprehensive, more interesting or more stimulating than another – and these possibilities are sufficient to explain the existence and perpetuation of artistic competitions. Such competitions are intelligible provided there is *some* measure of adjudication. They do not need full-scale objectivity, and those who take part in them can engage in rational reflection without supposing that there is just one 'right' choice. On the contrary, competition judges almost invariably believe that there can be legitimate and unresolvable differences of opinion about who the winner should be.

The same sort of rejoinder can be made about the need to refer to facts about the work. Any aesthetic interpretation must make reference to actual features of the work if it is to avoid arbitrariness. At the same time, all such interpretations are inevitably *underdetermined* by these features. Alternative interpretations can be equally faithful to the text, the painting or the score. In principle, Hamlet's words and actions could equally well be construed as weakness or scrupulosity. Furthermore, it is precisely because of this underdetermination that a critic can have a lot to say. Given the possibility of alternative constructions upon the evidence of the script or canvas, it is inevitable that elaborating an interpretation will have to be done at some length. Yet, when all that can be said has been said, the interpretation I elect to subscribe to will be one that expresses the meaning of the work *for me*. This is a function of the fact that I have to be touched, moved, attracted by a work of art. Otherwise it has failed – and so, despite the undeniable complexity of aesthetic appreciation, what it comes down to in the end is subjective preference – 'This is the interpretation I prefer, the one that means most to me'.

So far, then, it seems that subjectivists can overcome the difficulties that initially confront their view. But it is now time to ask what exactly the contrast between subjective and objective is supposed to be. Sometimes these words refer to the distinction between partiality and impartiality. If this is what is being referred to, however, there is no reason to think that aesthetic judgement is peculiarly subjective. Of course people *can* be partial and prejudiced about the arts, but so can they be with respect to issues in even the hardest sciences. The history of science provides plenty of instances when partiality and prejudice initially obstructed what eventually turned out to be the truth. Nor is it the case that there is less scope in the artworld for differentiating between partiality and impartiality. Indeed we do, and we ought to, try to arrive at impartial judgements in art and the aesthetic as much as anywhere else. Partiality – the introduction of irrelevant considerations arising from personal interests and prejudices – *clouds* judgement. That is why it is to be deplored and avoided in any exercise of the critical faculties – scientific, historical, philosophical, legal, practical *or* aesthetic. On this first interpretation of the distinction, then, we have as much reason to pursue the objective in art and art criticism as in any other aspect of life. All proper judgement must be arrived at in a spirit of critical open-mindedness, undeflected by personal bias.

Some determined subjectivists will accept the identification of subjectivity with partiality, and insist that art is essentially subjective because it is an arena in which it is impossible to escape personal bias. But this seems mere dogma. What evidence is there for it? Given the long history of art criticism and the vast amount of material over which it has ranged, we are not in a position to survey it all and thus be able to assert that partiality is everywhere, and unavoidable. Besides, if for some unexplained reason bias is inescapable in the arts, why is it not inescapable elsewhere? Here again some people are inclined to grasp the nettle and say that it is. This is global subjectivism – every point of view on everything is partial and biased. However, anyone who thinks that this helps the subjectivist case has failed to see that such a contention makes an important concession, and pretty soon becomes self-refuting. First, if every form of judgement is biased, bias is not a peculiar mark of the aesthetic, and any attempt to demarcate the special nature of aesthetic judgement along these lines has thus been undermined. Second, the general contention is itself subverted; by its own account the view that bias is inescapable must itself be the outcome of nothing better than bias. As a result, the objectivist alternative can assert itself with confidence. It too is the result of bias, perhaps, but since *everything* is, we have no choice but to look for some other differentiating feature.

For the most part those who believe in the essential subjectivity of the arts are not inclined to take this self-destructive path. The contrast they mean to draw between the objective and subjective is an epistemological rather than a psychological one, a contrast between knowledge versus opinion rather than prejudice versus open-mindedness. People who deploy this version of the distinction generally have this idea in mind. Any subject matter that is properly called 'objective' is such that when disputes arise, there is just one right answer (in principle at any rate). With respect to subjective matters, this is not the case.

What underlies and explains this difference? Hume's answer is that subjective matters cannot meet the requirement of correspondence with external 'reality'. He thus explains an epistemological distinction on the basis of a metaphysical one. But we have only to think of mathematics to see that this metaphysical requirement cannot be a necessary condition of objectivity in general. There are complex issues in the philosophy of mathematics (not to be entered into here) with which a fully adequate treatment of the subject would have to engage, but it seems fairly evident that the solution to a mathematical equation is not 'out there' in quite the way that the objects to which astronomical, historical or geographical hypotheses refer – the skies, the past, the earth – are 'out there'. So, at a minimum, and assuming that mathematics does admit of demonstrably right and wrong answers, it seems that it is not the failure of a correspondence relation that will, in the end, show aesthetic judgements to be essentially subjective, but something else. If mathematical propositions can be true, and shown to be such, but not in virtue of external realities to which they correspond, then failure to correspond cannot be the explanation of the subjectivity of aesthetic judgements.

What then does explain it? There is nothing to prevent the subjectivist conceding that there are manifestly erroneous interpretations of works of art. Importantly, though, once we have discounted those that fail to do justice to the actual text, script, canvas, score, etc., there will remain equally plausible alternatives. It seems, then, that the subjectivity of aesthetic judgement arises from this crucial claim about underdetermination.

What is this claim exactly? People can offer different interpretations of the same work. That is unquestionably true. But then, even the hardest science can generate alternative explanations of the same evidence. How does art differ? One answer is this: whereas in science, where there are two rival explanations of the same phenomena, we know that both cannot be correct, even if we do not (for the moment) know which is the better. In art criticism, by contrast, two rival interpretations need not be exclusive in this way; both can be illuminating of the work in question. Is *King Lear*, for instance, about nemesis or redemption? Substantial evidence from the text can be called upon on either side, and both constitute interesting ways of reading and producing the play. It is well known of Shakespearean drama that the same script can generate radically different productions. We are not forced to conclude, however, that one of them *must* be mistaken. Indeed, even the evidence of the text is not rigidly fixed; particular lines admit of varying interpretation – I read it this way, you read it that. We have a certain licence with words and notes and images that we do not have with particles, microbes, electrons and the like.

Now to express the point this way reveals a striking feature of modern criticism – in all the arts – namely its insistence upon the availability of alternative 'readings'. No one (serious) thinks that we can make of a text whatever we like. The claim, rather, is that after certain constraints have been observed, there remains an indefinite area of interpretative licence. But what are these constraints? So far we have mentioned only faithfulness to the text, canvas, etc. This accords with what some commentators have observed to be a striking feature of contemporary criticism, one that reveals an important shift in emphasis compared with earlier periods, a shift from author to reader. What matters now is not what the maker meant, but what the recipient makes of it.

But if we widen the focus again to include the author/painter/composer, a further constraint comes in to play – the author's intention. Since works of art are intentional creations it seems that any adequate interpretation of a work must take account of the originating intention of the author (or painter, or composer) as well as the perceptions of the reader (or spectator, or listener). Whatever meaning we the audience choose to attribute to it, there is a further independent question as to what its creator actually meant. And here, it appears, we have a new point of reference by which different interpretations may be judged good or bad; do they accurately capture the artist's intention?

The artist's intention and the 'intentional fallacy'

The question of the artist's intention and its role in understanding and evaluating art is another important topic in aesthetics, one which has received a great deal of philosophical attention. On the face of it, the relevance of the artist's intention is plain. Consider a simple case. I commend a child on her drawing of an elephant, say, only to be told that she meant to draw a hippopotamus. Had she meant to draw an elephant, I would have been right in my identification and the result would have been commendable; given that she meant to draw a hippopotamus, in *fact*, I am wrong, and it is not a very good drawing; it looks like an elephant, not like a hippopotamus, and is to this extent a failure, even if I very much like the final result. (We may leave aside here another possibility, that the child was mistaken and misidentified an elephant and a hippopotamus.)

There are more sophisticated examples that make the same point. In the sixth stanza of Yeats's *Among School Children*, the first four lines run:

> Plato thought nature but a spume that plays
> Upon a ghostly paradigm of things;
> Solider Aristotle played the taws
> Upon the bottom of a king of kings;

In the first printed edition of this poem, the typesetter put 'soldier' instead of 'solider'. Though some critics found 'Soldier Aristotle' intelligible, even ingenious, it is plausible to think that the military allusion makes little sense in the context of the whole, and is thus a poetic flaw. But this judgement on the poem's merits is overturned once we learn that this is *not* what Yeats intended. In short, it seems it is not only the poem and what we make of it that matters; the poet's intention is also relevant to an aesthetic assessment. Indeed in this case it is not merely relevant but crucial.

The same point may be made in a different way about music. In judging the merits of a composition it seems essential to ask (for instance) about the instruments on which the composer intended it to be played. The 'authenticity' movement in music insists that music should only ever be played on the instruments for which it was composed and, where necessary, these should be reconstructed. We need not go to this extreme to agree that a work intended to explore the timbre of one instrument should not be judged on its suitability for another, which might, of course, be a similar instrument of later date and design. What was written for the violin might not sound so very good on the tuba.

It is natural to generalize from examples like these, and conclude that there is more to interpreting a work of art than merely putting a construction upon its observable features and thereby giving it 'meaning'. We also have to know about the intention of its author, what he or she meant. Very many critics, indeed, have gone much further, and insisted that a wide range of biographical material is relevant to critical interpretation – family relationships, educational influences and so on. Still others (notably Marxist critics, of course) have held that knowledge of the social and historical context in which a work was created is also of the first importance in 'reading' it correctly. If any of this is true, then the freedom of the audience to find its own meaning in the work is severely constrained; an audience is no more free to make what it will of a play or a painting than a historian is free to construe the outcome of a battle in favour of whichever side he happens to favour; the Roundheads defeated the Cavaliers whether I like it or not.

How far do these additional factors, and especially the artist's intention, constrain aesthetic interpretation and evaluation? Is it comparable to the degree to which science and history are constrained by evidence? Can we make a mistake about a work of art in something like the same way we can make a mistake about a biological function? If we can, then it follows that the *essential* subjectivity of interpretation is an illusion, brought about, perhaps, by the contingent fact that there is more debate about art than there is about science, in large part because people feel free to offer opinions about books, plays and so on, where they would not feel free to offer an opinion in a scientific debate. Subjectivism is most plausible when we confine ourselves to 'reader response', but a properly critical approach to interpretation requires us to move beyond this. And if the artist's intention truly is crucial, then this means engaging in inquiry into what the poet or painter actually *meant*.

It is important to note that there are two different contentions to be distinguished here. Although the practice of drawing upon the artist's psychological history as an aid to interpreting his or her work is commonplace, especially among literary critics (though it has its adherents in musicology and fine art too), the claim that *biographical material* is relevant (or crucial) is rather more ambitious than the simpler claim that artistic *intention* is relevant to interpretation. Indeed the possibility of insisting upon a radical distinction between the two claims is importantly illustrated by the example of Collingwood, for whom the mind of the artist is central but who, as we noted in Chapter 3, is scathing about criticism that has been reduced to 'grubbing around for historical titbits'.

It is the second claim – about specific artistic intention rather than historical biography – with which we are chiefly concerned here. This is partly because the significance of the artist's intention has figured prominently in philosophical discussion. The starting place for much of that discussion is a famous essay by W. K. Wimsatt and M. C. Beardsley entitled 'The Intentional Fallacy'. As the title of their essay suggests, Wimsatt and Beardsley are *anti*-intentionalists. That is to say, they hold that any evidence of the artist's intention drawn from outside the text is aesthetically irrelevant.

Wimsatt and Beardsley's essay, as many commentators upon it have pointed out, is concerned with several distinguishable themes, some of which the authors are inclined to conflate. For instance, they are at pains to distinguish literary *criticism* from literary *history* and to make the former autonomous from the latter. But as we have just seen, it is consistent both to stress the centrality of the artist's intention and discount other biographical material. A further feature of Wimsatt and Beardsley's essay is that it constitutes a sustained assertion of a point of view rather than an argument properly so called; it never sets out clearly the fallacy it means to expose, or explains quite what makes it a fallacy.

Despite these uncertainties, their essay has attracted attention because they present those who think that the artist's intention is crucial with an important dilemma. *Either* the artist's intention is successfully realized in the work, in which case we need not look outside the text at all, *or* it is *not*, in which case the intention has failed, and cannot therefore illuminate our understanding of the resultant work. A work of art ought, from the point of view of criticism, to be relatively free-standing. We have to be able to understand and appreciate works of whose *originating* intention we know nothing. Our knowledge of Chaucer's or Piers Plowman's artistic intention can only be informed by the text, since we have no other source. Even where we do know something of the author's state of mind at the time of composition, in the end the justification of any interpretation must depend on the evidence of the text/canvas/score. (Wimsatt and Beardsley are exclusively concerned with literature, but it is not difficult to extend their claim to artworks in general.) This is confirmed by the fact that there could be no real ground to prefer an arcane interpretation, which relies on biography but fits rather ill with the text, over a plainer reading, which makes most sense of the text as it stands. Aesthetic judgement may be underdetermined by the text – which is why intentionalists seek other constraints on interpretation – but it is to the text, nonetheless, that it must finally answer.

Such is the burden of Wimsatt and Beardsley's essay. Yet the dilemma they present does not completely rule out the value of independent information about the artist's intention. Such information may set the parameters of interpretation by, for example, establishing just what the text *is*, what instruments the score is *for*; this is only a starting point. This is what the example from Yeats illustrates. The defence of an interpretation must draw its evidence from the text, but we may first have to establish a common text (which is why the origins of the solider/soldier variation are important). A further point of some importance is this. 'The content' of a work is not always written on its surface appearance. Art, like science, history and philosophy, is a tradition of activity. Artists of all kinds employ conventional devices of expression and representation. Moreover, they are often highly conscious of the tradition in which they work. T. S. Eliot is a particularly marked case. To understand his poetry we have to know a good deal of the poetry (and other literature) that preceded it. This constitutes another reference point by which to discriminate between good and bad interpretations: the good ones are those that are alive to the resonances of the tradition; the bad ones are those that are deaf to them. Whether I 'like' one interpretation better than another, I can only claim to have understood the work if I can take proper account in the reading I give of the detectable, and determinable, references it contains. No amount of freedom in attributing a personal 'meaning' detracts from this necessity.

There are then important facts to be accommodated and incorporated in arriving at a plausible interpretation of a work, and this puts limits on the claims of 'subjectivity'. Personal taste is not the only or even the main consideration. Even so, it cannot be denied that there is evidently the possibility, indeed the recorded reality, of different (and incompatible) readings, each consistent with the text, score, etc., upon which all are agreed, and all (apparently) taking account of the extra-textual elements of intention, convention and tradition. It might seem consequently, for all that has been said, that even making allowance for the role of artistic intention, we have still to admit the essential subjectivity of aesthetic judgement. In the end we can only call upon our personal preferences. Does this really follow? What *are* we to make of different 'readings', and how, if at all, are we to adjudicate between such competitors?

A further feature of the subjective/objective dichotomy is its all or nothing character. If we question this, then the possibility and perhaps eliminability of alternative 'readings' need not imply the subjectivist view. To begin with, objectivism only requires a distinction between 'better' and 'worse' readings/interpretations. Some readings of texts are strained, and silly; some performances of music are distorting; some interpretations of paintings are farfetched; some theatrical productions are failures. These possibilities are compatible with a number of readings/performances/interpretations being equally good, but this neither shows that we must retreat to subjectivity – after all they are equally *good* – nor does it reveal a peculiarity of art and the aesthetic. Underdetermination can occur in the sciences. Some philosophers think it unavoidable, but whether it is or not, so far as present evidence goes, several scientific explanations can be equally good. The possibility of several equally good interpretations of an artwork only shows that, *as yet*, there is no definitive interpretation. Perhaps the future will produce one that can be seen to supersede all the rest. Or not.

The important point is this: art is not different to science or history in this respect. The common picture of science (or empirical history) as invariably producing one right answer is a misperception of the reality. Even pure mathematicians, whose sphere is pre-eminently the 'provable', dispute and disagree, and often they have to leave the issues about which they disagree unsettled. Sometimes certainty is possible, sometimes it is not, in maths and science no less than in aesthetic interpretation and evaluation. Mathematical investigation, scientific explanation, historical inquiry and aesthetic interpretation can all be conceived as the pursuit of truth provided that we understand this as striving for *better* proofs, theories, narratives, interpretations, and not for some final 'best'. No sphere of critical inquiry rests upon the idea, or supposes in practice, that the last word has been said.

It might be replied that this overlooks the fact of logical exclusivity. We may not, as a matter of fact, know which of two competing scientific explanations is correct, but we know that they cannot both be since they logically exclude each other. Alternative interpretations of a work of art are not exclusive in this way. These are plausible claims to make, but their implications can be overestimated. Take a particular example. Very many cellists have performed and recorded Bach's 'cello suites', in a variety of styles and with varying degrees of success, all of which are available for us to listen to according to preference. Yet it is widely agreed, however, that the cellist Pablo Casals has made a recording that trumps all the rest, a recording that may be said to be definitive – to date at any rate. Of course this is a judgement that can only be sustained by musical critique, and in the absence of such a critique I can only assert it. What seems to me true is that excellent though many of these other recordings and performances are, Casals provides us with an interpretative performance that shows how Bach's composition is best heard. (The same claim might be made for Jacqueline Dupré's famous recording of Elgar's *Cello Concerto*.) Of course it remains the case that many of the others are worth listening to. In this sense they are not *excluded* by Casals's interpretation. But in so far as it is true that his is the best, they can be expected to lose some of their original attraction in its light. This is what it means, in my view, to say that his is the best, and though it does not sustain a conception of strict exclusivity, it allows us to say as much here as in many scientific cases. The best explanation need not exclude others, in the sense that they can be persisted with compatibly with the relevant evidence; but in the light of a better explanation, these alternatives lose a lot of their original plausibility.

In short, the subjectivist is mistaken not in believing that artworks admit of alternative readings, but in supposing that this undoubted fact is peculiar to art and that it implies admission of failure in the pursuit of objective inquiry into artistic excellence. The only thing that would show subjectivism to be true is the impossibility of deciding between the better and the worse, and the unintelligibility of the idea that there could ever be a 'best' interpretation (allowing for the interpretative impact of different contexts). Yet a familiarity with the real business of criticism in painting, literature, music and so on shows there to be ample scope for just such decisions. The literary critic writes, and the musicologist comments, on the presupposition that what he or she has to say sheds new light on hitherto unremarked parts of the text, composition or performance. Any other presupposition would make nonsense of their activities; it takes no special expertise to 'swap' opinions, and mere opinions have in any case no special claim upon our attention.

Aristotle remarks in one place that we ought not to demand of any inquiry more precision than it allows. This is a cautionary reminder. Art is not science; philosophy is not history; politics is not mechanical engineering; theology is not commercial law. Equally cautionary, though, is the reminder that we should not assume radical differences where we have no good reason to. The aesthetic is no more susceptible to ultimate rational adjudication than most other areas of human inquiry and reflection – and no less. Art critics, musicians, theatrical producers, scholars of literature and so on frequently dispute and disagree. So do scientists, mathematicians, historians and philosophers. Sometimes, especially in the sciences, explanations are rendered wholly redundant by further inquiry. In the arts this is less common, though not unknown. But so too is it in philosophy and history. Bearing this in mind, we have good reason both to acknowledge the provisional nature of aesthetic judgement, and to deny the contention that, in the end, it is all a matter of subjective preference.

The subjectivist, however, has a further arrow in the quiver. The argument to this point has relied to a considerable degree upon the idea of meaning. What, the critic asks, is the meaning of this work? How ought it to be interpreted? The answer lies in an attempt to construe it in a way that makes it intelligible, and to render it as intelligible (and interesting) as possible. What, though, of those things to which it makes no sense to attribute a meaning, but which, nonetheless, seem to invite aesthetic judgement? Are there such things? It seems that there are, namely natural objects. Surely some of the things we value aesthetically – objects in nature – could have no meaning. We speak easily enough of beautiful faces and physiques, landscapes, sunsets and so on. How are we to accommodate the aesthetic appreciation of nature within the framework of a philosophy of art that gives pride of place to intentional meaning and cognitive value?

The aesthetics of nature

It is an interesting fact about philosophical aesthetics that, while in some historical periods nature as an object of aesthetic judgement has occupied a central place, at others it has been almost wholly ignored. In the eighteenth century, for instance, nature was taken to be the pre-eminent object of aesthetic evaluation and what we call 'art' only secondarily so. As was observed in Chapter 2, it was Kant who developed this line of inquiry to its most sophisticated level in the idea of 'the aesthetic' as a distinct contemplative attitude revealed in the activity of mind that dwells upon, for example, the form and colour of a rose (one of Kant's own examples in fact). In the following century, however, aesthetics came to focus almost exclusively on humanly created art and indeed it may be said that, thanks in part to Hegel, by the mid-nineteenth century aesthetics and the philosophy of art were identical, or at least co-extensive. In the latter part of the twentieth century, interest in the philosophical investigation of an aesthetic appreciation of nature returned. An influential paper by R. W. Hepburn entitled 'Contemporary Aesthetics and the Neglect of Natural Beauty' revived interest in the subject, and this interest was considerably boosted by the rise of environmental philosophy and with it 'environmental aesthetics'. In the light of the history of ideas, then, there is some doubt as to whether nature is or is not a proper object of aesthetic attention and judgement.

In the eighteenth century, it was British writers and philosophers – notably the Scottish philosopher Francis Hutcheson (1694–1746) – who first took the appreciation of nature to be the purest form of aesthetic attention. Their central idea was similar to the Kantian aesthetic from which the modern concept of 'the aesthetic attitude' is derived. They thought that the enjoyment from looking at nature arises from a certain sort of 'disinterestedness' that sets aside personal, economic, moral (and religious) concerns. For many people this 'disinterested attention' is a matter of apprehending the visual *beauty* of nature, and hence appreciating it properly, but the eighteenth-century authors came to develop a distinction between 'the beautiful' and 'the sublime'. To appreciate the sublime in nature is to apprehend its power and majesty, its awesomeness we might say, while distancing ourselves from the sense of fear and foreboding that dramatic landscapes, snowstorms, thunder and lightning, violent winds, spectacular sunsets and so on naturally prompt in us. Such a disinterested attention to the sublime is to be contrasted with an appreciation of 'the beautiful' in art, that is the intentional production of the 'delightful' with words, paint or music. Beauty in this sense is the outcome of a designing intelligence; nature (if we ignore theological conceptions) has no such intention behind it, and consequently in nature the disinterestedness characteristic of the aesthetic can only apprehend the sublime.

There are a number of problems with this account of the aesthetic appreciation of nature. First, is this attitude of disinterestedness actually possible? Of course we can describe a process of abstraction, the process of setting aside all practical concerns and personal connections as we look at a landscape. But it does not follow that what this process results in is a distinct, or even a positive, attitude of mind; perhaps its logical extension is complete disengagement rather than disinterestedness. Indeed it is plausible to think that taken to its furthermost extreme this is exactly what will result, since if every purpose and interest that we may have is excluded, what is there left to hold our attention? At a sufficient level of abstraction, disinterestedness and sheer lack of interest seem to come to the same thing.

Second, even if there is some clearly distinguishable attitude called 'disinterestedness', is this the attitude we *ought* to bring to nature? To appreciate nature properly, it is arguable, we have to be engaged with it by seeing ourselves as part of it. Human beings are themselves part of nature, and so it is a mistake to draw a distinction between the human mind and the natural world such that the first is merely the contemplator of the second. By thus removing us from the natural world, the 'disinterested' attitude confines us to our own mentality and does not allow us to reach across the boundary between the human and the natural. Yet it is only when we cross this (artificial) boundary, it may be argued, that we come to appreciate nature properly.

A third difficulty is this. Even if the disinterested attitude is possible, and even if it is not susceptible to the objection just considered, why call it 'aesthetic'? This term, in its historical and contemporary use, is plainly applicable to works of art. If there is an aesthetics of nature, then it is also applicable to natural objects and, some have held, it is indeed refined and purified when it is extended in this way. But what is the connection between the two? What makes both attention to art and attention to nature modes of *aesthetic* appreciation? As we saw in the discussion of Kant, it is not easy to answer this question. 'Disinterested delight' seems to be the exclusive province of the spectator; it is the mind of the spectator that bestows the 'aesthetic' character on that which it contemplates. If so, the 'genius' of the creative artist is connected with it only contingently; we may happen to bring an aesthetic attitude to their creations, or we may not. For similar reasons 'beauty' is too thin an aesthetic concept to do much work here. Certainly, landscapes (and other natural objects) can be beautiful, but as we saw in an earlier chapter, beauty is one feature of the aesthetic but neither its only nor its distinguishing feature.

In fact, the gap between artistic production and aesthetic appreciation construed as disinterestedness seems to be wider even than these remarks imply. The productions of artists have intentional meaning. They arise from deliberative purposes which common human understanding can grasp or fail to do so. How then *could* we take an attitude to them of human disinterestedness? It is for some such reason that there arose an alternative, slightly later eighteenth-century conception, one that forged a connection between art and nature with the concept of 'the picturesque'. As the term itself might be thought to imply, to construe the beauties of the natural world as picturesque, and thereby make them available for aesthetic appreciation, is to interpret them as pictures in the making. In other words, we can appreciate nature aesthetically in so far as we can view it as a series of pictures such as an artist might paint. Accordingly, *landscapes* are aesthetically appreciable in just the same way that *pictures* of landscapes are – in terms of harmony of colours, shapes and perspective.

The 'picturesque' understanding of nature certainly forges a connection with art and the aesthetic. However, it seems by that very fact to eliminate the very thing that could be thought to constitute an appreciation of nature – its independence of human intervention (and invention), which is what the concept of 'the sublime' sought to secure. If a landscape is only aesthetically appreciable in so far as it has harmony, perspective and so on, then it seems that these things are to be secured by deliberately bestowing them upon it, by painting them or (at a later date) capturing them photographically. The landscape painter and the photographer bring to the vista before us a perspective, a way of viewing it. The result is that, in the end, what is to be appreciated is not the natural landscape itself, but this painter's or photographer's way of looking at it.

Alternatively, natural processes might themselves be used as artistic materials. The eighteenth century was the great era of an art form that has not been mentioned hitherto – landscape gardening. One way to think of landscape gardening is as the creation of the picturesque in the ultimate unification of art and nature. Landscape gardening uses nature and natural properties as an artistic medium. By a means more intimately connected with the forces of nature than landscape *painting*, it imbues terrain and vegetation with intentional meaning. But it does so only by giving the natural an order and a harmony that it does not have when left to its own devices. What results is not a piece of nature, but a painting composed of natural phenomena – streams, trees, grass and so on. Even in a medium that uses the processes of nature itself, then, nature is not the ultimate object of aesthetic appreciation after all. In any case, this may not be the right way to think of landscape gardening, which has some claims to be regarded as a form of architecture rather than painting, or even a performing art, since its maintenance requires a constant gardener as well as the original landscaper.

Landscape painting rose to considerable prominence in the late eighteenth and nineteenth centuries. It is notable that many of these artistic productions included human subjects, either human beings and their dwellings (especially castles), or objects of special interest in human pursuits (Landseer's *The Stag at Bay*, for instance). By the turn of the century, however, an alternative conception began to gather favour. This made much of the idea that the proper object of painting and photography was nature *untouched* by human intervention and interest, and a notable instance of art inspired by this conception is to be found in the work of the American naturalist John Muir. Muir's paintings aim not merely to represent nature but to *disclose* it, and to do so precisely by excluding the (deleterious) impact of human activity upon the landscape.

Does such disclosure result in the possibility of *aesthetic* appreciation? Even if it makes sense to suppose that we can abstract from the perspective chosen and provided by the artist, and thus infer that what is presented to us is (in some sense) the vista itself, aesthetic appreciation seems to require more than merely savouring the beauty of the landscape depicted in a painting or captured in a photograph. We need to be able to explore and investigate its properties. This, after all, is just what we aim to do with works of art, and what gives substance to the idea of aesthetic *judgement*. But *how* are we to do this in the absence of intentional meaning or expressive properties bestowed upon it by the painter or the photographer? The most recent answer to this important question is that an appreciation of harmony, balance and so on in nature, is to be supplied by science, especially ecology. This is where 'environmental aesthetics' comes into play.

'Environmentalism' means many things, but in this context we may take it to mean an understanding of the world in terms of interrelatedness, or perhaps interdependence. The basic thrust of environmental philosophy lies in the claim that a proper understanding of the natural world, of which we are ourselves a part, must take account of ecology, the science which alerts us to the interconnectedness of seemingly independent features of the world. This is a theme with which the philosopher Allen Carlson is especially associated. The idea is this. In art the backdrop that makes aesthetic appreciation possible is knowledge of the artist's intention, the history of painting, music, literature and so on, as well as the conventional problems and devices with which artists work. In the case of nature, a comparable backdrop is to be found in our expanding scientific understanding of ecological interconnection. The landscape artist *imposes* harmony on the natural world. To appreciate and understand landscapes as such we need to focus on their *own* harmony, and close attention to ecological relationships reveals just such a harmony. Aesthetic appreciation endeavours to discover an organic unity in humanly created works of art, and it can seek a similar, ecological harmony in nature. Unlike the first, this second harmony derives from features independent of human action and intervention. But that is precisely how it should be; the aim, after all, is to lend to the aesthetic in nature an independence from the creative purposes of human beings.

Now there is nothing wrong, as it seems to me, with calling this appreciation of ecological relationships 'aesthetic', but we ought to be clear about just what this implies. It has long been remarked that there can be a kind of beauty about scientific theories, especially those whose universality is such that they bring a huge range of physical phenomena within the terms of a relatively simple law. Similarly, mathematical proofs can rightly be described as having beauty and elegance. Furthermore, this beauty is part of their attraction. It is what compels our attention, and persuades us to continue to explore them even in the face of apparent snags and difficulties. Yet we cannot seriously be in doubt that their significance lies, not in their beauty, but in their scientific and mathematical power. This itself may prompt a sense of wonder by causing us to marvel at the astonishing sweep of understanding suddenly revealed to us. But the beauty and the wonder are essentially secondary. There is nothing wrong, or even linguistically odd, about referring to these as the *aesthetic* dimension of science or maths; scientists often do talk about a 'beautiful' theory. Where we do fall into error, however, is when we allow this linguistic usage to mislead us into thinking that it is beauty rather than truth that is of primary importance.

A similar conclusion seems to apply to the ecologically informed appreciation of nature. What this uncovers is the remarkable interconnectedness of things, the striking equilibrium in which the great diversity of nature – land, water, climate, animal and plant life – is held. Eighteenth-century deists, had they known of it, would have found here still more evidence of the wonderful 'contrivances' of nature, but they could think of them as contrivances, and in this sense works of art, primarily because they thought of them as supplying insights into the divine mind, the marvellous designs and purposes of God. If we abandon this theological context (as rightly or wrongly most modern thinkers do), and rest content with seeing them as ecological outcomes of evolution, then even if we stand in wonder, this is at most a by-product of the scientific understanding we have achieved. On this account, consequently, the aesthetics of nature is an epiphenomenon; it does not enter directly into our understanding of and judgements about nature in the way that it plays a central role in our understanding of art.

Those for whom there seems something wrong about an account which makes the aesthetics of nature peripheral or epiphenomenal to the scientific understanding which underwrites it, sometimes seek another alternative: they become nature mystics. That is to say, they believe that abandoning the Christian conception of God and His creation does not oblige us to abandon religious or spiritual values *in toto*:

> [P]eople also find sustenance in natural beauty. If contemporary materialist philosophers are reluctant to identify that sustenance as

> religious or spiritual . . . it is because they too easily identify Christianity with all religion and reject the latter because of their problems with the former. Once spirituality is unhooked from its particular Western Christian version, by contrast, nature may appear as the repository of transcendent values.
>
> (Kemal and Gaskin 1993: 5)

So it may, I am inclined to say. Indeed, it is interesting that by means of a concern with 'the environment' the notion of 'the sublime' should have re-entered contemporary philosophical aesthetics. Yet I do not think that this appeal to transcendent values and spiritual sustenance can in the end serve to substantiate the idea of an aesthetics of nature. This is for much the same reason that the appeal to an ecological underpinning cannot do so. In both cases the aesthetic becomes secondary, in the first to science and knowledge, in the second to spiritual or religious enlightenment. There is a parallel in the way music has often been thought to open up access to God. If music does open the door to the transcendental, this gives music additional value. But it does not explain its value *as music*. Similarly, though we may take spiritual inspiration from natural landscapes and vistas, this cannot be an adequate explanation of their value as a kind of art.

Chapter 4 defended a cognitivist account of art which emphasizes the ability of the artist to create images which illuminate our experience of the human condition and our understanding of human nature. What the discussion of the aesthetics of nature in this chapter shows, is that nature itself, unsullied and unrefined, does not provide us with such images. In literature, painting and photography, or more directly through landscape gardening, it can provide the materials out of which such images are fashioned but only by the subjection of the world of nature to human intention and artistic purpose. In this sense, though the world of the natural may be beautiful, interesting and inspiring, it cannot in and of itself, after the manner of poetry or music, supply something aesthetic to the mind.

Summary

We began this chapter with a question: can aesthetics be a matter of objective judgement, or is it merely a matter of subjective feeling? Despite the general dominance of subjectivism in aesthetics, the common practices of art criticism and artistic competition run counter to it. Though further responses can be made to these difficulties, there is the constant risk that they collapse into a global subjectivism that says nothing about art and aesthetics in particular, and is self-undermining.

An important counter to subjectivism lies in the observation that works of art are *made*; they do not simply spring into existence as objects freely available for unconstrained personal interpretation. Interesting and intelligible aesthetic judgements must take into account the point of view of the writer, composer or painter as well as the reader, audience and spectator. Works of art are intentional creations, deploying the traditions, conventions and resources of the practices which give them life and meaning. Perhaps, as the authors of 'The Intentional Fallacy' claim, works of art are importantly independent of such factors; literary criticism is not literary history. Nevertheless, they are objects with a meaning, and this implies that they are not entirely at the disposal of the 'free play of the imagination' of those who choose to look at them. This implies that, while there can evidently be alternative, equally good, readings and interpretations, it always makes sense to strive for a yet more intelligible, more comprehensive, more illuminating interpretation. This gives an objectivist view of aesthetic judgement an edge over the subjectivist account which dominates so much contemporary thinking about the arts.

This conclusion rests, of course, upon the contention that art has a meaning. What then of nature? Surely there can be aesthetic appreciation of the natural world in which (leaving theological conceptions aside) there is nothing intentional? Upon investigation, however, it proves difficult both to secure the independence of the natural and to forge a connection with aesthetic judgement as it applies in art. One way of doing so is to replace the intentional context from which works of art derive their intelligibility and depth with the scientific context that ecology supplies. In the end, though, this must make the aesthetics of nature secondary and derivative. We may wonder at the far-reaching and impressive balance of forces that nature exhibits, but it is scientific and not aesthetic judgement that reveals this to us.

The themes of this chapter were prompted by the need to sustain the normative approach to aesthetics that this book has adopted by an examination, and in the end a defence, of the objectivity of aesthetic judgement. There is, however, yet one more question to be explored. Is this normative approach really preferable to the others on offer? This is the topic of our final chapter. It takes us into the realms of somewhat abstruse theory and, though it is *logically* crucial to the cogency of the book as a whole, the chapter is one that readers whose primary interest is in the arts may reasonably feel no need to grapple with.

Suggested further reading

Advanced introductory reading

Routledge Companion to Aesthetics (second edition), Chapter 42
Oxford Handbook of Aesthetics, Chapters 1, 2, 6, 15, 39

Classic writings

R. W. Hepburn, 'Contemporary Aesthetics and the Neglect of Natural Beauty'
Aldo Leopold, *A Sand County Almanac*

Major contemporary works

Allen Carlson, *Aesthetics and the Environment* (2000)
Salim Kemal and Ivan Gaskin (eds), *Landscape, Natural Beauty and the Arts* (1993)

12

Theories of art

The question with which we began was normative: 'What is valuable about art?' This question has been used to guide us through, and adjudicate between, the competing claims of hedonism, aestheticism, expressivism and cognitivism, and the arguments of major philosophers associated with these positions. But now we must return to the logically more fundamental question which was suspended in the introduction. Is a normative approach the best one to take in aesthetics?

This question arises for two reasons. First, the normative approach to art is not the commonest. Traditionally philosophical aesthetics has been concerned with the definition of art, of trying to say what art is, rather than why it is valuable, and consequently, some defence must be made of taking a different approach. Second (and more important), contemporary art theory, of which aesthetics more narrowly defined is a branch, is marked by the great variety of methodologies that different writers adopt. These are not just alternatives; they are usually in express competition. The highly influential ideas about art and literature described as Marxism, structuralism, deconstructionism or postmodernism purport to have revolutionized the subject in a way that makes philosophical aesthetics outmoded and renders it redundant. If this is true, almost all of the argument in preceding chapters is seriously undermined. So we need to ask whether it *is* true, and this means that we have to examine the basis of theories of art. Let us begin with those traditional theories which seek to define art.

Defining art

The aim of philosophical theories of art that try to define and analyse the concept of art was perhaps most uncompromisingly stated by Clive Bell, who though not himself primarily a philosopher, was an influential figure in twentieth-century aesthetics, and is best known for the elaboration of one such theory:

> if we can discover some quality common and peculiar to all the objects that provoke it, we shall have solved what I take to be the central problem of aesthetics. We shall have discovered the essential quality in a work of art, the quality that distinguishes works of art from all other classes of objects.

Bell then goes on to say:

> [e]ither all works of visual art have some common quality, or when we speak of 'works of art' we gibber. Every one speaks of 'art', making a mental classification by which he distinguishes the class 'works of art' from all other classes. What is the justification of this classification? What is the quality common and peculiar to all members of this class? Whatever it be, no doubt it is often found in company with other qualities; but they are adventitious – it is essential. What is this quality? What quality is shared by all objects that provoke our aesthetic emotions? What quality is common to Sta Sophia and the windows at Chartres, Mexican sculpture, a Persian bowl, Chinese carpets, Giotto's frescoes at Padua and the masterpieces of Poussin, Piero della Francesca, and Cezanne?
>
> (Bell in Neill and Ridley 1995: 100)

Bell's answer to his own question is that what is shared by all works of art is 'significant form', but what he takes to be 'the central problem of aesthetics' is of primary concern here. Bell is interested chiefly, perhaps exclusively, in the visual arts. Even so, he gives expression to a general aim found in many writers, namely, the hope of formulating a definition of art that will state the necessary and sufficient conditions for something's being properly classified as a work of art.

To state the necessary and sufficient conditions of art is to set out the properties something must have in order to be a work of art, and the properties it does have which will guarantee that it is. It is in the spirit of the same endeavour that the American philosopher Suzanne K. Langer, also a leading figure in twentieth-century aesthetics, 'make[s] bold to offer a definition of art, which serves to distinguish a "work of art" from anything else in the world . . .: Art is the creation of forms symbolic of human feeling' (Langer 1953: 53). So too, as we saw in Chapter 3, the Italian philosopher Benedetto Croce advances the simple, if somewhat obscure, theory that art is 'the expression of intuition', and clearly he offers this formula as an account of necessity and sufficiency.

A British philosopher, E. F. Carrit, who was impressed by Croce's view as getting 'nearer the root of the matter than any previous philosopher', concluded that '[i]f we find ourselves unable to accept it . . . we should have either to say that the explanation of beauty is still undiscovered or to accept the alternative . . . that beautiful things have no other common and peculiar quality which makes them beautiful . . .' (Carrit 1932: 88). Carrit assumes that theory in aesthetics can take only the form of specifying a defining characteristic, and that if no such theory can be formulated satisfactorily, aesthetics has failed.

This assumption that a theory of art must be a definition of the concept 'art' characterizes a whole approach to philosophical aesthetics. Under the general label 'aesthetics' philosophers have been engaged in many different things, but it is the pursuit of a distinguishing definition that has dominated philosophical aesthetics in the period since the work of Immanuel Kant. Indeed, although philosophers since Plato have talked about art, and have frequently followed Plato in the search for philosophical definitions, it would not be an exaggeration to say that Kant was the founder of *aesthetics* as it has generally been understood.

Kant's major work on aesthetics is entitled *The Critique of Judgement* (discussed in some detail in Chapter 2). It is not in fact a freestanding work on aesthetics, but part of a much broader 'Idealist' philosophy, which he elaborated in three lengthy *Critiques*, and Kantian Idealism can be found still at work in a good deal of aesthetics. Sometimes philosophical aesthetics, understood as the search for a necessary and sufficient definition of art, has been thought inextricably tied to Idealism, which is at heart the belief that philosophy is the understanding of the abstract ideas of the intellect rather than of objects experienced in the world around us. W. B. Gallie, for instance, argues that all definitional theories are 'vitiated through and through by the "essentialist fallacy": they presume that whenever we are in a position to define a substance or activity, we must know its essence or ultimate nature – and know this by methods that are entirely different from those used in the experimental and mathematical sciences' (Gallie 1948: 302).

However, the stated task of philosophical aesthetics – to arrive at a definition, conception or characterization of art that makes explicit the necessary and sufficient conditions for something's being a work of art – does not need to be and as a matter of fact is not always accompanied by Idealist metaphysics. Contrary to Gallie's claim, in other writers, the search for the defining characteristic of art is more readily construed as empirical or factual, a survey of the facts about art as we know it, one which *does* use something like the methods of the sciences. John Hospers, for instance, thinks the expression theory of art (which was examined in Chapter 3) is to be construed in this way. The famous essay in which he scrutinizes the claim that 'all art must be expressive of something or other, so much so that a non-expressive work of art is a contradiction in terms' criticizes it for failing to fit relevant facts.

> If the [expression] theory is presented not as an *a priori* pronouncement but as an actual account of the creative process in artists, it will have to stand the empirical test, namely: in all cases of admitted works

> of art, was the process of its creation such as the expression theory describes? And I do not see any evidence that it holds true in all cases.
> (Hospers 1955: 315)

That the generally opposing philosophical doctrines of Idealism and empiricism may *both* accommodate the traditional project of aesthetics is clear testimony to how dominant an approach this has been. Indeed, according to Morris Weitz (who does not take into account Marxist or other sociological theories), the aim of arriving at a definition of art is common to all the major aesthetic theories of the modern period.

> Each of the great theories of art [he says] – Formalism, Voluntarism, Emotionalism, Intellectualism, Intuitionism, Organicism – converges on the attempt to state the defining properties of art. Each claims that it is the true theory because it has formulated correctly into a real definition the nature of art; and that the others are false because they have left out some necessary or sufficient property.
> (Weitz in Neill and Ridley 1995: 183–4)

It is Weitz's belief that all such theories fail. He shares Gallie's view that this search for definition is essentialist and therefore impossible, although he thinks it may still serve a purpose. But essentialist or not, the marks of its failure are unmistakable: no theory of this sort has met with universal, or even very widespread, approval. Kant's definition of the aesthetic (not quite the same, admittedly, as a definition of art) as 'purposiveness without purpose', Croce's 'intuitionism', Bell's 'significant form' or Langer's 'symbolic feeling' have all had as many critics as advocates. Philosophical fashion has for a time seized upon some favoured theory, but almost at the same time problems inherent in this same theory have been detected.

Problems with a theory do not constitute a conclusive objection to the enterprise; much the same may be said about every branch of philosophy. More important here is the reason for each theory of this sort being rejected. It is very easy, too easy in fact, to counter any of these general claims about 'Art', as Hospers counters expressionism, by pointing out recognized art forms or works of art that the theory simply cannot accommodate. For instance, many works of literature appear to have significant content as well as significant form. It seems plainly perverse to hold, in the spirit of Kant or Bell, that architecture has purposiveness but no purpose (though Kant himself acknowledged the essential utility of architecture). Again while poetry and drama, and representational works in general, may easily be thought to be expressive – a love poem is an obvious example – it is difficult (and may be impossible) to say what, or even whether, absolute music (music without words) could be said to express. Absolute music and abstract art can be made to fit the 'significant form' theory better, and so perhaps can ballet, but films cannot because they are usually made up of scenes and actions and tell a story. And opera, which is in many ways an amalgam of all the arts, can always be relied upon to produce counterexamples to any definitional theory. In short, philosophical definitions of 'art' invariably involve unwarranted generalization. This is the first major objection. There are, it is true, rejoinders that can be made on behalf of all these theories, but their uniform and manifest failure to fit the facts about art is a major difficulty for philosophical aesthetics as a whole.

In response to this difficulty, philosophers have sometimes made an important and interesting move. If a form or a work of art does not fit their preferred definition, they claim it is not 'art proper' or 'true art'. The validity of invoking this distinction needs to be considered closely. It has often been regarded as a bit of cheating, a way of bending the theory to fit the facts. But what it actually does is to convert a *descriptive* definition of art into a *prescriptive* or normative one, and there is no reason not to attempt the express formulation of a normative conception of art. The difference is that the aim of a descriptive definition is to include all the things called art; the aim of a normative one is to sort out from among the things known as art those that truly deserve the label. Normative conceptions of art is a topic to which we will be returning at the end of this chapter. For the moment, however, let us remain with descriptive definitions and see what other difficulties they present.

Croce, who offers one such descriptive definition of art, sees that there will be cases it cannot cover, but he argues that since the different art forms simply cannot be everywhere distinguished one from another clearly – there is no sharp division between fine art and jewellery, for instance – we have no choice but to resort to generalization. It is not only legitimate but inevitable, and not peculiar to aesthetics. A clear distinction between 'light' and 'dark', for example, will not encompass the 'partially lighted'. But even if Croce is right in this, there is a further deeper difficulty: what is the generalization to be about?

This is the second major difficulty confronting philosophical aesthetics. In the history of the subject since Kant, there has been continual uncertainty as to whether the subject matter of art theory is a subjective state of mind – the 'aesthetic attitude' (discussed at some length in Chapter 3). That is to say, do we theorize about the mentality of the auditor/spectator; or is the subject matter objectively existing artefacts, the works of art themselves? In other words, is a theory of art a theory about the kind of human judgement and/or perception that arises when we are confronted with a work of art, or is it a theory about actual objects – paintings, poems, plays, pieces of music and so on? The origin of this uncertainty is found in Kant himself. While Kant is primarily interested in the way the mind operates when it calls an object beautiful, he also has a theory of what it means for something to be a work of art, and the relation between the state of mind and the external object itself is very uncertain.

Arguably this uncertainty has plagued philosophical aesthetics ever since Kant. Despite the opening words of the passage from Clive Bell quoted above, the theory of 'significant form' has for obvious reasons focused attention on created objects – it is the form of the objects which matters – while expressivism, and more specifically Romanticism, have tended to give pride of place to states of mind of both artist and spectator. The problem has been compounded by the emergence of a third possibility. Functionalist and institutional theories of art tend to focus on neither the aesthetic attitude nor on individual works, but on the general activity of art making and art viewing, and on their social role. The result of all this is that aesthetics has in part come to be a dispute about what it should dispute about, and what one theorist regards as central another will regard as irrelevant. In addition to the problem of unwarranted generalization then, philosophical definitions of art have a problem about subject matter. Are we seeking a definition or generalization about attitudes or artefacts or functions or activities?

Even if both these difficulties could be overcome, and many writers have thought they can be, there is a third. This is the objection that most alternative sociological theories have made their starting point. It arises from the observation that every language is a cultural product with a history, and that consequently concepts themselves have a history. When philosophers have spoken about 'Art', this objection runs, they have implicitly supposed that there is some object or category or activity or attitude which finds universal application and is indifferent to cultural context and historical development. But socio-historical investigation seems to show this to be false. One sociologist of art, Janet Wolff, puts it this way:

> The social history of art shows, first, that it is accidental that certain types of artefact are constituted as 'art'. . . . Secondly, it forces us to question distinctions traditionally made between art and non-art . . . for it is clear that there is nothing in the nature of the work or of the activity which distinguishes it from other work and activities with which it may have a good deal in common.
>
> (Wolff 1988: 14)

Her point is that what is regarded as art at any one time is the outcome of social influences, not of the nature of the art objects themselves. This important fact, according to Wolff, will not be overcome by appeal to the accepted conclusions of art criticism:

> aesthetics can find no guarantee of any corpus of works or canon in art criticism or literary criticism. These discourses, too, are the historically specific product of social relations and practices, and hence as partial and contingent as art and literature themselves.
>
> (*ibid.*)

In other words, the mind of the art critic, or the reading public for that matter, is not itself immune to social interest and conditioning. Art critics do compile lists of 'classic' works, but this list is as subject to historical influence and change as the concept of art itself.

The precise force of the sociological objection to traditional aesthetics will be considered more closely a little later on. For the moment, it is enough to observe that something in this sociological line of thought is incontestable. What is to be called 'Art' is not even today universally agreed upon, and we do not have to look very far to see that the concept of 'Art with a capital A' does not have application in many other times and places. The distinction between art and craft, for example, brought to prominence in modern aesthetics by Collingwood (whose version of expressivism was examined in Chapter 3), cannot be translated into the language of Plato and Aristotle. Nor is it easy to relate this distinction to that which was made during the eighteenth century between fine and mechanical arts. This way of thinking about language and concepts reveals that philosophical aesthetics, even if it is not essentialist, is Platonist. Plato held that everything has an eternal unchanging 'Form' which the things we see around us mirror or imitate, and in a similar way, it can be argued, philosophical aesthetics supposes that there is a universal unchanging form called 'Art', which can be apprehended at any and every time. But the truth is, or so the sociologist of art holds, that the practice, the criticism and the institutions of art are all social products, and have to be understood in terms of historical development. They are not fixed or final, and they differ in both time and place. If this is true, philosophical aesthetics is not merely using the wrong methods, but seeking to explain the non-existent.

To summarize: philosophical aesthetics as inspired by Kant seems to suffer from three major difficulties. First, it proceeds on the basis of a certain generalizing which, whether or not it is informed by the essentialism of Idealist metaphysics, seeks the defining characteristic of art when there is no warrant to suppose that there is any one property or feature which all works of art must or do share. Inevitably, every definition fails to accommodate all the facts, because the facts are just too various. Second, philosophical aesthetics has a deep-seated uncertainty about what the possessor of this characteristic is, even if it could be found. Is it the work, the attitude we bring to it, or the whole complex of activity of which these are both part? Third, approaching art in the traditional manner of philosophical aesthetics ignores the incontrovertible fact that the concept of art is not an unchanging 'Form' laid up for all eternity but a socially and historically determined conception whose application, if it has one, is correspondingly limited.

There are further rejoinders to all these objections, but it is not germane to consider them here, for the purpose of this chapter is merely to describe the thinking that has determined where the battle lines between modern art theories are drawn. Whether or not these rejoinders are sufficient to overcome the difficulties, the fact is that serious doubts have been raised about philosophical aesthetics, and this gives us good reason to consider more closely its rivals.

Art as an institution

There is one theory of art which has commanded attention and which can be thought of as occupying a middle position between the philosophical and the sociological. This is the institutional theory, whose best-known exponent is the American philosopher George Dickie, though Jerrold Levinson is another prominent exponent of a similar idea. The institutional theory is an alternative to the Kantian 'aesthetic attitude' (which Dickie thinks a myth, as we saw in Chapter 2) and it takes seriously the idea by which sociologists of art are motivated, namely, that what counts as a work of art can differ over time and place. But it is also an exercise in traditional aesthetics, because the institutional theory aims to make this fact the basis of a philosophical definition of art.

Dickie originally formulated his definition as follows:

> A work of art in the classificatory sense is (1) an artefact (2) a set of the aspects of which has had conferred upon it the status of candidate for appreciation by some person or persons acting on behalf of a certain social institution (the artworld).
>
> (Dickie 1974: 34)

This is a convoluted definition, and it is one that Dickie himself later abandoned (see Dickie in Neill and Ridley 1995: 213–23). Nevertheless it captures a general idea which continues to have its attractions and can be stated more simply as follows: an artefact becomes a work of art if relevant critics regard it as being a candidate for this status. Art is what the artworld decides it is. This social definition of a work of art has certain advantages over a purely conceptual or *a priori* definition. A definition arrived at independently of the real artworld, based perhaps like Kant's on a general philosophical system, can in principle be wholly at odds with what is commonly thought of as art. But if what philosophy tells us is art is not what the world of artists, critics and audiences regards as art, what possible interest could the philosophical definition have? By defining art in the way he does, Dickie avoids any such disparity.

This advantage accrues to the institutional theory because it pays full attention to the social context of art, the feature the sociologists are keen to stress. Even so, the institutional theory has met with even more contention than other definitions. Three problems have emerged as being especially intractable. First, the definition appears to suffer from circularity. A work of art is defined in terms of the artworld. But how is the artworld to be defined if not as the world concerned with works of art? Not all circularity is vicious, and Dickie has defended his view on the grounds that his definition, though circular, is not viciously circular. Even if he is correct in thinking this, two other objections are not so easily met.

The idea of a social institution that has the power to confer status is neither unfamiliar nor peculiar to art. The law, for instance, is a much plainer example. An action's being a crime is a matter determined entirely by the institutions of law declaring it to be so. Crime is whatever the legal system says it is. Similarly, someone's being a priest is a result of a bishop's having bestowed this status. But both these examples refer to institutions with known and established authorities. In the case of the 'artworld' there are no such authorities. Who exactly is it that confers the status 'work of art' and by what authority do they do so? The 'artworld' is neither sufficiently corporate nor does it have recognized procedures for bestowing status. The crucial point is that people in anything plausibly called 'the artworld' often disagree about the value and status of a work. This possibility is illustrated by the example of Duchamp's urinal, discussed at length in Chapter 10. First, established critics rejected it as a work of art; later, for whatever reason, equally established critics came to regard it as such. Since the same object must either be or not be a work of art, this implies that one of the groups of critics was mistaken. But then nothing about its status as art follows from *either* response.

The consequence of the artworld's being mistaken is different from that of the law's being mistaken, and this reveals a crucial difference between the two institutions. Although judges and legislators can make mistakes, their doing so does not eliminate the authority of their decisions. Until the law is changed or the judicial decision reversed, the status of crime and criminal remain, even though a mistake has been made. What this shows is that social authority derives not from opinion, however well informed, but from recognized social function. What Dickie's 'artworld' lacks is not so much the function he attributes to it, as the social recognition of some 'invested' authority it would need to have for his theory to work.

This leads to the third objection. We might agree with Dickie that the artworld has a function, but to assume that this function is that of bestowing status is to accept the artworld on its own terms. It may be true that artists and critics think that they are the determiners of what is and is not art. Why should we accept their own estimation of themselves? To begin with, this would make for a deep conservatism in the arts – anything which the artworld does not accept becomes unacceptable. Furthermore, it takes too narrow a view of the social context of art. The artworld, if indeed it does make sense to speak of such a thing, is not a distinct and isolated entity, but a complex of institutions and activities bound up with society as a whole. To understand art in its social context properly requires us to take into account this wider context, and in doing so we may well discover that art has functions different from those the people engaged in it claim for it or are willing to admit. Dickie has taken a step in the right direction by focusing upon the social institution of art, but his focus is too narrow. It is this thought that leads us on to broader theories which I have here labelled sociological.

Marxism and the sociology of art

Sociological alternatives to philosophical aesthetics may be grouped under a variety of labels: Marxist aesthetics, structuralism, critical theory, deconstructionism, postmodernism. These are all familiar terms in contemporary art criticism, but the precision of these labels is slightly misleading since there is a good deal of overlap between the ideas they represent. However, Marxism, structuralism, deconstructionism, and so on, are convenient names for some highly influential movements in twentieth-century thought about the arts, and it is important that they be considered.

Let us begin with Marxism. There are recognizably Marxist theories of art, but since Marx himself had little to say about art, these theories consist of an extension of basic Marxist concepts. Indeed if Louis Althusser, once a leading French Marxist theorist, is right, a proper understanding of art can only come about through understanding fundamental Marxist conceptions.

> [T]he only way we can hope to reach a real knowledge of art, to go deeper into the specificity of the work of art, to know the mechanisms which produce the 'aesthetic effect', is precisely to spend a long time and pay the greatest attention to the '*basic principles of Marxism*'.
>
> (Althusser 1971: 227)

On this view,

> in order to answer most of the questions posed for us by the existence and specific nature of art, we are forced to produce an adequate (scientific) knowledge of the processes which produce the 'aesthetic effect' of a work of art.
>
> (*ibid.* 225)

Althusser is here effectively generalizing the approach Lenin took in an essay on Tolstoy:

> The contradictions in Tolstoy's views are not those of his strictly personal thinking; they are the reflection of the social conditions and influences, of the historic conditions . . . that determined the psychology of the different classes and different strata of Russian society at the time . . .
>
> (Lenin 1968: 293)

Of course, from the Marxist perspective, the purpose of intellectual activity is not merely to understand the world but to change it, and for this reason

Marxists have also been interested in the practical effect of art, both conservative and revolutionary. The history of Marxist art theory as summarized by Tony Bennett, himself a Marxist critic, reflects these two aims. (Bennett is talking about literature, but his description can legitimately be extended to art in general.)

> [W]ithin the context of the topography of 'base' and 'superstructure' mapped out by Marx, there has been a sustained attempt to explain the form and content of literary texts by referring them to the economic, political and ideological relationships within which they are set. In addition, Marxist critics have always sought to calculate what sort of political effects might be attributed to literary works and accordingly, to judge for or against different types of literary practice.
> (Bennett 1979: 104)

Bennett detects a third concern in Marxist aesthetics, to which we will return. The two he identifies here – interest in the socio-economic context of art, and in its political effects – have led to a theory of art as falling between ideology on the one hand and science on the other. 'Science' and 'ideology' are terms from Marxist social theory according to which science is the true perception and understanding of reality while ideology is the false and distorting set of ideas in which reality is presented by those who have a vested interest in resisting radical change. To say that art is halfway between the two, therefore, is to say that it has a dual nature. On the one hand, we do find a reflection of the world in art, but not as it really *is* so much as how people *take it to be*. Art expresses, in part, the historically limited perceptions of each particular society and period. To this extent art is ideological because it disguises reality. On the other hand, art is recognized as art. That is to say, it is understood to be the outcome of imagination, not scientific inquiry, and because it is understood in this way it can also reveal the *unreality* of the ideological world, show it to be made up of ideas and images. In this way art inclines to science because it tells us something about the world of capitalism and thereby increases real understanding. Althusser expresses this Marxist conception of art as a mixture of the ideological and the scientific when he says, 'the peculiarity of art is to "make us see", "make us perceive", "make us feel" something which *alludes* to reality' (Althusser 1971: 222, emphasis original).

In revolutionary art the element of *alluding to* reality will be evident. Art as an instrument of radical social change shows something about reality by shaking the ideological false-consciousness of the spectator. It is for this reason that Althusser praises the painter Cremonini, because 'his painting denies the spectator the complicities of communion in the complacent breaking of the humanist bread, the complicity which confirms the spectator in his spontaneous ideology by depicting it'. This abstruse remark means that revolutionary art does not represent things in familiar and comfortable ways, which most art does, but in unfamiliar and hence disturbing guises. By implication, non-revolutionary art, which in the view of most Marxists includes all forms of naturalist 'copying', leaves ideological images of the world undisturbed. It thus plays its part in sustaining the status quo. In bourgeois art, most Marxists would contend, the element of allusion escapes both artist and spectator, who are accordingly deceived. Similarly deceived are the critics, notably the so-called New Critics of the 1950s, who supposed their inquiries to be what the Marxist literary theorist Terry Eagleton calls 'innocent': that is, quite without social or political presupposition or interest. Such critics take artworks at face value and imagine themselves to be commenting impartially upon what they 'find' in them. But mere 'finding' assumes an impossible neutrality; no one can stand completely free, above and outside their own social allegiances.

This understanding of art is typically Marxist. An example is the work of the Hungarian writer Georg Lukács who, although a dissident, has had considerable influence in Marxist aesthetics. Lukács draws an evaluative distinction between 'narration' and 'description'. 'The real epic poet', Lukács tells us, 'does not describe objects but expresses their function in the mesh of human destinies' whereas 'the decisive ideological weakness of the writers of the descriptive method is their passive capitulation' (Lukács 1970: 146). His point is that real poets play a part in social struggle; those who purport merely to 'describe' are in fact allying themselves with forces of oppression.

The Marxist theory of art ascribes to art both intellectual and practical importance. Compared with science, it is a defective form of understanding but one that can serve either to maintain the established political order, or to disturb it. The accuracy of this view of art is clearly bound up with, and in fact rests upon, the truth of the Marxist theory of history and society of which it is only a part. It might be thought therefore that we can only examine the Marxist theory of art if we examine Marxism in general, and since this would involve a large number of important issues in politics, history and philosophy, the task of assessing the Marxist theory of art seems very extensive. Fortunately for present purposes we can ignore these larger questions. The truth of the Marxist theory of historical materialism is a *necessary* condition of the truth of Marxist theories of art, but it is not a *sufficient* condition. That is to say, if Marxist social theory is false, then the Marxist theory of art is false. But even if Marxist social theory is true, the application to art can still be erroneous. In other words, we can investigate the plausibility of the Marxist theory of art independently of Marxist theory as a whole.

When we do, even considered on its own terms the Marxist approach to art encounters an important problem, a problem encapsulated in the question: What is the Marxist theory of art a theory *of*? The Marxist alternative to philosophical aesthetics as traditionally pursued arises, it will be recalled, because of dissatisfaction with the ahistorical essentialism of Kantian aesthetics. Marxism finds here just the same fault that Marx found with Hegel's theory of the State. 'Art', like 'the State', is one of those 'abstract determinations which in no way really ripen to true social reality' (Marx 1970: 40). Yet in the elaboration of their views, the idea of something called 'Art' (as well as several related abstract concepts) is employed by Althusser, Lukács, Bennett and many other Marxists nonetheless. Indeed, references to 'Art' are no less frequent in the writings of Marxist theorists than in the writings of philosophical aestheticians. Nor is this surprising because it is hard to see how *any* such theory could be elaborated without relying on some abstract conception of 'Art'. Furthermore, it is clear from the examples the Marxists use that they are drawing precisely the sort of distinction between art and non-art that Wolff claims social investigation has exploded.

According to Bennett the continued use of this discredited abstract concept 'Art' arises from the fact that in addition to the two aims he cites in the passage quoted above, Marxists have a third incompatible one:

> with the possible exception of Brecht's work, every major phase in the development of Marxist criticism has been an enterprise in aesthetics. It has attempted to construct a theory of the specific nature of aesthetic objects. . . . Indeed, if there is a single dominant thread running through the history of Marxist criticism it is the attempt to reconcile . . . two sets of concerns: the one consistent with the historical and materialist premises of Marxism and with its political motivation, and the other inherited from bourgeois aesthetics.
>
> (Bennett 1979: 104)

Bennett holds, rightly in my view, that these two elements in Marxist criticism cannot be reconciled.

> The inheritance of the conceptual equipment which goes with the concerns of aesthetics constitutes the single most effective impediment to the development of a consistently historical and materialist approach.
>
> (*ibid.*)

The remainder of Bennett's book is, consequently, an attempt to develop such an approach. The net effect of his impressive efforts in this direction is instructive. Bennett's more consistent Marxism results in what might be called the disappearance of art (or in Bennett's case, the literary text). Since the very idea of 'a work' is one of the categories of aesthetics, the Marxist cannot consistently maintain that 'works' either reflect, reveal, sustain or subvert social reality.

> It is rather *Marxist criticism* which, through an active and critical intervention, so 'works' upon the texts concerned as to *make them* 'reveal' or 'distance' the dominant ideological forms to which they are

> *made to* 'allude'. The signification of ideology that they are thus said to have is not somehow 'natural' to them; it is not a pre-given signification which criticism passively mirrors but it is a signification they are *made to have* by the operations of Marxist criticism upon them.
>
> (Bennett 1979: 156, emphasis original)

This way of speaking is not easy to understand. What Bennett means to say is that if the importance and true meaning of works of art is their social function, this is brought out not by an examination of their internal content, but by a Marxist analysis of the place of art in a culture. Possibly he is correct in thinking that this is the inevitable conclusion of a consistent attempt to abandon the abstractions of philosophical aesthetics, but if so, a very high price is exacted. This is not so much because the concept of a work of art must be given up, but because if *all* the work is done on the part of Marxist criticism, the object of that criticism may be anything whatsoever. Marxist critics may as readily, and perhaps more satisfactorily, create their own material as rely on anything those commonly called artists may produce.

This drastic result is well illustrated towards the end of Bennett's book. There he refers approvingly to a work by Renée Balibar in which he says, 'the decisive theoretical break is finally located'. Balibar offers two contrasting texts of a passage from George Sand's *The Devil's Pool*. One is an edited (1914) version for use in schools, the other the text of a 1962 critical edition. The two differ widely, but because all that matters to the Marxist critic is how they differ in social function and effect, according to Bennett, 'neither one of these is the "original" or "true" text'. If this is correct, we are forced to the conclusion that *from the point of view of Marxist criticism*, what Sand wrote, or indeed whether she wrote anything at all, is a matter of indifference. The text not only means but *is* whatever Marxist criticism says it is.

Bennett is happy to accept this conclusion, and perhaps consistency requires this of him. The point to be made here, however, is that there is no special connection between his consistent version of Marxist criticism and any known phenomena commonly called art, no matter how broadly that label may be applied. As a result, we have no reason to regard Bennett's version of Marxist criticism as an exercise in the theory of art at all. Since 'Art' is a false abstraction which should be abandoned, there cannot be any theory of it, Marxist or otherwise. Marxism, pushed to its logical conclusion, does not mean a different or better way of doing what philosophical aesthetics has done badly, but a total abandonment of any such enterprise. Bennett concludes that 'there are no such things as works or texts which exist independently of the functions which they serve' (*ibid.* p. 157). If so, the theory of art must be replaced by the analysis of society.

This is not an outcome that many Marxist theorists have expressly accepted, and it is important to note that so far this conclusion has been found to derive only from the views of Althusser and Lukács. Other Marxist theorists have had slightly different conceptions of art. The exploration of these might have different implications. For instance, Terry Eagleton, one of the best-known Marxist literary theorists, holds that texts do not reflect or express ideological conceptions of social reality, but are rather themselves products of that reality. Consequently the task of criticism

> is to show the text as it cannot know itself, to manifest those conditions of its making (inscribed in its very letter) about which it is necessarily silent. . . . To achieve such a showing, criticism must break with its ideological prehistory, situating itself outside the space of the text on the alternative terrain of scientific knowledge.
>
> (Eagleton 1978: 43)

It is not altogether easy to understand what Eagleton means by this, but if the proper object of criticism is something about which the text or work is *necessarily* silent and if criticism must put itself 'outside the space of the text', there does seem a distinct possibility of the disappearance of art here too. One response to this lies in interpreting Eagleton's endeavour as a matter not of ignoring the text but, so to speak, reading past it in the same way perhaps that natural science goes beyond bare experimental data and constructs a theory to explain the data, or that anthropology offers interpretations of myths and rituals which go beyond the level of mere observation. Though neither analogy is perfect, this way of putting it draws attention to similarities between Eagleton's line of thought and some other more general structuralist conceptions. Accepting for the moment that consistent Marxism means the end of aesthetics rather than its mere revision, it is the associated structuralist approach which now needs to be explored.

Lévi-Strauss and structuralism

Structuralism made its first appearance in the field of linguistics, and it would be true to say that the role of language in human thought and understanding remains of central importance. Moreover, the extension of the role of language to art in general generates a conception of music, painting, architecture, and so on, that preserves several linguistic concepts by viewing these as systems of signs and signifiers somewhat comparable to natural languages. In linguistics the pioneer of structuralism was the Swiss linguist Ferdinand de Saussure (1857–1913). Saussure made the now famous distinction between *parole* – utterance – and *langue* – the unspoken and inaudible system of language which determines the structure and meaning of an utterance. The things we say are constructed out of and depend for their meaning upon a grammar and vocabulary that is not itself expressed, and generally is not explicitly known by language speakers. The task of linguistics as Saussure conceived it, is to construct or deduce the *langue* from its realization in *parole*.

Two features of this way of thinking are especially worth noting. First, the hidden *langue* behind a manifest *parole* is not to be thought of as something existing apart from language as it is used. Although the hidden *langue* may be distinguished from concrete utterances, nonetheless it can only manifest itself in these same utterances. The grammar of a natural language for instance is not identical to grammatical utterances themselves, yet it can be realized only in real spoken sentences. The distinction at the heart of structuralism thus holds out the promise of something which in a sense all intellectual endeavour strives for – the detection of reality behind appearance – while at the same time invoking no occult or strangely metaphysical entities. This explains much of structuralism's attraction in a wide variety of fields, social anthropology as well as the study of language, for instance. Second, structural linguistics opens up the possibility of theoretical explanation, that is to say, explanation of linguistic phenomena in terms of the internal nature of language and thought, and not merely their appearance or development as seen in varying time and place. Sometimes this is expressed by saying that structuralism allows for synchronic (simultaneous) and not merely diachronic (historical) explanation. In other words it provides a way of understanding appearances *via* an ever-present structuring system and not merely by means of a historical process of development. It was for this reason that structural linguistics seemed to provide a source of theoretical liberation from the mere recording of historical changes which had marked the study of language hitherto.

Given the intellectual attractiveness of structuralism it is not surprising to find the basic ideas of linguistic structuralism extended into wider spheres of inquiry. Most notable of these is anthropology as it was developed by Claude Lévi-Strauss (1908–92). Lévi-Strauss himself seems to have thought of his employment of ideas from the field of linguistics merely as an extension and not a special adaptation of them, for he says, '[W]e conceive anthropology as the *bona fide* occupant of that domain of semiology which linguistics has not already claimed for its own' (Lévi-Strauss 1978: 9–10). The effect of this extension, however, was to give the concept of underlying structure a more abstract form, and hence one that allowed it to be applied to systems other than language. In his view, '[E]ven the simplest techniques of any primitive society take on the character of a system that can be analyzed in terms of a more general system' (*ibid*. p. 11).

Lévi-Strauss's definition of a suitable object for structuralist analysis is as follows:

> An arrangement is structured which meets but two conditions: that it be a system revealed by an internal cohesiveness, and that this cohesiveness, inaccessible to observation in an isolated system, be

> revealed in the study of transformations through which similar properties are recognized in apparently different systems.
>
> (Lévi-Strauss 1978: 18)

It is not difficult to see that such abstract conditions can be applied to art and art making. Indeed Lévi-Strauss himself was one of the first to make this connection in the field of anthropology, by drawing attention to work on fairy tales by the Russian Vladimir Propp. Propp thought that certain constant functions and spheres of action, delineated by character types such as 'the villain', 'the provider', 'the sought for person', and so on, can be detected in the various characters of particular tales. More abstract and ambitious still was the approach of Tzvetan Todorov, who employed a close parallel between grammatical and literary structures so that characters were seen as 'nouns', their attributes as 'adjectives' and their actions as 'verbs', with 'rules' again conceived on the model of grammar, which of course determine the combinations of the parts of speech.

The most important implication of the structuralist approaches to literature was the creation of a new view of literature itself, namely, that in it we find not merely the manifestation of an underlying structure, but a conscious or partly conscious reflection upon the structure itself. To use the terminology of linguistics, the field in which this development began, contrary to other forms of writing, in literature we do not find a clear distinction between signifier (words) and signified (the objects the words refer to). Rather, in literary compositions the signified *is* the signifier itself, and the effect of this identification is to draw the attention of the reader, not to an external reference, but to the very means of reference themselves. It is this function that the semi-technical term 'foregrounding' aims to capture.

> The function of poetic language consists in the maximum of foregrounding of the utterance . . . it is not used in the services of communication, but in order to place in the foreground the act of expression, the act of speech itself.
>
> (Jan Mukarovsky, 'Standard Language and Poetic Language', quoted in Hawkes 1977: 75)

The impact of structuralism in thinking about the arts has clearly been greatest in literary theory, no doubt because of its origins in the study of language. But it is not hard to see how the extension to other arts is to be made. Lévi-Strauss's two conditions for the existence of a structured system make no explicit reference to language, and it seems quite plausible to conceive of art forms other than literature as structured arrangements analysable in terms of constants and variables. Indeed it is natural and quite common for artists and art critics to speak in this way. Thus, painting can be understood as a way of foregrounding the visual, architects often speak of an architectural 'vocabulary', and it is difficult to talk about music at all without referring to the structure of a composition.

Structuralist ways of thinking, then, can be made to generate an understanding of the arts in general and not simply of poetic function. The resulting view plainly has connections with Marxism, as many writers have acknowledged. There is a crucial difference between the two, however. On structuralist theories properly so called, the systems of meaning and perceptions that are self-reflected in art are universal and for the most part fixed. That is to say, structures of the sort Lévi-Strauss describes, even if ultimately subject to change, are atemporal 'grammars' manifested in particular historical cultures. In Marxism, by contrast, everything is subject to historical change and especially, perhaps, social and cultural structures.

Derrida, deconstruction and postmodernism

Structuralism has its difficulties of course. In fact, it is probably correct to claim, as Edith Kurzweil does in *The Age of Structuralism* (1980), that the age of structuralism is over. The reasons for its decline may have as much to do with intellectual fashion as with its intellectual problems, but for present purposes it is instructive to explore some of these problems.

First, and in some ways least interestingly, no one has been successful in actually deriving a convincing structure of axioms and rules of transformation. Lévi-Strauss's universal system of binary opposites (light/dark, good/bad, and so on), after a promising start, ran into innumerable difficulties which could only be resolved by retreating to a degree of complexity that removed most of its theoretical power. And Lévi-Strauss himself, despite an abiding admiration for the pioneering nature of Propp's work on fairy tales, revealed considerable weaknesses in his treatment of the same. In short, in none of the spheres over which structuralist theorists have ranged has anything like a 'grammar' emerged.

Second, it will have been clear, even from this brief exposition, that the move from structural linguistics through anthropology to a structuralist theory of literature and finally art is questionable. To treat music, for instance, as comparable to a natural language is mistaken, as we saw in Chapter 5. But even if we accept the legitimacy of this extension, the resulting view seems to encounter precisely the same objection as we found in philosophical aesthetics. That is, we end up with something called *the* function of poetic language, *the* role of literature. These are ways of talking which seem just as subject to sociological objection as the pursuit of a Platonic definition of art or poetry or literature.

But third and most importantly, the theories that emerge from structuralism appear to contradict its originating thought. This is the line of objection developed by the French literary theorist Jacques Derrida (1930–2004), perhaps the major influence on post-structuralist thought. Derrida's corpus of writing is very large, hard to understand, still harder to generalize about and impossible to summarize. Here I shall elaborate his criticisms of structuralism as they appear in the essays 'Force and Signification' and 'Structure, Sign and Play in the Human Sciences', both of which appear in the collection of essays entitled *Writing and Difference* (Derrida 1990).

Derrida thinks that structuralism arises from and reflects an important 'rupture' in the history of human thought, a final break with Platonism of the sort some people have detected in philosophical aesthetics. A Platonist view of language thinks of words and signs as substitutes for the things they signify, and further thinks that these transcendental objects are the fixed centre on which structures of thought and language are built. But the crucial rupture in the history of thought consisted in a recognition that:

> the substitute does not substitute for anything which has somehow existed before it. Henceforth, it was necessary to begin thinking that there was no centre ... that [the centre] was not a fixed locus but a function, a sort of nonlocus in which an infinite number of sign-substitutions come into play. This was ... the moment when in the absence of a centre or origin everything becomes discourse.
>
> (Derrida 1990: 280)

What Derrida is saying here is that whereas most theorists have thought of human language and the external world as two distinct entities related by correspondence, structuralism sees that the underlying reality is not some fixed world, but rather the structure of thought and language itself. It is upon this recognition that the whole of structuralism rests, but according to Derrida its proponents (in these two essays he refers chiefly to Lévi-Strauss and the literary critic Jean Rousset) do not pursue the basic insight of structuralism to its logical conclusion. 'Structuralism', he says, 'lives within and on the difference between its promise and its practice' (*ibid.* p. 27). Structuralism denies the independent existence of the structures upon which it rests. To this extent it treats 'parole' (the utterance) as basic and has no place for reified or concretized Platonic forms. Yet instead of recognizing that if everything has become discourse, a series of utterances, 'structure' is itself a metaphor, structuralists continue to treat 'structure' as a sign in the Platonic fashion, as an existing entity upon which theories may be built. Thus despite pretensions and appearances of being a radical alternative to Western philosophy, 'modern structuralism [is] a tributary of the most purely traditional stream of Western philosophy, which, above and beyond its anti-Platonism, leads from Husserl back to Plato' (Derrida 1990: 27).

> For as long as the metaphorical sense of the notion of structure is not acknowledged as such, that is to say interrogated and even destroyed as concerns its figurative quality ... one runs the risk through a kind of

> sliding as unnoticed as it is efficacious, of confusing meaning with . . . its model. One runs the risk of being interested in the figure itself to the detriment of the play going on within it.
>
> (*ibid.* p. 16)

This notion of 'play' is important in Derrida, but before looking at it further we should note that Derrida acknowledges the extreme difficulty of recognizing fully the implications of the 'rupture'. To express, or even merely to signal, our abandonment of traditional ways of thinking requires us to use the language of tradition, and hence to run the risk of being recaptured by it. Derrida thinks this is what has happened to the structuralists as well as the literary and art critics who have pursued structuralist methods.

> [S]tructure, the framework of construction, morphological correlation becomes in fact and despite his theoretical intention the critic's sole preoccupation . . . no longer a method within the *ordo cognoscendi*, [the realm of knowing] no longer a relationship in the *ordo essendi*, [the realm of being] but the very being of the work.
>
> (*ibid.* p. 15)

It is arguable that this difficulty is of Derrida's own making and that it cannot in fact be overcome, because what he is demanding is that structuralists, and philosophers quite generally, speak in a wholly new language, when of course there cannot be any such thing. We could only invent a new language by translating terms and concepts we already employ. A less flatly contradictory interpretation is that Derrida does not demand a completely *new* language, but only that we use language in a different way, 'knowingly', which is to say, conscious of its limitations. In other words, there is a way out of the linguistic 'trap' if we stop trying to devise replacements for old theories and instead understand them in a different way.

> [W]hat I want to emphasize is simply that the passage beyond philosophy does not consist in turning the page of philosophy . . . but continuing to read philosophers *in a certain way*.
>
> (*ibid.* p. 288, emphasis original)

This alternative way of reading is to be contrasted with the older way of thinking, back into which structuralism slides. It is here that the notion of 'play' becomes important.

> There are thus two interpretations of interpretation, of structure, of sign, of play. The one seeks to decipher, dreams of deciphering a truth or an origin which escapes play . . . the other, which is no longer turned toward the origin, affirms play and tries to pass beyond man and humanism.
>
> (*ibid.* p. 292)

Faced with a work or a text or a myth or a story, then, we cannot hope to detect within it something which will determine for us *the* correct interpretation of it. We can only 'play' upon it, and a good deal of Derrida's later work consists precisely in 'play' of this sort, as does the work of critics inspired by similar thoughts. Such a prospect, he thinks, could be greeted negatively. Having lost all prospect of there existing a thought-determining centre or origin we may incline to the 'saddened, negative, nostalgic, guilty, Rousseauistic side of the thinking of play'. Or we might find instead a cause for

> the joyous affirmation of the play of the world and of the innocence of becoming, the affirmation of a world of signs without fault, without truth, and without origin which is offered to an active interpretation.
> (*ibid.* p. 294)

Derrida's conception of free interpretation has been taken up with enthusiasm by some students of literature, notably the American critics Hillis Miller and Paul de Man, though the same free interpretation could as easily be applied to paintings, drama or music. This sort of interpretation has come to be known as 'deconstruction', the sustained unravelling of 'imposed' structures. Literary criticism of this sort, as inspired by Derrida, seems to have capitalized on ideas arising from a number of different but contemporaneous sources. Derrida's distinction between two types of interpretation, for instance, bears a close similarity to Roland Barthes's distinction between *lisible* (readerly) and *scriptible* (writerly) texts. In the former, the reader is expected to be passive, to 'receive' a reading of the text and hence absorb an established view of the world. In the latter, the writer and the text itself (for it is not just a matter of intention but of style) acknowledges its malleability and involves the reader's interpretation as part of the creation of the work. Barthes seems to think that the most we can hope for from 'readerly' texts is pleasure, whereas from 'writerly' texts, which invite our active participation, we can expect something much more exhilarating – *jouissance* – a term deployed by the Marxist/post-structuralist theorist Lacan – something similar to Derrida's 'joyous affirmation of play'.

The point to be stressed in the thought of both thinkers is that a proper understanding of structuralism leads to a liberation from the very idea of structure itself. It leads to a certain sort of freedom, the freedom of indefinitely many 'readings'. These are to be teased out from the work in a host of different ways, and much of Derrida's later writing consists precisely in doing this (as does Hillis Miller's). The idea that must be abandoned is that of natural, innate or proper meaning, and interpretation must recognize that it moves in a world without fault, without truth, without origin.

But if this liberation from the idea of structure is complete, no interpretation can be wrong. (This is one reason that the influential German philosopher Habermas thinks the thoughts of Derrida, and Foucault, to be irrationalist.) Moreover, no distinction or discrimination can be *required* of us, and this includes the distinction between art and non-art and the discrimination between the aesthetically valuable and the aesthetically valueless. Derrida appears to recognize and to accept this implication when he anticipates an objection from Rousset.

> Does not one thus run the risk of identifying the work with original writing in general? Of dissolving the notion of art and the value of 'beauty' by which literature is currently distinguished from the letter in general? But perhaps by removing the specificity of beauty from aesthetic values, beauty is, on the contrary, liberated? Is there a specificity of beauty, and would beauty gain from this effort?
>
> (*ibid.* p. 13)

It is fairly clear what Derrida takes the answer to these rhetorical questions to be – there is no one thing that is aesthetic beauty, and once we see this we are freed to discover beauty everywhere and anywhere, not just in those things conventionally accepted as 'works of art'. This freedom is the mark of 'postmodernism'. While the modernist (at least on some uses of the term) strives to find 'the' right proportions and harmonies, the *post*modernist abandons any such attempt as futile, and thus opens up a world liberated from conventional and culturally relative constraints.

The terminology is confusing here since Derrida's conclusion seems to be deeply in accord with the art of the readymade discussed in Chapter 10 under the general heading 'modern' art. But the modernism to which Derrida's thought is 'post' is not the art of the avant-garde in general, but that movement in early twentieth-century architecture that thought of itself as penetrating the essentials of pure form. In fact, the expression 'postmodernism' makes its first appearance in architecture and is perhaps most easily understood in that context, since thereafter it assumed multiple meanings (one commentator having identified no fewer than fourteen!).

In the present context, 'postmodernism' is to be understood in the context of Derrida's account of structuralism and its aftermath, and we may reasonably raise questions about the cost of accepting this way of thinking. As with consistent Marxism, it seems to involve us in the abandonment of art theory altogether. Indeed worse than this. At least Marxism points us in the direction of an alternative type of inquiry, namely the socio-historical, whereas for Derridian studies everything, and hence anything, goes. Thus, should literary critics choose to interpret the railway timetable, or art critics 'explore' the wrapping from a takeaway hamburger, there is nothing to be said about the fitness or unfitness of the objects of their attention. We can ask only whether joyful affirmation in a system of signs is possible, whether the result is '*jouissance*'.

It is open to Derrida, Barthes and those who think in this way to accept this conclusion and regard it as an honest recognition of the wholly unconstrained or liberated condition in which critics find themselves. But there are at least two further points to be made. First, in the work of the deconstructionists there is a measure of the same tension between promise and practice which they allege is to be found in structuralism. Although it is impossible to classify Derrida as a philosopher, critic or social theorist because he refuses, on theoretical grounds, to work within these traditional distinctions, he does nevertheless discuss almost exclusively the work of philosophers, critics and anthropologists. He does not discuss the scribbles of race-track punters or the instructions on packages of medicine (though Barthes does examine 'literary' works such as these). In other words, distinctions *are* being made within the sphere of 'the letter in general', even if these distinctions are not the most familiar and are treated with a greater degree of flexibility than the study of literature has traditionally done.

Second, it is hard to see how this could conceivably be avoided. Indeed a certain measure of Platonic realism seems to lurk in Derrida's thought itself and to be for this reason inescapable. It seems tempting to express his view by saying, for instance, that those critics who persist in looking for a centre or an origin do not acknowledge the *fact* of their condition, that their criticism is *really* free. To speak in this way, however, is to reintroduce the idea of an independent reality against which understanding and interpretation are to be tested.

What exactly is wrong with speaking in this way? Some version of the Marxist idea of 'false-consciousness' runs through nearly all of the critical attacks on philosophical aesthetics we have been considering. Essentialism, unwarranted generalization, Platonism or the failure to recognize the mind-dependent structures upon which systems of meanings depend, the transformation of 'structure' itself into a centre or origin – the error in each of these philosophies is said to lie in the assumption that there is a 'given' which can determine our understanding for us, whereas, according to the deconstructionist, the interpretative mind is free to 'play'. However, there must be a serious doubt whether the thrust of this criticism can be sustained. As I have suggested, some kind of Platonic realism seems inescapable if we are to speak of this assumption as an error, for 'error' suggests that these philosophies misrepresent how things really are. But suppose traditional metaphysics is erroneous in this regard. Even so, if the motivation behind deconstruction and its forerunners is to free critical interpretation from the imaginary metaphysical constraints, another line of thought deploying a different conception of constraint can be seen to open up.

Normative theory of art

If there is to be such a thing as theory of art, we must be able to distinguish art from non-art. Let us agree, however, that Platonism about art is false.

There is no such thing as an essential 'Form' or universal 'Idea' called 'Art' which those things properly called works of art realize. Consequently this distinction between art and non-art is not a reflection of a reality independent of our thinking about art, and the words 'art' and 'non-art' are not substitutes for, or signs of, something that pre-exists them. However, to accept this does not carry the implication that we have to cease making the distinction. It only means that we cannot interpret the distinction descriptively; there is nothing to prevent us interpreting it *normatively*. That is to say, applying the distinction between art and non-art does not signal a *discovery*, but a *recommendation*. Thinking of art theory in this way not only avoids the strictures imposed by Wolff, Eagleton, Todorov, Derrida and others, but also resolves an ambiguity, noted earlier, which runs through a great deal of aesthetics, an ambiguity in the term 'work of art'.

Is 'work of art' a descriptive or an evaluative label? The only plausible answer, given the way the term is used, is 'It is both.' When, for instance, experts testify in court, on behalf of artists or writers, that a particular painting or novel is not pornography but a work of art, they mean not simply to say what it is, but to give it a certain evaluative or normative status. Be its content what it may, the force of their testimony is that there is a value in it other than the value pornography has. To call something a 'work of art' in these circumstances is not merely to classify it but to exonerate it. Most of the definitions of 'art' which have been devised in philosophical aesthetics treat 'art' as a neutral classification, but sooner or later this leads to the sort of Platonic essentialism or empirical generalization which, as we have seen, contemporary critics find so objectionable. The solution, however, is not to abandon all attempts at distinguishing between art and non-art, as some of these critics have done, but only to set aside the idea of 'art' as a neutral classification. A theory of art which explicitly and self-consciously sets out to recommend a distinction between art and non-art in terms of relative value would avoid most of the problems we have considered.

We can make the point in Derridian language. It is a mistake to think that we can discover, in the nature of things as it were, interpretative rules by which to 'play'. But this does not mean that we cannot *devise* rules of 'play' and proceed to recommend them for the purposes of discussing art. Such rules would, of course, be mere stipulations unless there were rational grounds for recommending these rather than some other set of rules. But there is nothing in any of the critiques we have been considering that excludes the possibility of rationally recommended norms of criticism. All that has been ruled out is a certain kind of metaphysical realism.

Deconstruction could itself be rationally grounded in this way. We might, for instance, recommend Barthesian rules on the grounds that they lead to greater '*jouissance*'. A parallel with a more straightforward example of 'play' will make the point clearer. Consider the game of chess. There is indeed a sense in which we 'discover' what the rules of chess are, but anyone who supposed that this means the rules are, so to speak, 'laid up in heaven' would have made a metaphysical error. The force of the error (or so critics allege) is that it leads to the rules being regarded as unalterable. On the other hand, acknowledging their alterability (or 'contingency' as some writers call it) does not imply that we can play chess any way we choose. It means rather that we can make rationally grounded alterations in the rules. The grounds for altering them will have to do with improving the game from the point of view of the value we derive from playing it. Rules establish norms – how games *ought* to be played – and these norms are to be assessed according to their effectiveness in realizing values – pleasure is one such value. A rule can increase or diminish the pleasure of a game, and its ability to do so is a reason for or against adopting it.

Similarly, to distinguish art from non-art, or kitsch from art proper, need not be thought of as an attempt to unveil a metaphysical difference. At the same time, this does not mean that the distinction can be applied arbitrarily in any way we choose. If there is too great a measure of latitude we will end by making no distinctions at all. What we need, once the deficiencies of essentialist and sociological theories of art have been uncovered, are grounds for identifying art proper in one way rather than another; in other words, we need normative recommendations.

This suggests an alternative approach to aesthetics and art theory, one which ceases to strive for philosophical or sociological neutrality, and expressly aims to formulate a reasoned conception of 'art proper', a conception that can then be applied in judging the objects and activities which lay claim to the status of art. Instead of seeking a definition of art in terms of necessary and sufficient properties, or trying to isolate its distinctive social function, such a theory is intended to help us grasp the values music, or painting, or poetry can embody, and how valuable this form of embodiment is.

Such an approach to art is not a novelty. It is true that for the most part philosophers in the modern period have treated aesthetics as a branch of ontology (the nature of being or existence) and the philosophy of mind, chiefly because of Kant's influence. But the much older Greek tradition established by Plato and Aristotle was evaluative rather than metaphysical in character. Monroe C. Beardsley, one of the best-known American philosophers of art, makes this point:

> the dominant movement of Plato's thought about art, taking it all in all, is strongly moralistic in a broad sense . . . it insists that the final evaluation of any work of art . . . must take into account the all important ends and values of the whole society.
>
> (Beardsley 1975: 48–9)

The normative approach is not exclusive to the Greeks. It is to be found for instance in Alexander Baumgarten's *Reflections on Poetry* (1735), the work to which, as far as one can tell, we owe the very term 'aesthetics'. Baumgarten's treatment of poetry could hardly be called 'moralistic' in even the broadest sense. But it *is* evaluative, implicitly if not explicitly. Baumgarten's concern is not to discover the essence of poetry but, like Aristotle long before him, to establish principles of good poetry. He seems to have in mind the model of logic. Logical formulae do not distil the metaphysical essence of thought but establish rules for what is valid thinking. In a similar fashion Baumgarten's reflections, made largely upon his reading of the Latin poet Horace, are intended to provide a concept of 'true' poetry, or poetry proper, in the light of which we may judge any poem presented for our consideration.

Amongst the major philosophers of the modern period, it is Hegel (as we saw in Chapter 4) who develops a recognizably normative philosophy of art to a more sophisticated level. Hegel's theory of art is what he refers to in the *Science of Logic* as a 'determination'. The difference between a definition and a determination is explained by Stephen Bungay as follows:

> A determination is not a definition because a definition excludes possible examples by delimiting the object at the outset [which is what Hospers complains of]. A determination is a theory, a framework of universal explanation, which then must demonstrate its own explanatory power through its differences and its instantiation.
>
> (Bungay 1987: 25, material in brackets added)

Hegel's own theory of art follows this conception. It does not consist in generalization drawn from an examination of acknowledged works of art, and it does not seek to discover what is essential in the aesthetic attitude. Rather, in the elaboration of an encyclopaedic account of knowledge and understanding, something called art is allocated a place. As we saw in Chapter 4, for Hegel art stands somewhere between intellectual understanding and experience of the senses, and its distinguishing character is thus what Hegel calls 'sensual presentation of the Idea', or the presentation of the idea of a thing by means of the senses. 'Sensual presentation of the Idea' is something art makes possible through its ability to identify the form of a thing (Idea), which we grasp intellectually, and its content (appearance), which we encounter through the senses.

This line of thought owes a good deal to Kant's treatment of art in his third *Critique*, but it does not describe our everyday experience. Hegel does indeed *begin* with '*Vorstellungen*', that is things as they are presented to us in our consciousness, but the aim of the whole of his philosophy – and not just his aesthetics – is to reconstruct these *Vorstellungen* critically in thought. Hegel is engaged in formulating a philosophy of 'the Absolute', which is to say a complete philosophical understanding of everything, and it is this

Absolute which determines finally what the conceptual character of art is. Once we have grasped its place in the Absolute, the Idea of art can be used to order and explain our experience of art. Strictly, this last step is not philosophy, according to Hegel, since the application of the Ideal to the actual products of the people thought to be artists requires judgement and not merely philosophical theorizing. However, the adequacy of the philosophical theory must in part be proved by the explanations and discriminations it allows us to make, and in the *Aesthetics*, Hegel does go on (not altogether satisfactorily) to apply his philosophy in an examination of architecture, music and literature.

This critical way of thinking about art has much to commend it, but with Hegel the chief difficulty lies not so much in what he has to say about art, as in his ambitious metaphysical enterprise, of which the theory of art is just one part. A slightly more accessible approach of the same kind is to be found in the works of Hegel's great contemporary rival, Arthur Schopenhauer (1788–1860).

For Schopenhauer there is no distinction between 'art' and 'art proper'. True works of art are to be understood as having a distinctive value within human consciousness, and for any work claiming this status, the only question is whether it realizes this value. A work of art aspires to achieve something, and the task for philosophical reflection is to decide what the proper object of this aspiration should be. Schopenhauer's account of artistic value and how it is realized in different art forms is largely cognitivist. That is to say, it is what art allows us to see and to understand about human experience that lends it significance and makes it valuable. The cognitivist theory of art was examined in some detail in Chapter 4, and along with Hegel, Schopenhauer is another instance of a major philosophical author who clearly offers a normative theory of art along cognitivist lines.

A plainer example yet of normative theory, this time expressivist rather than cognitivist, is to be found in Collingwood's *The Principles of Art*, where 'art proper' is systematically distinguished from art as craft, entertainment and magic in terms of the peculiar value it embodies. As we saw in Chapter 3, Collingwood thinks that the value of art lies in its character as the expression of feeling, rather than some special apprehension of reality. Exploration of his version of expressivism showed that it easily gives way to Schopenhauer's type of cognitivism, but whether this is correct or not, Collingwood and Schopenhauer both believe that the chief task of aesthetics is to explain the *value* and *importance* of art.

The same ambition is to be found in several modern-day writers. Roger Scruton, a prominent contemporary philosopher of art, tells us that 'philosophy aims at the discovery of value. The only interesting philosophical account of aesthetic experience is the account which shows its importance' (Scruton 1979: 3) and Malcolm Budd, another British philosopher, opens his book *Values of Art* by saying that 'The central question in the philosophy of art is, What is the value of art?' (Budd 1995: 1). Normative philosophy of art, then, is neither a novelty nor an aberration, but a promising theoretical approach to the arts. It is an approach that the preceding chapters have taken, and what this chapter has shown is that at a deeper philosophical level it has advantages over its traditional and sociological rivals.

Summary

Philosophical aesthetics has traditionally tried to formulate a definition of art which will serve as a neutral classification. Such definitions easily become stipulative, and in an attempt to avoid stipulation appeal has usually been made to Platonic essentialism or empirical generalization. But neither view can properly accommodate the social context of art. The institutional theory formulated by George Dickie tries to define art in terms of the social 'artworld', but it fails because it leads on naturally to a more radical sociological approach. The danger in this approach, however, whether in Marxist, structuralist or post-structuralist forms, is that the distinction between art and non-art disappears, so that there remains no subject to theorize about.

We can avoid both sets of difficulties if we take an expressly normative approach to art, of the sort we find in Hegel, Schopenhauer and Collingwood. Normative theories of art concern themselves not with the definition of the nature of art but with its value. Sociological theories explain this value in terms of the historically specific functions that art has performed in different cultures. But the fact is that generation after generation, and a wide variety of cultures, have all attributed a special value to certain works and activities. This suggests that some of the things we call art have an abiding value. Consequently, the socio-historical approach to art is importantly limited. Marx himself observed this in a remark about the art of antiquity.

> [T]he difficulty lies not in understanding that Greek art and the epic are linked to certain forms of social development. The difficulty is that that they still afford us artistic pleasure and that in a certain respect they count as a norm and as an unattainable model.
>
> (Marx 1973: 110–11)

The last few words of this quotation are crucial. People in different periods have abiding ideas about the *norms* of art, just as they have abiding ideas about what is and what is not a valid logical inference. And, just as logic can investigate the extent to which these ideas are correct, not by revealing metaphysical truth but by devising systems of rules, so an interest in the ideal of art can investigate the evaluative basis upon which that ideal might be founded. In this way, objectionable essentialism is avoided, but so is anxiety about the Derridian 'rupture'. Furthermore, by being self-conscious about its evaluative character, philosophy of art can be made to escape Eagleton's charge of seeking an impossible 'innocence' (see *Criticism and Ideology*). Other writers have seen this. Janet Wolff, whose views on art and sociology were quoted earlier in this chapter, argues that sociology of art, no less than philosophical aesthetics, has sought a similarly impossible neutrality, and closes her book by saying this:

> The sociology of art involves critical judgements about art. The solution to this, however, is not to try even harder for a value-free sociology and a more refined notion of aesthetic neutrality; it is to engage directly with the question of aesthetic value. This means, first, taking as a topic of investigation that value already bestowed on works by their contemporaries and subsequent critics and audiences. Secondly, it means bringing into the open those aesthetic categories and judgements which locate and inform the researcher's project. And lastly, it means recognising the autonomy of the question of the particular kind of pleasure involved in past and present appreciation of the works themselves.
>
> (Wolff 1988: 106)

What Wolff means to say is that the sociological study of art can only proceed successfully if we identify what is to count as artistically significant. This requires us to make critical judgements. The possibility of such judgements was explored at some length in the previous chapter, and in turn led us to consider normativity in art theory more generally. Normative investigation of the meaning and value of art, we have now seen reason to think, is a more promising approach than either of its two major rivals – philosophical definition and the study of social function. In fact, Wolff, who favours the second of these, nevertheless makes an implicit assumption of just the sort that this normative approach to art ought to investigate. She supposes, in what she says, that the 'value already bestowed on works by their audiences' will find its validation in 'the particular kind of pleasure' works of art supply. In short, Wolff implies that the value of art proper lies in the pleasure it provides. This is itself, in a simple way, a normative theory of art, widely held. Yet we cannot *assume* its truth; it is a claim that has to be investigated and its investigation launches us upon the course of inquiry in which this book has been engaged.

Our subject has thus come full circle. We have seen how an examination of the philosophical basis of rival theories of art leads to a question about the connection between art and pleasure. Appropriately enough, this was the topic with which the first chapter of our study began.

Suggested further reading

Advanced introductory reading

Routledge Companion to Aesthetics (second edition), Chapters 17, 18
Oxford Handbook of Aesthetics, Chapters 2, 7, 47, 48

Classic writings

Morris Weitz, 'The Role of Theory in Aesthetics'
George Dickie, *Art and the Aesthetic: an Institutional Analysis*
Claude Lévi-Strauss, *Structural Anthropology*
Jacques Derrida, *Writing and Difference*

Major contemporary works

Stephen Davies, *Definitions of Art* (1991)
Terry Eagleton, *The Ideology of the Aesthetic* (1990)

Finding examples

It is important for anyone studying the philosophy of art to have a good knowledge of examples from a number of art forms. It is also essential that examples used in the text to illustrate the argument should be known or available to the reader. The development of the internet makes accomplishing both of these things far easier than it ever was before. There are now a great many very high quality collections that are easy to access. The following are just a few that will be found useful.

Architecture Through the Ages – http://library.advanced.org/10098/
Art History Network – http://www.arthistory.net/artist.html
Art History Resources on the Web – http://witcombe.bcpw.sbc.edu/ARTHLinks.html
Art Nouveau World Wide – http://art-nouveau.kubos.org/en/an.htm
Classical Midi Archives – http://www.prs.net/midi.html
Digital Archive of European Architecture – http://www.bc.edu/bc_org/avp/cas/fnart/arch/
Global Music Network – http://www.gmn.com/
Great Buildings Collection, the – http://www.greatbuildings.com/
National Gallery of Art – http://www.nga.gov/
New York Public Library – http://www.nypl.org/
Renaissance and Baroque Architecture: Architectural History 102 – http://www.lib.virginia.edu/dic/colls/arh102/index.html

Bibliography

Alperson, P. (ed.) *The Philosophy of the Visual Arts*, New York, Oxford University Press, 1992

—— (ed.) *What is Music? An introduction to the philosophy of music*, Philadelphia, Pennsylvania State University Press, 1994

Althusser, L. 'Letter on Art' in *Lenin and Philosophy and Other Essays*, trans. Ben Brewster, London, New Left Books, 1971. Originally published in *La Nouvelle Critique*, 1966

Aristotle, *Poetics*, trans. Malcolm Heather, London, Penguin Books, 2004

Arnheim, R. *Film as Art*, London, Faber and Faber, 1958

Baumgarten, A. G. *Reflections on Poetry* (1735), trans. K. Aschenbrenner and W. B. Hatthner, Berkeley, University of California Press, 1954

Bazin, A. *What is Cinema?*, Vol. I, trans. Hugh Gray, Berkeley, University of California Press, 1967

Beardsley, M. C. *Aesthetics: Problems in the Philosophy of Criticism*, New York, Harcourt Brace, 1958

—— *Aesthetics: from Classical Greece to the Present*, Tuscaloosa, University of Alabama Press, 1975

Beiser, F. C. (ed.) *The Cambridge Companion to Hegel*, Cambridge, Cambridge University Press, 1993

Bell, C. *Art*, Oxford, Oxford University Press, 1987

Bennett, T. *Formalism and Marxism*, New York, Methuen, 1979

Brooks, C. *The Well Wrought Urn*, New York, Harcourt Brace, 1947

Bryson, N., M. Holly and K. Moxey (eds) *Visual Theory*, Cambridge, Polity Press, 1991

Budd, M. *Music and the Emotions*, London, Routledge & Kegan Paul, 1985

—— *Values of Art*, Harmondsworth, Penguin, 1995

Bungay, S. *Beauty and Truth: a Study of Hegel's Aesthetics*, Oxford, Clarendon Press, 1987

Bürger, P. *Theory of the Avant-garde*, Minneapolis, University of Minnesota Press, 1984

Carlson, A. *Aesthetics and the Environment*, London, Routledge, 2000

Carrit, E. F. *What is Beauty?*, Oxford, Clarendon Press, 1932

Carroll, N. *Philosophical Problems of Classical Film Theory*, Princeton NJ, Princeton University Press, 1988

—— *The Philosophy of Horror*, New York, Routledge, 1990

Cavell, S. *Must We Mean What We Say?*, Cambridge, Cambridge University Press, 1969

Cherry, D. 'Tracy Emins Bed', SHARP 2.0 www.sussex.ac.uk/ Units/arthist/sharp

Chilvers, I. and Osborne, H. (eds) *Oxford Dictionary of Art*, Oxford, Oxford University Press, 1997

Chipp, H. B. *Theories of Modern Art*, Berkeley, University of California Press, 1968
Collingwood, R. G. *The Principles of Art*, Oxford, Clarendon Press, 1938
Cooke, D. *The Language of Music*, Oxford, Clarendon Press, 1957
Cothey, A. L. *The Nature of Art*, London, Routledge, 1990
Croce, B. *Aesthetic*, trans. D. Ainslie, London, Peter Owen, 1953
—— *Guide to Aesthetics*, trans. Patrick Romanell, Indianapolis, Library of Liberal Arts, 1965
Currie, G. *Image and Mind: Film, Philosophy and Cognitive Science*, Cambridge, Cambridge University Press, 1995
Danto, Arthur C. *The Transfiguration of the Commonplace*, Cambridge MA, Harvard University Press, 1981
—— *After the End of Art: Contemporary Art and the Pale of History*, Princeton NJ, Princeton University Press, 1997
Davies, S. *Definitions of Art*, Ithaca NY, Cornell University Press, 1991
Derrida, J. *Writing and Difference*, trans. A. Bass, London, Routledge, 1990
Dickie, G. 'The Myth of the Aesthetic Attitude', *American Philosophical Quarterly*, 1, 1964, pp. 56–65
—— *Art and the Aesthetic: an Institutional Analysis*, Ithaca NY, Cornell University Press, 1974
Eagleton, T. *Criticism and Ideology*, London, Verso, 1978
—— *The Ideology of the Aesthetic*, London, Blackwell, 1990
Eisenstein, S. *The Film Sense*, London, Faber and Faber, 1943
Freeland, C. *But is it Art?*, New York, Oxford University Press, 2001
Gadamer, H.-G. *The Relevance of the Beautiful and Other Essays*, trans. N. Walker; ed. Robert Bernasconi, Cambridge, Cambridge University Press, 1986
Gallie, W. B. 'The Function of Philosophical Aesthetics', *Mind*, 57, 1948, pp. 302–21
Gardner, H. *Religion and Literature*, Oxford, Oxford University Press, 1983
Gaut, B. and D. M. Lopes *Routledge Companion to Aesthetics* (second edition), London, Routledge, 2005
Goldwater, R. and M. Treves (eds) *Artists on Art*, London, John Murray, 1976
Gombrich, E. H. *Art and Illusion* (fifth edition), London, Phaidon, 1977
—— *The Story of Art* (fifteenth edition), London, Phaidon, 1987
Goodman, N. *The Languages of Art*, Indianapolis, Bobbs-Merrill, 1968
—— *Ways of World Making*, Indianapolis, Hackett, 1978
—— 'How Buildings Mean' in Philip Alperson (ed.) *The Philosophy of the Visual Arts*, New York, Oxford University Press, 1992
Hanslick, E. *On the Musically Beautiful*, trans. G. Payzant, Indianapolis, Hackett, 1986
Harries, K. *The Ethical Function of Architecture*, Cambridge MA, MIT Press, 1997
Hawkes, T. *Structuralism and Semiotics*, London, Methuen, 1977
Hegel, G. W. F. *Science of Logic*, trans. Johnston and Struthers, London, Allen and Unwin, 1929
—— *Aesthetics*, trans. T. M. Knox, Oxford, Clarendon Press, 1975
Hepburn, R. W. 'Contemporary Aesthetics and the Neglect of Natural Beauty' in *British Analytical Philosophy*, ed. Williams and Montefiore, London, Routledge & Kegan Paul, 1966
Hospers, J. 'The Concept of Artistic Expression', *Proceedings of the Aristotelian Society*, 55, 1955, pp. 313–44 (also in Hospers, *Introductory Readings in Aesthetics*)
Hospers, J. *Introductory Readings in Aesthetics*, New York, The Free Press, 1969
Hume, D. *Essays, Moral, Political and Literary*, Oxford, Oxford University Press, 1963

Ingarden, R. 'Artistic and Aesthetic Values' in H. Osborne (ed.) *Aesthetics*, Oxford, Oxford University Press, 1972
Inwood, M. *A Hegel Dictionary*, Oxford, Basil Blackwell, 1992
Isenberg, A. *Aesthetics and the Theory of Criticism*, Chicago, University of Chicago Press, 1973
Johnson, S. *Lives of the Poets*, Vol. 1, Oxford, World Classics, 1906
Jones, E. *The Origins of Shakespeare*, Oxford, Oxford University Press, 1978
Kandinsky, W. *Concerning the Spiritual in Art*, New York, George Wittenborn Inc., 1947
Kant, I. *The Critique of Judgement*, trans. W. S. Pluhar, Indianapolis, Hackett, 1987
Kemal, S. and Gaskin I. (eds) *Landscape, Natural Beauty and the Arts*, Cambridge, Cambridge University Press, 1993
Kivy, P. *The Corded Shell: Reflections on Musical Expression*, Princeton NJ, Princeton University Press, 1980
—— *Music Alone*, Ithaca NY, Cornell University Press, 1990
—— *Osmin's Rage: Reflections on Opera, Drama and Text*, Ithaca NY, Cornell University Press, 1999
Kurzweil, E. *The Age of Structuralism: Levi-Strauss to Foucault*, New York, Columbia University Press, 1980
Lamarque, P. V. and S. H. Olsen *Truth, Fiction and Literature*, Oxford, Clarendon Press, 1994
Langer, S. K. *Feeling and Form*, London, Routledge & Kegan Paul, 1953
Lenin, V. I. *Collected Works*, Vol. XIV, London, Lawrence and Wishart, 1968
Leopold, A. *A Sand County Almanac*, New York, Oxford University Press, 1949
Levinson, J. *Music, Art and Metaphysics*, Ithaca NY, Cornell University Press, 1990
—— *The Pleasures of Aesthetics*, Ithaca NY, Cornell University Press, 1996
—— (ed.) *Oxford Handbook of Aesthetics*, Oxford and New York, Oxford University Press, 2002
Lévi-Strauss, C. *Structural Anthropology*, Vol. II, Harmondsworth, Penguin, 1978
Locke, J. *Essay Concerning Human Understanding*, Vol. II, Oxford, Clarendon Press, 1896
Lopes, D. *Understanding Pictures*, Oxford, Clarendon Press, 1996
Lukács, G. *Writer and Critic and Other Essays*, trans. A. Kahn, London, Merlin Press, 1970
Lynton, N. *The Story of Modern Art*, Oxford, Phaidon, 1980
MacDowell, J. 'Aesthetic Value, Objectivity, and the Fabric of the World' in E. Schaper (ed.) *Pleasure, Preference and Value*, Cambridge, Cambridge University Press, 1983
Margolis, J. (ed.) *Philosophy Looks at the Arts* (third edition), Philadelphia, Temple University Press, 1987
Marx, K. *Critique of Hegel's Philosophy of Right*, trans. Annette Jolin and Joseph O'Malley, Cambridge, Cambridge University Press, 1970
—— *Grundrisse*, trans. Martin Nicolaus, Harmondsworth, Penguin, 1973
Mayhead, R. *Understanding Literature*, Cambridge, Cambridge University Press, 1965
Mellers, W. *Man and His Music* (revised edition), London, Barrie and Rockliff, 1962
Mill, J. S. *Utilitarianism* (seventeenth impression), London, Fontana, 1985
Morgan, D. 'Must Art Tell the Truth?', *Journal of Aesthetics and Art Criticism*, 26, 1967, pp. 17–27 (also in Hospers, *Introductory Readings in Aesthetics*)
Neill, A. and A. Ridley (eds) *The Philosophy of Art: Readings Ancient and Modern*, New York, McGraw-Hill, 1995

Nietzsche, F. *The Birth of Tragedy*, ed. M. Tanner; trans. S. Whiteside, London, Penguin, 1993
Norris, C. *Deconstruction: Theory and Practice*, London, Methuen, 1982
Noverre, J.-G. *Letters on Dancing and Ballet*, trans. C. W. Beaumont, New York, Dance Horizons, 1966
Nussbaum, M. *Love's Knowledge: Essays on Philosophy and Literature*, New York, Oxford University Press, 1990
Nuttgens, P. *The Story of Architecture*, Oxford, Oxford University Press, 1983
Otto, R. *The Idea of the Holy*, trans. J. W. Harvey (second edition), Oxford, Oxford University Press, 1950
Perkins, V. F. *Film as Film*, Harmondsworth, Penguin, 1972
Pevsner, N. *An Outline of European Architecture* (revised edition), Harmondsworth, Penguin, 1963
—— *The Cities of London and Westminster: The Buildings of England*, Vol. 1, third edition, Harmondsworth, Penguin, 1972
Schaper, E. (ed.) *Pleasure, Preference and Value: Studies in Philosophical Aesthetics*, Cambridge, Cambridge University Press, 1983
Schopenhauer, A. *The World as Will and Representation*, trans. E. F. J. Payne, New York, Dover, 1966
Scruton, R. *Art and Imagination*, London, Methuen, 1974
—— *The Aesthetics of Architecture*, London, Methuen, 1979
—— *The Aesthetic Understanding: essays in the philosophy of art and culture*, London, Methuen, 1983
—— *The Aesthetics of Music*, Oxford, Clarendon Press, 1997
Soskice, J. M. *Metaphor and Religious Language*, Oxford, Clarendon Press, 1985
Storr, A. *Music and the Mind*, London, HarperCollins, 1993
Tolstoy, L. *What is Art?*, trans. A. Maude, Oxford, World Classics, 1930
Tormey, A. *The Concept of Expression*, Princeton NJ, Princeton University Press, 1971
Walton, K. *Mimesis as Make-Believe*, Cambridge MA, Harvard University Press, 1990
Watkin, D. *The Morality of Architecture*, Chicago, University of Chicago Press, 1984
Weitz, M. 'The Role of Theory in Aesthetics', *Journal of Aesthetics and Art Criticism*, 15, 1956, pp. 27–35
—— 'Truth in Literature' in Hospers, *Introductory Readings in Aesthetics*
Wimsatt, W. K. and M. C. Beardsley *The Verbal Icon*, Lexington, Kentucky University Press, 1954
Winters, Y. *In Defense of Reason*, Denver, Alan Swallow, 1947
Wolfe, T. *From Bauhaus to Our House*, New York, Farrer Strauss, 1981
Wolff, J. *Aesthetics and Sociology of Art*, London, Allen and Unwin, 1988
Wolffin, H. *Principles of Art History*, New York, Dover, 1986
Wollheim, R. *Painting as an Art*, London, Thames and Hudson, 1987
Young, J. *Nietzsche's Philosophy of Art*, Cambridge, Cambridge University Press, 1992

Index